Always Yours

memoir of an adopted child

C.F. Stice

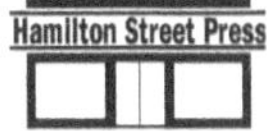

Published by C.F. Stice, Hamilton Street Press, 145 Harpeth Trace Smt., Nashville, TN 37221

ISBN printed book 978-0-692-84976-7

ISBN ebook 978-0-692-84977-4

Library of Congress Control Number 2017903485

Nonfiction/Biography and Autobiography/Personal Memoir

Nonfiction/Family and Relationships/Adoption and Fostering

Publication managed by Lystra Books & Literary Services, lystrabooks.com

~

For R.P. and S.K.,
who understand the importance
of history, family, and family history

~

Whatever you choose to claim
of me is always yours:
nothing is truly mine
except my name.

*— from the poem
"Passing Through"
by Stanly Kunitz*

Contents

Prologue 1

PART *1*: Who Am I? 3

   1. Lightning Strikes 4

   2. Blood Poisoning 14

   3. The Trouble with Travel 18

   4. A Bastard in the Family 30

   5. At Home in the City 38

   6. The City at Christmas 46

   7. Of Lice and Lies. 53

   8. About Cousins. 61

   9. Siblings for Six Weeks 69

  10. Crisis of Faith 80

  11. Piano Lessons Plus 86

  12. Another Moving Experience 105

  13. Reassurance 119

  14. Adolescent Humiliations 125

  15. Unwilling Transplant 133

PART *2*: Moving On 145

  16. Culture Shock 146

  17. Other Shocks that Flesh Is Heir to. 167

  18. Chicken, Chicken! Pluck, Pluck, Pluck. . . 176

19. My Worst Fear 183

20. More Trouble with Men 194

21. Kissing Bill Goodbye 214

PART *3: Losing Mom & Dad* 223

22. A Question of Roots 224

23. Gone Fishing 239

24. Mama's Hawk 245

25. With His Boots On 252

26. Re-searching 258

PART *4: Relative Strangers* 265

27. Becoming Alex Haley 266

28. My Half-Siblings 282

29. Drawing Conclusions 298

30. Except My Name 307

Epilogue 320

Kirchner Family Tree 321

Pugh Family Tree 322

Prologue

New York Avenue
Nashville, Tennessee
February 1943, 4:45 a.m.

Liz slipped quietly out of bed, her small suitcase waiting in the closet, packed.

Twelve-year-old Geri stirred and opened her eyes. "Whatcha doin'?"

Light from the street lamp outside cast a pink halo through Liz's fiery red curls.

"Shush." Liz patted her little sister's head. "Go back to sleep."

Geri propped herself on one elbow. "You got your good coat on. Where you going so early?" She reached for the light switch.

"Don't." Liz sat down on the bed, whispering so as not to wake the two little ones in the other bed. "I'm going up north where I can get me a really good job."

Geri sat upright. "You leaving home?"

"I got to, sugar."

Geri began to cry. "But why?"

Liz sighed. "I need to make more money to help out around here."

"What do you want me to tell Mama?"

"Don't tell her anything till she asks for me. Then say I've gone to a big city to work in an airplane factory. With this war on there's all kinds of good jobs for girls. Tell her I'll be sending money home soon as I can." Liz gave Geri a quick hug. "I gotta go. Somebody's waiting for me."

Geri padded along to the front door, sniffling and swiping her nose. "Please don't go." But Ann Elizabeth Pugh had already disappeared into the frigid winter morning. Down the street, a car engine started up.

"Where's Liz off to this time of morning?" Mama asked from the doorway. Geri jumped.

"To a big city," she said quickly, "to work in an airplane factory."

"What?" Mama peered past the porch railing. "Who with? Why didn't she tell me?"

"She'll be sending money home soon as she can." Geri started to cry again.

"Okay, okay. It's all right. Stop your bawling." Mama put her arm around Geri's shoulder. "I bet Liz will be back before you know it. This war can't last forever." She shut the door behind them. "Dry your eyes and go get dressed. Then come to the kitchen. They'll all be up soon enough. And somebody's going to have to tell your daddy about Elizabeth."

~

PART I

Who Am I ?

~

Lightning Strikes

When I was a little girl, I was struck by lightning. Not the billion-watt kind that kills you instantly, frying you where you stand, but the other kind, bright and buzzing. My family lived in a two-bedroom apartment above a drugstore— my mother, my father, my grandmother, and me—in Highland Park, Michigan. Other than hot, humid summer nights, I remember that apartment as large and comfortable and safe. I never expected we'd be struck by lightning.

Daddy has already left for work. He works nights. My mama, my grandma, and I are eating supper at our red and white enameled table. At the far end of the table the window is open. A breeze flaps Mama's starched and ironed, red and white café curtains.

Our dining room is small, just wide enough for the furniture and us. The walls are white. I sit on a booster seat at the end of the table in Daddy's place across from the window, where I can feel the breeze. The kitchen is behind me. I can see down the hall all the way to the bedroom I share with my grandmother. On my right side, I can see into the living room all the way to the front door. I hear thunder.

"Uh oh," Grandma says. "Storm's coming." She reaches out to lower the sash and—boom!—a blast of light hits the table. We all jump as static electricity surges around us and a glowing basketball of light tumbles across the table. It spills onto the floor and rolls into the living room where it dissolves in a fuzz of fading sparks against the front door.

Mama is on her feet, her eyes wide. "What in this world?" She lays her hand on my head. "It's a wonder we weren't all killed." She looks down at me. "You okay?"

I nod.

"Whew," Grandma says. "That was ball lightning." She plops back onto her chair. "It's harmless enough. I've seen it once before, but not this close."

"I want to see it again," I say.

One morning a few weeks later, just after my fourth birthday, Mama stands me in front of her and Daddy as they sit side by side in two kitchen chairs with the living room behind them. Mama's hands are folded in her lap, her long fingers tipped with candy-apple red nail polish. Daddy is wearing dark brown pants. The tabletop is just above eye level. He is drinking coffee and smoking. Daddy is always smoking. Mama's dressed for work.

"Now that you're a big four-year-old," Mama says, "your daddy and I have something to tell you."

She pauses and I wait. Maybe they have a surprise for me, another present. Maybe it's a puppy.

"You were adopted," Mama says. "That means you're special." She bends forward and strokes both my arms. "Other parents take whatever they get when they have children, but you were handpicked because we wanted you more than anything in the world. We brought you home when you were just ten days old. We love you very much." She kisses my cheek.

When she pulls back, her hazel-brown eyes have tears in them. Something about me has made her sad. That, more than not getting a puppy, is unsettling.

"Your daddy always wanted a little girl with big blue eyes and red hair and that's exactly what he got. We are very lucky."

Daddy doesn't say anything.

I glance at my grandmother, who's standing in front of the stove stirring something in a pot. I know she's listening, but she doesn't look at me. Mama is still talking. I wish she'd stop.

My parents' friends call my grandmother Mrs. Williams, or Mother Williams. I tried to say Williams, too, but it came out sounding something like Beo.

"Is she saying I have B.O.?" my grandmother asked.

"Now how would she know to say a thing like that?" Mama said.

They decided I was saying Bill, and now I call my grandmother Bill all the time. I think she likes it.

I love Bill very much. So, in my nightly prayers I bless Mama twice just in case she thinks I love Bill best. "Now I lay me down to sleep… God bless Mama, Daddy, Bill, and Mama."

Mama is not as huggable as Bill, not as soft. But she smells just as good, like coffee and cinnamon and vanilla, especially right after work. Mama manages a restaurant in downtown Detroit. Bill smells of baby powder and Ivory soap and sometimes pie dough. Bill came to visit the week after I was born, to help out, and now she lives with us all the time so Mama can work. Bill is my best friend.

After they tell me I am adopted, Mama goes to work and Daddy leaves to take care of business. That's what he says when is going to the racetrack. I usually play in my room while Bill does her chores, but today I don't want to play alone. My tummy feels like I swallowed a woolly worm. I go into the kitchen to find Bill.

"Read to me, Bill?"

She sighs and unties her apron. "All right. How about *The Story of Jesus?*"

"I want *The Little Red Hen* and *The Poky Little Puppy.*"

"Let's read all three. We can sit in the rocking chair and snuggle." She reads to me almost every day, but we only snuggled in the rocker sometimes.

When she finishes, I look up at her thick glasses and curly blue-white hair. "Bill?"

"What, honey?"

I feel my forehead scrunch. "I'm 'dopted?"

"Yes," she says, "but you just forget about that. Dr. Rosenthal told them to tell you now so you'd grow up always knowing." She closes the Little Golden Books and lays them aside. "But it doesn't make one iota of difference. Everything is fine just the way it is. It's nothing for you to worry about. Why don't you run on now and play some more while I bake a pie for supper? You'd like that, wouldn't you?"

"Chocolate or lemon?"

She laughs. "Lemon." Bill knows lemon is my favorite.

Later, in the kitchen, I lay my head against her leg while she works. Her hands are covered in flour. She dusts them off over the sink. Her cheeks sag like one of Mama's old powder puffs.

"Bill?"

"What, honey?"

"I don't think I want to be 'dopted."

I like the idea of being special, but I don't know what to think about being adopted. Most of the time, I manage not to think about it at all. But sometimes it's unavoidable.

One day, after I have turned five, we visit my daddy's niece who lives in a house nearby. Whenever we're there, I play with my cousin Mona in her room or in the backyard.

Today, we are playing dolls on the floor, because her bed is made and her mama does not allow anyone on the bed after it has been made. Mona is nine months older than me and she's smart. She just started first grade and she can already read. She was named Mona after my mother. Mona has straight dark hair like her daddy. She's also bigger than me. We don't look alike at all, but she's my favorite cousin.

"These are my babies," Mona says, rocking one of her dolls in her arms.

"I want that baby," I say, taking the doll she has already put to bed. "Did you know I'm 'dopted?" I say.

"Yes," she says.

"It means I'm special."

"It means your mama isn't your real mama," she says.

Mona may be smart, but I don't believe her. Of course, Mama is my mama. Isn't she? I want to go home. My stomach hurts, but I can't go home. We are all going to the zoo.

The next time Mama tells me to pick up my toys and put them in the box, I say, "If you aren't my real mama, do I still have to mind you?"

"Oh Lord!" She rolls her eyes at me and pulls me onto her lap. "Maybe we shouldn't have told you. Anyway, I'm your mama now, and for always, and yes, you do have to mind me."

I'm glad she said the "for always" part, but I don't understand. How can Mama not be my real mama? Do I have a real mama? If so, who is she? Where is she? Why isn't Mama my real mama?

I wonder about the whole handpicked scenario, too. Handpicked how? How did they find me? Where had I been? I think lots of questions and ask some.

When the family down the hall has a baby, I watch its coming with all the objective disinterest of any five-year-old.

"Mrs. Peacock's getting fat," I say.

"She's expecting," Bill says.

"Expecting what?" I ask.

"A baby."

"Oh."

"Bill, where do babies come from?"

"They grow in their mother's tummies," she says.

I am not sure that's true, but something was certainly growing in Mrs. Peacock's tummy.

The Peacocks invite us over to meet the newly arrived infant. They seem overjoyed with him, but to me he's red-faced and wrinkled and ugly. They name him Leonard and don't seem to care one bit that he wasn't "handpicked" because surely they had not gotten Leonard on purpose. Maybe Mrs. Peacock doesn't know she doesn't have to settle for any old baby who just happened to show up. I decide to explain it to her.

"Mrs. Peacock," I say, "I was 'dopted. My mommy and daddy picked me out from all the rest of the babies because I was the prettiest one."

"I know that, Carole Faye," she says.

"If you want a pretty baby," I say, "you should take Leonard back and get a better one. You can do that, you know."

Bill gasps and tries to drag me, apologetically, from their apartment while Mrs. Peacock thanks me for the information but says they think they will keep Leonard anyway. "We imagine he'll improve with age," she says.

Seems risky to me. We don't see the Peacocks very much after that.

If people can handpick their babies, why did the Peacocks settle for Leonard? And why, if I'm so pretty, did my "real" mama not keep me? Did she trade me for an even better baby? No one said she hadn't.

Sometimes I ask Bill questions when we are alone, especially when we are out of the house by ourselves at the park or the playground. Most Saturdays we go to the movies and some days we take our lunch to the park. Before we eat I swing and play on the merry-go-round. Afterward, we sit at a picnic table and eat. I like to lean against Bill and look at her wrinkled arm close up. There's a lump just below her elbow where her arm got caught in the wringer washing machine when she was a girl. She lets me feel it. Bill is blind in her left eye. So when we go out I have to stay on her right side and hold her right hand so she always knows where I am.

Over liverwurst sandwiches with pickles and New Era potato chips, I ask her why my real mama gave me away. Even asking that questions makes me feel funny inside.

"Oh honey, your mother was just so young. She didn't have any choice. She had red hair and blue eyes just like you do. She was so pretty. That's what your daddy wanted—a red-haired baby girl with big blue eyes. And that's just what he got."

How did Mama and Daddy know my real mother was pretty? They must have seen her. And how did they know I would grow red hair eventually, because in all the pictures I'd ever seen of me as a baby, and there were plenty, I was as bald as my father's bowling ball. Not a red hair in sight. Maybe my "real" mother didn't want a bald baby. Was that it?

"If I didn't grow red hair, would Mama and Daddy have given me back?"

Bill stops eating. "Of course not." Her eyes look like olives through her thick bifocals. "They never wanted any other baby but you. They would love you just the way you are no matter what, but your daddy does like your red hair. He had a red-headed grandfather he loved very much."

I stopped asking so many questions after that. The

Carole, age 3 months, with Daddy.

whole notion of being adopted was very confusing and I didn't want to think about it. If a new question occurred to me I'd usually just keep it to myself.

Some questions were subconscious, because I was too young to formulate and articulate them, but they were in the back of my mind from what seems like the very start. What was my "real" mother like? Did Mama and Daddy like her? Where is she now? What about Daddy? Is he not my "real" Daddy? Maybe he is. We both have blue eyes. Does my "real" mother know who I am and where I live? Does she have other children? Is she sorry she gave me away? Are Mama and Daddy glad they picked me? What would have happened to *me* if they hadn't wanted me?

If Bill knew the answers to questions I asked out loud, she would tell me some, though not always all, of the story. Occasionally, when I'd ask about my "real" mother, Bill would change the subject. When I'd ask Mama, she'd say, "You'll understand when you're older." Then she'd change the subject, too. By adolescence, I had stopped

asking Mama any questions at all, but I never fully stopped asking Bill and I never stopped wondering. Eventually, I understood that I had another mother and another father somewhere else, people I did not know and never could. I didn't want to have another mother and father. Why did *I* have another mother and father somewhere? No one else I knew did. Sometimes I felt like I was standing on thin ice over deep water.

My parents could not have children of their own, so they adopted late in life when Mama was thirty-eight and Daddy was thirty-five. Whenever I thought about being given away, like a pair of unwanted shoes, it was like being zapped by ball lightning. It almost stung and made my stomach sink. Even so, I never thought of Mama and Daddy as anything other than my mama and my daddy. They were mine and I was theirs forever. Anything else was too frightening to contemplate.

Still, the older I grew, the stickier my unasked questions became. They chaffed like grains of sand in an oyster's shell. What was wrong with me that my birth parents didn't want me? What if another family had adopted me? Bill said other couples had wanted me. How would my life have been different if some other couple got me? Is my being here rather than someplace else, part of a larger plan? What would my "real" name be if my "real" mother hadn't given me away? Does a person's name make a difference? If it does, then who am I really and how would I be different with the name my "real" mother would have given me? How come mamas and daddies can give their babies away like that? Is anyone in charge of what happens to people on this planet?

Blood Poisoning

"Tell it again," I beg. We are sitting on our scratchy red sofa in the living room of our apartment above the drugstore. I am not yet six, but I can count. Mama has thirteen egg-shaped scars on her right leg.

"I don't know why you like that story so much," she says. "It's a terrible story."

"Tell it anyway," I say.

She sighs. "Oh, all right. When I was three years old, I stepped on a rusty nail. It went through my shoe and punctured deep into my foot, causing blood poisoning. This was before tetanus vaccine so I was very sick. They thought I was going to die, but I fooled them. The doctor said the only hope was to amputate my leg at the hip."

In the telling, this is where Bill chimes in. "I stood in the cabin door and stopped that old horse doctor from cutting off your mama's little leg," Bill says. "I told her papa I'd rather lose her than condemn her to such an awful life. We had no way to care for a child with one leg. Besides, there were no anesthetics back then, no penicillin either. I always believed if we'd have put her through such agony she'd have died anyway. I just wasn't going to let him cut on my baby like that. I put it in God's hands."

Bill's part of the story gives me goose bumps. "What happened next?" I say.

"I was bed-ridden for a whole year."

"You can see where she developed a bit of a spinal curve because of lying in bed so long when her bones were still growing," Bill says.

"That was the summer of 1908," Mama says. "Your grandmother had to drain the pockets of puss and clean the sores on my leg every other day. The smell was terrible. The doctor had her use carbolic acid to clean out the sores, and then she'd put fresh cloth bandages on my whole leg. I'd cry and cry because it hurt so much. Mama and Papa would comfort me the best they could."

"And every night your papa would light a little coal oil lamp by your bed so you were never in the dark," I say.

"That's right. I think he was afraid I'd die some night while he was asleep, and he didn't want me to die alone in the dark."

Since she didn't die, I try not to think about that. I look at her red lipstick and her dark wavy hair. She is so beautiful.

"The best part," she says, "was when Papa would come in to see me of an evening. He'd feed me supper and read to me and rock me. I loved my papa so much. I looked just like him, they said."

"I look like my daddy, too," I say. "We both have blue eyes."

"You certainly do," Bill says.

Bill snorts. "That old doctor said her little leg would shrink up and never develop properly. Even if she lived, he said, she'd hobble on a dwarfed and crooked leg for the rest of her life. Just goes to show what doctors knew back then. The old fool."

Mama stands, hikes up her flowered skirt, sticks her leg out, and turns it this way and that. "As you can see, my leg is fine," she says. "You hardly notice the scars unless you look real close. They don't tan though, so in the summer they show more."

Carole, age 2½, with Mama and Bill in Palmer Park.

"I never got a hurt foot, did I?" I say.

"No, but you had your tonsils out last year in the hospital," Mama says.

I remember that. My throat hurt. Did Mama's leg hurt more than that?

"When your mama was fifteen, I took her to visit the doctor who had wanted to amputate. He was retired and living in Topeka with his son who had taken over his practice. We heard him say, 'Bring her in here, son. I want to see that young lady.' He was seated at a big roll-top desk in a side room off the living room. He was old when he treated your mama, so he was really old then, but he remembered her case very well."

"He asked me to walk away and turn around," Mama says, "which I did."

"When he saw how soundly her leg had healed," Bill says, "he broke down, buried his face in his hands, and cried like a baby."

I had goose bumps. I loved Mama's terrible story. I'm not sure why. Maybe it's because it connected me to her when she was a little girl like me. Or maybe it's because I was trying to understand how life worked—planned and patterned or random and happenstance—even though I could not have articulated such a thought when I was young. Still, I hung on every word of every story, the painful and the funny, as though desperate for anything that bound me to them, especially to Mama.

These stories bound us all together as tightly as blood. Bridging the generations and binding family together is what family stories are designed to do. I still recall some of mine in my mother's voice or in Bill's. But mostly, I remember on my own, complete with the images that go with them.

$\sim$ *3* $\sim$

The Trouble with Travel

It's July 4, 1949. Mama is taking Joey, a neighbor's child, and me to the Independence Day parade in downtown Detroit. Joey and I are both almost six.

"It's going to be crowded," Mama says. "So you two stay close to me. I don't want us to get separated."

We walk in the bright sunshine three blocks from our apartment on Hamilton to Woodward Avenue to catch the downtown streetcar. Getting to Woodward means crossing two very busy streets—Second and Third Avenues, the one-way arteries to and from downtown, with two lanes of traffic each. We stop at each light and peer down the street. When the light turns red and the traffic stops, we cross.

The parade—with its marching bands and holiday floats, crowds of excited onlookers, and American flags flying in every hand—is thrilling. The bands play so loud I feel every drumbeat and cymbal crash in my chest and legs. Afterward, on the ride back, Joey and I are so excited we can hardly sit still.

When we hop off the streetcar and reach the curb at the corner of Woodward Avenue and Highland Street, we break free of Mama's grasp and run. I love to run and usually have the skinned knees to prove it. I wanted the hot

Carole at the Fourth of July parade in downtown Detroit.

wind in my face, and to feel the wild abandon and joy of forward motion. I almost believe I can run fast enough to take off and fly. Oblivious to the danger of falling and unaware of the wall of oncoming traffic hurtling toward us, we run headlong across both Second and Third Avenues without looking or even slowing down. We manage to run between the oncoming cars and trucks, with Mama behind us screaming for us to stop, running as fast as she can in her hat and high heels. She chases us all three blocks before nabbing us, just as we are about to dash across Hamilton, the widest and busiest of all three streets. She jerks us both off our feet, me by my dress collar and Joey by one arm.

"Don't you dare move another muscle," she pants. "Joey, you stand right there. I'm telling your mother and I hope she whips you within an inch of your life." Mama wheezes as she spanks me with what strength she has left.

She probably wants to beat Joey, too, but doesn't dare. The spanking surprises me more than it hurts.

"Just look at what you've done to my heels." She shows me the blisters ballooning on the backs of her ankles where her shoes rubbed as she ran. "You are the most stubborn, willful, and headstrong child I've ever seen."

Sometimes she calls me obstreperous. "How can she be so sweet one minute and so obstreperous the next?" she says. I'm not sure what that means, but it doesn't sound good. Mama is really mad this time. But hasn't she ever wanted to run like the wind? Isn't that why she likes to ride horses?

Back in the apartment, when she tells my father what I've done, he looks up from *The Detroit Free Press.* "We'll have to break her of that," he says.

"I'll tell you one darn thing," Mama says, rubbing her ankle, "I'll never take two children anywhere by myself again." She turns to me. "I'm just glad you never ran away from your grandmother like that. You could give her a heart attack."

"Oh, I wouldn't run away from Bill," I say.

"Why not?" Mama's hands are on her hips. She still looks plenty mad.

"Because that wouldn't be fair," I say. "She can't run as good as you can."

A few days later, Bill and I are on a train heading west. Mama and Daddy have decided the city is no place for a child in the summer.

We take the train rather than the bus because Bill says the bus is too confining and I am too wiggly. We board the train in Detroit, change in Chicago to the streamlined Zephyr, and ride it across the plains and through the Rockies, all the way to Grand Junction, Colorado, where

LEFT: *Aunt Bessie and Mama.* RIGHT: *Uncle Reggie in Grand Junction, Colorado.*

my aunt Bessie, my mama's older sister, and her husband, my uncle Reggie, live. I love sleeping on the train with Bill. It's cozy and the sound of the wheels talks me to sleep.

Aunt Bessie and Uncle Reggie meet us at the station. On the way to their house, I get to ride in the back of the truck with the suitcases. They live in a small two-bedroom house on a piece of irrigated desert among cowboys and horses, wheat farmers and cattle ranchers. Their little house is at the edge of pastures that smell of freshly mowed hay with fruit orchards full of peach and pear trees and mountains along the horizon in three directions. From their front porch I can see the Book Cliffs across the state line in Utah, and from the backyard I can see Grand Mesa to the southeast. Bill says that's the largest flat-topped mountain in North America. I wonder what happened to its top.

Almost as soon as we arrive in Grand Junction, I meet Charlotte Jenkins, the little girl who lives on the adjoining

farm. She's a year older than me and knows all about horses and mules. We get together every few days to play.

Life here is different from life in our apartment back
in the city. For one thing, it never rains in Grand Junction
in the summer. The sky is always a clear, bright blue, and
endless. The sky over Detroit is often clogged and cloudy,
smoky and mingled with mist seeping up from around
manhole covers. In Grand Junction, I can play outside
all day, and Bill can watch me better. But life in Colorado
is not easier or safer than in the city, no matter what my
parents think. There are canals on two sides of the house
filled with swiftly moving water. I am warned repeatedly
not to go near them by myself. I also have to watch out for
snakes, tarantulas, scorpions, and cars.

At my aunt and uncle's house, I get to be around animals.
There are horses and cows on the other side of every
fence, and everyone has dogs and cats. My aunt also keeps
chickens. Sometimes I walk down the dirt road that runs
in front of their house between the two canals to visit their
neighbor, Mary. She is an artist, like my aunt, and Mary
has dogs. Without a railing, the bridge over the big canal
is scary. If a car comes by, sometimes the dust is so thick I
can hardly see.

Like Mary, Aunt Bessie paints in oils, mostly pictures of
the mountains, flowers, and various kinds of cacti. Aunt
Bessie's paintings are stacked against walls and hanging
all over the house. She paints mostly in the winter. Every
Saturday she cleans the Pear Park Baptist Church at the
other end of their road, polishing the wood and glass until
the little church shines. During the warm months she also
works in a fruit canning plant.

My aunt and uncle grow wheat, and in the summer,
they pick fruit—pears and peaches mostly. Sometimes my

uncle prospects for gold and uranium. Once, he gave me a rock with a vein of pitch blend in it. It makes his Geiger counter thrum. Uncle Reggie has thinning red hair and wears cowboy boots, bib overalls, and plaid shirts. He plays the guitar and sings "Big Rock Candy Mountain" until I know all the words and can sing along. He teases me and makes me laugh. He can wiggle his ears, and when he tickles my knees I collapse on the floor laughing.

Aunt Bessie's chickens, mostly white leghorns, lay eggs that we collect every day. The spring before my second visit, one of the chickens was born blind. As soon as I arrive, I tell everyone she is mine; she's my first pet and I name her Snowflake. I love my little blind chicken as only a small child can love an injured fellow creature. I stroke her and feed her. When I'm not carrying Snowflake in my arms, she follows me around whenever I'm outside.

One day, I can't find her. Aunt Bessie says she died during the night. I don't know why she died. She wasn't sick. Snowflake never got to see the mountains, or the sky, or other chickens, or me. It isn't fair.

A few days later, as I am building a house in the backyard with some of Uncle Reggie's rocks, Aunt Bessie grabs a chicken pecking in the dirt and wrings its head off, twisting it by its head around in the air until the chicken's headless body flops onto the dirt where its body keeps moving. The stump of its neck spews blood in all directions. My aunt jerks the body up by its feet, plunks it in a pot of boiling water over an open fire. It stinks. She lifts the chicken out of the water and begins ripping its feathers off, each feather leaving a small, evenly spaced red hole in the bird's yellowish skin. The sound of ripped feathers is like the tearing of thick cloth. White feathers fly at my face as I stand there, stunned. What kind of person twists the head off a defenseless, harmless bird and rips out its feathers? Did Aunt Bessie do that to Snowflake?

I look down. Blood has splattered on my legs and white socks. I run down the road to Mary's and hide on her front porch. After that, I am afraid of feathers.

After my birthday, Bill and I prepare to leave Grand Junction to go to Topeka, Kansas, to visit Bill's mother and sisters and brothers. But before we go, we are invited to Sunday dinner with the Barleys. They live on a nearby ranch. Anna Barley is one of Uncle Reggie's cousins.

After lunch, Mr. Barley is asked to entertain me while the women clean up the kitchen and Uncle Reggie naps in the living room. Mr. Barley wears cowboy boots and Levis, a western shirt and a cowboy hat. He is a bigger rancher than my uncle, Bill says. Mr. Barley is a rough-faced man with sandy-colored hair white around the edges. When he suggests taking me out back to show me his prize chickens, I hesitate.

"We have cows and pigs and horses and ducks and dogs and cats," Anna Barley says.

"He won't kill a chicken, will he?" I ask. Aunt Bessie gives me a dirty look and mutters something under her breath, but Mrs. Barley and Bill just laugh. Anna Barley assures me her husband will do no such thing and shoos us both out the back door.

After rubbing the velvety noses of their calves and helping Mr. Barley water several horses in the corral, we enter the chicken coop at the side of the barn. With the smell of warm milk and green grass clinging to us, he latches the gate behind me.

Small black and white speckled chickens peck around my feet. I stand very still so I won't step on one. I reach down to touch one. It lets me pet it.

"Can I hold it?" I ask Mr. Barley.

"Sure." He bends down and scoops up one of smallest chickens. "You like animals, don't you," he says.

I nod. "I love animals."

He places the little creature in my arms. I stroke it and think of Snowflake.

"These are prize chickens," he says. "Do you like them?"

"They're so soft."

"You like soft things, do you?"

I nod, while I'm still looking at the chicken in my hands.

"Better put her down now. We don't want to scare her. They're not really used to being handled."

I gently set the chicken on her feet, sad to have to let her go, and watch them for a minute longer, while Mr. Barley remains silent.

"How about giving your Uncle Barley a little kiss then," he says. "You're such a pretty little girl."

I turn my face up expecting a chicken-like peck on the cheek. Instead, he puts his hand on the back of my head, mashes my face to his, and sticks his tongue in my mouth. I gag and can't breathe. I struggle to pull away. When he lets me go, I cough and wipe my mouth. His tongue felt like a big bumpy lizard trying to wiggle down my throat. Why did he do that?

"Now that was just a little kiss, wasn't it," he says.

No. It wasn't just a little kiss. I know what kisses are. But I nod and he unlatches the coop door.

At my aunt and uncle's house later that night, Bill and I get ready for bed. All I have to do is pee and brush my teeth. Since it is so hot, I sleep in my underwear, but Bill sleeps in a nightgown. Our little bedroom is off the kitchen. Bill goes out to get a drink of water. When she comes back I think I'll tell her about Mr. Barley.

She folds her underclothes and puts them on a chair. She reaches for a hanger to hang up her dress.

"Bill, what's a little kiss?"

She pauses and looks at me. Her dress falls from the hanger. She picks it up. "What are you talking about?"

"When somebody says, give me a little kiss, what does that mean?"

She does not look happy. "Why are you asking such a question?" Maybe I should not have said anything, but it's too late now. So I tell her what happened.

She flops down onto the edge of the bed. She doesn't want to believe me.

"Are you sure?"

I guess no one ever stuck his big fat tongue down her throat or else she would know—you can't be wrong about a thing like that.

She rubs her hand over her mouth. "I never thought Will Barley would do such a thing." She shakes her head. "Don't tell your Aunt Bessie. She'd probably beat him half to death. You just forget about it. I'll take care of it."

Maybe my aunt likes me better than I thought. I am seriously tempted to tell her, just to see what she'll do, but I don't.

The day before we are scheduled to leave on the train for Topeka is the hottest so far. Charlotte comes over to say good-bye and swim in the big canal. Tethered by ropes to a cottonwood tree that stands along the bank and under the watchful eye of my aunt and grandmother, we are safe enough, even though the water is swift and deep and very cold. It is summer run-off from melting snow at the higher elevations, my aunt says. It is so cold, in fact, that when we first jump in, our squeals and shrieks are reduced to gasps and sputters. This is our third swim in the big canal and a perfect end to my visit.

Charlotte is the first person I've ever seen with white-blond hair and pale blue eyes. Once she offered to teach me to horseback ride, but when I got close to the pony, all I wanted to do was rub its nose and feed it carrots. As far as I'm concerned, all horses are too big.

Almost without exception, the only time Charlotte comes to visit me is when we plan to go swimming or on a trip to town or the mountains. Other times, I am invited to her house to play. I'm not sure why. Maybe it's because Charlotte has so many chores to do living on a working ranch and farm. She has a playhouse under an enormous weeping willow tree in a corner of one of the pastures. We spend lots of time there in the shade playing pretend.

Years later, I found out why I went to Charlotte's house more than she came to my aunt's house. It was because her parents knew Aunt Bessie better than I did. Mama said,

"Your aunt is a little crazy, but she's a good soul. She's had problems since she was a child." Mama explained that every summer after we would leave, Aunt Bessie would scrub the house from floor to ceiling and boils our sheets and blankets. Mama knew because Uncle Reggie told her.

My aunt thought Bill and I were infected with tiny bugs. She was convinced bugs were crawling all over her, brought into her house by other people. No wonder she acted so weird and standoffish around me. Doctors call it formication, an extreme version of obsessive-compulsive disorder. For my aunt, it caused a sensation like ants crawling all over her body, for which a mild sedative was the only treatment back then.

Before she died, she developed macular degeneration and thought bugs were eating out her eyeballs. I can't imagine how terrible that must have been for her. I am amazed she managed to live as normal-appearing a life as she did. Being around her when I was a child was often tense and uncomfortable. After I understood about her OCD and that she thought I carried vermin into her house, I coped better, but when I was little, I didn't know what the problem was. I only knew she was hard-hearted and unhappy and that she never touched me and didn't seem to like me being there. I decided it was because I was not her "real" niece. And yet, Bill did say she would have beaten up Mr. Barley if she'd known what he did.

Back in Detroit, I told my parents that Aunt Bessie killed a chicken in front of me. Then Daddy discovered I was terrified of white feathers. That gave him a new weapon in his arsenal and he used it, keeping one long white feather lying in plain sight on the coffee table. "Time for bed," he'd say, casting a glance at the feather. Whenever I saw a white feather, I'd flash on a honeycomb of red and oozing holes in yellowish skin and shudder in a wave of nausea I could not control. Though I never wanted to go to bed before ten, he got no argument from me. For years, I gave that hateful white feather a very wide berth.

~ *4* ~

A Bastard in the Family

Our visits with Bill's mother and two sisters in Topeka are very different from our time in Grand Junction. Bill's mother, my great grandmother, lives in town, on Elm Street in a three-story, white clapboard house with a wide front porch and a swing across one end. Billowing blue hydrangeas frame the porch. Between the clothes line and the red rose bushes, the backyard is too full to play in, but I love the backyard because it smells good—green grass, freshly laundered sheets on the line, and roses in full bloom, but I like the front yard, too.

Elm Street is made entirely of hand-laid bricks. The street is lined with majestic elm trees spreading their branches to form a canopy over the pavement in both directions as far as my eye can see. It's the most beautiful house and street I've ever seen.

Great Grandma Johnson lives with Bill's other sisters, my great aunts Eva and Effie. Grandma Johnson is in her nineties. The aunts are younger than Bill, but I don't know how much younger. Bill is seventy-four. Aunt Eva seldom smiles because she has buckteeth. She wears sensible, clunky shoes and clomps across the floor when she walks. Bill says she sounds like she's stomping out a brush fire. To me Aunt Eva seems very determined. Aunt Effie is more bird-like and only taps when she walks, as though she

30

*Great Grandma Johnson, Great Aunt Eva, Great Aunt Effie, Bill,
Mama, Mama's nephew Rudy, Aunt Bessie, and Great Grandma's
sister-in-law in Topeka.*

still retains some youthful dream of becoming a ballerina. Whenever our eyes meet, Aunt Effie smiles at me, and often winks. Sometimes, when I walk into a room, she gasps, startled by the presence of a child among them, or by anyone who notices she is still there, too. She sneaks me pieces of hard candy, especially when I seem bored or sad. She presses the candy into my palm and whispers, "Don't tell Eva or Mandy." Mandy is what all her brothers and sisters call my grandmother, whose first name is actually Amanda.

I whisper thank you to Aunt Effie for the candy, though it's usually something I don't much like: licorice or horehound or root beer barrels or strong peppermint. But once in a while it's butterscotch, so I always take it just in case. I save the others for my cousin Karen. Sometimes she comes to Topeka with her family while I'm there.

Both Aunt Effie and Aunt Eva had tuberculosis when they were younger, which at the time was largely a disease of the malnourished, Bill says. Aunt Effie is in remission, and Aunt Eva is well. Aunt Effie is afraid to hug or touch me for fear she might make me sick. I don't get a lot of hugging during the two months Bill and I are out west. Aunt Effie wants to hug me. That's what Bill says, anyway. Aunt Eva doesn't want to hug anyone. Aunt Effie is very delicate and I think she's beautiful.

Bill says Aunt Effie and Aunt Eva are spinsters. According to Bill, one young man of modest means and limited prospects came calling on Aunt Effie when she was a girl and she fancied him very much, but her father said he wasn't good enough and ran the boy off, leaving Effie broken-hearted.

When Bill and I visit, we share Aunt Effie's little bedroom. I sleep on a cot under the window. Aunt Effie sleeps in Aunt Eva's room. My great grandmother's room is the big bedroom off the kitchen. The kitchen is small but pretty, white with pink-flowered wallpaper. A small round breakfast table with four chairs sits in one corner near the back door where painted steps lead down to the basement.

Dark furniture with stiff chairs and a sofa, crocheted doilies, and a glass-shaded lamp fill the seldom-used living room. Flowered area rugs cover the wooden floors. This is the biggest house I've ever been in. To me, the house is both enormous and mysterious. I want to explore it, but Aunt Eva, who is not really fond of children, says no. Even though it's my great grandmother's house, Aunt Eva is in charge.

Great Grandmother Johnson keeps to her bed most days. She has failing eyesight, though her hearing is acute. Aunt Eva likes the house dark and quiet. I am told to go outside to play in the backyard or on the front porch and to be quiet, but my great grandmother comes to my defense.

"I can hear you, don't think I can't," my great grandmother says from where she is propped up in her bed. "You all stop fussing at that child. Carole Faye is not hurting one thing in this old house. Leave her be." After that, I am freer to roam. I love my great grandmother.

The second floor of the house has been converted into an apartment that my great grandmother rents to a single, middle-aged lady art teacher who, from time to time, invites me to come to her kitchen to finger paint and play with watercolors. I paint scenes of empty stages with purple curtains along the sides and across the top. When I tire of that, I paint underwater scenes with colorful little fish hiding among tall brown and green seaweed. Bill saves most of my artwork in a box she keeps under her bed. She asks me why I paint the same scenes over and over.

"Because I know how to make them look right," I say. It never occurs to me to wonder how that's possible, or why my pictures have no people in them, or why all the fish are hiding among waving stalks of kelp-like plants.

The third floor is my favorite part of the house. It's a large attic containing glass-front cabinets filled with figurines, china, and colored glassware. Trunks and boxes, stacked neatly in sections, are filled with discarded clothing, household items, some books, and old photographs. The remainder of the space contains discarded furniture. I am told I may look but not touch anything. I disobey and rummage in one of the trunks for clothes so I can play dress-up. I open one of the curio cabinets to lay my hand on a piece of cool green glass. I like the green glassware best and take a bowl to the window where I hold it up in streaming sunlight. Green light washes over the entire attic and I pretend I'm Dorothy in the Emerald City.

At mealtime, both aunts drink weak tea and there is never as much food as Bill and I have when we are home. My father says they slice their meat so thin a person could read the newspaper through every piece. Bill says they are frugal.

They have slender fingers like Mama, but where Mama's nails are manicured and painted, theirs are short and unpolished. Age spots mottle their skin and bulging blue veins web the backs of their hands. Bill's hands remind me of tree or plant roots. Looking at Aunt Eva's hands reminds me of the story about the time she slapped one of her more unruly students. Before retiring, she taught high school math and did not put up with foolishness. They said he came back to see her after he graduated from college and thanked her for straightening him out. Aunt Eva means business, Bill says. She scares me almost as much as Aunt Bessie does, but between them, I know Aunt Eva and Aunt Effie take very good care of Great Grandma Johnson.

Of Bill's living brothers, Will and his family live in the old farmhouse near Marysville, Kansas, in the northeast corner of the state. They still work the family farm. Bill's brother Sid lives in a big house on the main street in Marysville. He has a wife and three daughters, though his daughters are all grown, and two are living elsewhere. According to Bill, compared to the farmhouse, the houses in Topeka and Marysville are practically brand new, merely dating back to the 1890s. The farmhouse is much older. I always look forward to our visits to Marysville mostly because my Great Uncle Sid is a tease and a story teller.

That first summer in Topeka, Bill and I go with the aunts to visit the state capitol. Aunt Eva says they have been talking about going there ever since they learned we were coming. She wants to show me that beautiful and historic building. Aunt Effie says they want to do it before more relatives arrive and the group would be too big. Bill says when the leaves are off the trees in the winter a person can see the capitol dome from the front upstairs windows of the house on Elm Street.

My aunts and Bill all wear flowered dresses, sturdy low-heeled shoes, and their Sunday hats. Aunt Effie has on white lace gloves, though it's a hot summer day. I have on a Sunday dress that ties in the back and my best black patent leather shoes with white socks fringed in lace. Bill has learned how to make my hair look like Shirley Temple's, the way my daddy likes it, although since he isn't here I don't know why we have to bother. Aunt Eva opens the heavy front door for us and we file past to go inside. She is taller than both Aunt Effie and Bill.

From the floor of the rotunda, I look up all the way to the top of the dome. A metal scaffold around the base of the dome leads to an outside balcony, Aunt Eva says. We look around the rotunda, at pictures of old men on the walls, and Bill reads signs and plaques about the history of the state of Kansas that I am too short to see. Then we enter an elevator. When we step out we are on that metal grid. I peer through the slats at the marble floor below and am instantly terrified. I plop down, grab hold of the railing, and refuse to budge.

"Oh for heaven's sake, stand up," Aunt Eva snaps, clasping her hands in front of her stomach. She tucks her chin, which makes it disappear altogether. "I said stand up."

"Come on, Carole Faye," Bill coaxes. "It's perfectly safe. You can't fall through."

"No," I cry. "I want to go down. I want to go down."

"Well, you can't," Aunt Eva says, tapping her foot. "We're going to the top. You can either come with us or stay here."

"I don't want to stay here. I want to go down. Please."

"Hush," Bill says.

"This is ridiculous," Aunt Eva says. "Just leave her."

In the background as always, Aunt Effie remains silent. She looks unhappy and I wonder if she is afraid of high places, too. I begin to sniffle.

"All right." Bill turns to me. "Don't you dare cry! You're embarrassing me."

"I just want to go down," I wail.

"You stay right here and don't you dare move until I come back," she says. "And be quiet. You're perfectly fine."

"Don't leave me," I wail. My grandmother holds up one hand like she's stopping traffic. She turns on her heel, clicking on the metal platform, and walks away. I could die if I fall through. I can't believe they've all left me. I'm afraid to move. The floor below is hard and cold and far away. I wish now I'd gone with them to the top, but I didn't. All I can do is cower, wait it out, and hope I don't wet my pants.

When they finally come back to get me, Aunt Eva says I'm spoiled. Bill says I'll be all right when we get home and that she doesn't want to hear another word about it.

No one mentions it again.

After spending the morning in vacation bible school at the church down the street, where I listen to a Bible story about birds and flowers and poke dozens of whole cloves into an apple until my fingers hurt, I hurry home where it is a little cooler. I sneak down the basement steps and sit there in the dark. The basement is always cool since it's below ground and the steps are on a side of the house the sun never reaches.

My aunts keep cases of soft drinks, Pepsi and Grape Nehi mostly, on the steps and even though I know Aunt Eva counts the bottles every day, I am determined to sneak one. Aunt Eva is in the kitchen visiting with a neighbor lady so I have to be very quiet and wait until they leave. As I hold a cool bottle to my face, I hear my aunt say, "Well, I never thought we'd have a bastard in the family." Her voice is hushed, but I hear my name, too, and I'm startled. What did she say? Never thought we'd have a bastard in the family? I'd heard my father use that word. It's not a nice word. But how does it apply to me? Is it because she thinks I'm spoiled? What does being spoiled mean, any- way? Is that the same as being a bastard? Aunt Eva may like me less even than Aunt Bessie.

I slide the unopened bottle back in its wooden case and when my aunt goes to the front door with her lady-friend, I go looking for Bill.

She's taking a nap, so I sit down to color until she wakes up. Then I tell her what Aunt Eva said.

Carole, age 6, with Bill in Kansas.

Bill straightens the bedspread on her bed and plumps the pillows. "Are you sure you heard her right? You're sure she was talking about you?"

"I think so," I say.

Bill stands up straight. Her mouth is twisted funny and she looks mad.

"What were you doing on the basement steps where you could eavesdrop on someone else's conversation?"

"It's cool there," I say. I am not about to tell her the truth.

Bill grunts. "Aunt Eva's just jealous because she never had any children of her own."

"If she wanted a baby, she could have adopted one," I say.

"No, she couldn't. Aunt Eva never married, remember?"

Oh. So a person has to be married to adopt a baby. I didn't know that. "Are all adopted babies bastards?"

"I don't want to talk about it anymore," Bill says. "You just forget you ever heard that word. Aunt Eva didn't mean it in a bad way."

Nothing sets a concept more firmly in the mind of a child than being told not to think about it. And how else could she have meant it if not in a bad way?

$\sim 5 \sim$

At Home in the City

Bill and I usually arrive back in Detroit the week before Labor Day. The task of getting me ready for the new school year takes time. Mama gauges how much I've grown over the summer and then we shop for school clothes. According to Mama, I'm hard to buy for.

I like dresses made from polished cotton with a black background. I had one once, with pink flowers, made from feed-sack fabric Aunt Bessie sent us. The flowers were so pretty against the glossy blackness, but Mama didn't think it appropriate for little girls to wear black. I don't know why.

I am hard to sew for, too, Mama says.

"Why can't you be taller or slimmer? No patterns fit you quite right and everything we buy has to be altered. It's so irritating."

That hurts my feelings.

"At least she's not one of those skinny, frail children who are sick every time you turn around," Bill says.

"That's true," Mama says. "Carole hasn't been really sick since we had her tonsils taken out."

"If we buy three dresses and make three," Bill says, "that will be enough.

"Put pockets in my dresses," I say when Mama is inspecting fabric.

"Pockets are hard," she says, but she agrees to try if there is enough material. They have to buy one more piece of fabric. I want the brown one with the zebras on it. Mama doesn't like that one, either.

Highland Park is a quiet, tree-lined neighborhood in mid-town Detroit. It has a mix of houses and apartment buildings, grocery stores, a movie theater, a park, and three schools. Ferris Elementary School has a swimming pool in the basement so every child can learn to swim. We wear ugly red or blue cotton tank suits when we swim, provided by the school system. At least my parents don't have to buy swimsuits for me each year.

The school also has science equipment, a large gym, and a well-stocked library. The building has a low-slung steel chain-link fence along the front. The heavy chain hangs between short brick pillars and provides a place for the smaller children to sit and swing their legs before and after school. A tall metal fence forms the perimeter of the dirt playground. Before school, and after, the older kids gather on the front steps or behind the building, while the younger kids huddle in small groups playing marbles in the dirt.

I like school because that's where the kids are. Ferris School is three-and-a-half blocks from our apartment. So every weekday morning, either Mama or Daddy walk me to school on their way to catch the streetcar to work. Bill comes to get me every afternoon. Less than a month after school starts, on a rare day when Daddy picks me up and walks me home before going to work, he asks me how my day was and what I learned. I mope and don't answer him.

He peers down at me. "Come on. What happened?"

"The teacher wouldn't let me go to recess," I say, looking for sympathy.

"Why not?" Daddy has stopped walking.

"Because some little girl tore up my paper and I had to stay in and do it over."

"That doesn't sound fair," he says.

"That's what I thought."

The next morning Daddy insists on walking me *to* school. He is going to speak to my teacher. He does not approve of punishing me for something another little girl did. "No siree," he says, "I don't like that one little bit. We'll just see about this."

He holds my hand as we walk. I am becoming more nervous with each step, even though I am too young to fully grasp the difference between the truth and a small, political-style spin on reality.

When Daddy finishes talking to my teacher, a conversation lasting all of about fifteen seconds, he comes to get me where I have been told to wait in the hallway. "You didn't tell me the truth," he says. His face is dark as he shakes his head at me. "You tore up your own paper. Then you said some little girl did it."

"Well, I'm some little girl, aren't I?" My father is not amused. Later, though, he does seem to enjoy repeating the story to others.

My first-grade teacher is Mrs. Hope, an elderly, short, gray-haired woman with gray skin and a cloudy disposition. She's old and doesn't like children very much any more, if she ever did. When a child misbehaves or fails to pay attention, Mrs. Hope digs her long, right-hand thumbnail into that child's chin and bangs his or her head against the blackboard. This is designed to obtain the child's undivided attention or drive a point home, so to speak. Most kids just *hope* they get out of her room alive.

Having been around so many old people, however, I have acquired certain survival skills, which I happily employ. I am quiet and never talk back. I answer her questions loudly and look her in the eye. I ask how she is feeling and never run in the hallways when she might be watching. Nearly every other child has his or her head banged or chin gouged, but not me. I thrive in her classroom. Still, recess is always a welcome respite from the tension of being in Mrs. Hope's aggravated presence.

Once that fall, as I am swinging near the edge of the playground during recess, I notice a lady in a long dark coat, white scarf, and dark glasses standing beside a nearby tree. She is watching the children on the playground and I am convinced she is looking directly at me. The next day, there she is again. Maybe she's my "real" mother, I think, come to check on me, to see how I am doing. The third day, she appears again wearing the same glasses and scarf. Maybe my real mother is a movie star, or princess who couldn't keep me for mysterious but unavoidable reasons.

I swing higher, leaning back to let my hair drag the ground so she sees how daring I am. I sit up straight and pump harder and swing higher and higher until the chains go slack and I nearly fall. By the time the swing has bucked and slowed enough so I can jump off safely, the recess bell is ringing and the lady in the scarf is gone. She had watched us, or me, for the entire recess. I hope she will come again tomorrow. If she does, I will wave hello and maybe go over to the fence and talk to her.

But she does not come back. I watch and wait for her for weeks. If she is my "real" mother, is she sorry she didn't keep me? I don't want to be with her, but I definitely want her to want me, to regret having given me away only to find out now that it's too late to get me back. I think that might make me very happy. Still, I never tell anyone about the lady in the white scarf. Not even Bill.

Carole, age 5, performing on the radio at Christmas.

More than anything, I want that lady to be my "real" mother. I want her to want me and not be able to have me. Either that, or I want the whole adoption thing to be untrue. Everyone who doesn't know I'm adopted says I look just like my daddy. Maybe I actually belonged to him, just not to Mama. I'm pretty sure that's possible. I am less certain about the details.

People say I'm smart, though. I can recite from memory the complete Little Golden Book *The Story of Jesus*. I even performed it on the radio once at Christmas. Bill read aloud to me the same stories over and over until I had two of them memorized. *The Story of Jesus*, "One night many hundreds of years ago..." and *The Littlest Angel*, "Once upon a time—oh many, many years ago as time is calculated by men, but which was only yesterday..."

When my grandmother realized I knew most of the

words "by heart" she made me practice until I could say every word in both books upon demand. Each recitation takes about fifteen minutes, not counting the occasional cough or sneeze, hiccup or burp. When the minister at our church heard me (apparently he had not quite believed my grandmother when she told him), he asked if I would perform *The Story of Jesus* for the church's Christmas pageant. Bill said I would. After that, ministers from several other churches call asking me to perform for their pageants, too. Turns out, I am quite the little entertainer.

From the time I am four years old until I am seven, Mama dolls me up like Shirley Temple, my father's favorite child-star, and I make the circuit at Christmas and Easter. Mama, Daddy, and Bill never miss a performance. After that, either no one wants to hear an eight-year-old recite or there isn't a church left in the neighborhood that hasn't.

Bill says a good memory is mostly inherited. Maybe if the lady by the tree knew about my good memory and the fact that I had been on the radio, she'd be sorry she gave me away. But I can't tell her if she doesn't come back. She never does.

The winter I was in kindergarten, Daddy went deer hunting in the Upper Peninsula and brought home a stray cat. The cat adopted Daddy, following him around until he picked her up and began petting her. She was cold and hungry and he fed her. When she snuggled against him and began to purr, he was hooked.

She has gray eyes and the softest gray-striped fur with a nose the color of an eraser. I name her Suzie.

I dress her in doll clothes, a bonnet and booties and little shirts, and include her in my Sunday afternoon sermons. I preach to my stuffed animals and dolls, sermons similar to the one in church that morning. Bill says I'm the best hellfire-and-brimstone preacher she has ever heard. I'm not quite sure what that means, but I think it means I can talk loud and threaten my congregation with the fires of hell if they aren't good.

Some days I put doll clothes on Suzie and take her with me into my cave under the big dining room table that stands at one end of our living room. Suzie sleeps with me, curled up by my side. While I'm at school, I leave her asleep on a pillow in my doll buggy. When I come home she is the first thing I see, peeking up over the edge of the buggy when I open the front door.

One day, about two months after Suzie arrives, I come home from school and find her gone. Mama says they had to give her away.

"Why?" I cry. "Why did you give my cat away without telling me?"

"I'm really sorry," Mama says. "Your daddy should never have brought her home. I just can't stand the smell of that litter box. I gag when I have to clean it and nothing helps, not even baking soda and perfume mixed into the sand. I've tried everything. And it's such a mess in the bathroom, and taking the dirty litter out to the garbage. It's all too much."

"But I didn't even get to say good-bye."

"It's better this way," Mama says. "We found her a good home in the country."

I stop crying. "Is she close by? Can I go see her?"

"That would just upset you, and Suzie wouldn't understand." Mama gives me milk and cookies, but I want my cat. It isn't fair. Suzie will never know I didn't want to give her away. She will always think I didn't care, that I didn't love her. I go into my room and cry for a long time. I would rather have been spanked every day for a year than have my parents give my cat away. I hope they found her a really good home, one that was handpicked just for her.

As an adult, I understand the dilemma Mama faced. This was 1950. There were no plastic trash bags, no absorbent kitty litter with chlorophyll and baking soda. Mama, with the nose of an FBI bloodhound, was highly sensitive to odors. She hated the smell and the mess of a cat box. And she and Bill would not let me clean it up.

I didn't associate losing Suzie with being given away myself. If the connection was there, it was deeply subconscious. But I never forget Suzie, or how much it hurt to lose her.

The City at Christmas

With Christmas less than a week away, the clink of pots and pans tells me Bill is hiding dirty breakfast dishes in the oven again. No one else knows she does that. It's our secret. My father is still asleep and does not like to see dirty breakfast dishes in the sink when he wakes up, but Bill and I are in a hurry. She is taking me Christmas shopping and to visit Santa. I turned six in August, but I still believe in Santa Claus and the presents he brings. My family always exchanges presents on Christmas Eve. The gift from Santa arrives during the night and is the only one I open on Christmas morning.

Last year, I bought Bill two fancy lace handkerchiefs to take with her to church and Mama got her a box of flowered stationary for sending letters to the relatives back in Kansas and Colorado. This year, Mama takes me to see Mr. Pierce in the drugstore downstairs. He suggests she buy Bill a bottle of Evening in Paris cologne, and she does. I get her the smaller ink-blue bottle of Evening in Paris perfume with the silky tassel on the end. Bill will like that, and she'll give me the bottle when it's empty.

Bill dons her winter coat, a wool scarf at her throat. Her slightly crooked hat is held in place by one long hat pin, as hand in hand we venture out into the falling snow. Snow has whitewashed dirty city streets and turned Detroit into a winter wonderland. Music fills the air at every street corner. The city loves itself during Christmas.

"What do you want to buy for your daddy?" Bill's breath fogs the air between us when she speaks so as I look up I can't quite make out her face.

"He likes things he can use," I say. "Let's go see Mr. Turpentine. I can find something for Daddy there."

Bill says his name isn't really Mr. Turpentine, but when we redecorated our apartment two years ago, Daddy bought so much paint and thinner from him, at his hardware store on the corner, I thought his name was Turpentine, and I have called him Mr. Turpentine ever since. He seems not to mind.

"Hi, Mr. Turpentine," I say as we enter the wooden-floored shop to the jingling of a bell. I stomp my slick red boots and shake the snow off my curls. Steam rises from our wet wool coats. The face behind the counter lifts into a cheery grin.

"My, aren't you two out early."

Mr. Turpentine and Bill talk while I shove my hands wrist deep in bins of nails and nuts and bolts—a metal sea. I am mesmerized by the cold, rough sensations against my skin.

"And what can I do for you, young lady?" Mr. Turpentine says, peering down at me.

"I want a present for my daddy." Holding up a black and white folded yardstick, I show it to Bill. "Do you think he'd like one of these?" I unfold it awkwardly.

"He has one," Bill says, taking the thing away from me before I pinch my fingers.

Bright colors catch my eye and I go to take a closer look. It's fishing tackle, and my daddy is a fisherman. At six-and-a-half years old, I am tall enough to see directly into trays of purple rubber worms, golden spinners with slick black feathers, little wooden fish in polka dots or stripes, and heavy teardrop-shaped leaden sinkers of various sizes. "I want one of each," I say.

"The yellow worm glows in the dark," Mr. Turpentine says with a wink.

I hold the yellow worm carefully by one end to avoid the hooks. It jiggles and shines like sunlight trapped in Jell-O that never melts. I want to lick it and wonder if it tastes like lemons or like worms. "Watch out for the hooks," Bill says. She retrieves the yellow wiggler and hands it to Mr. Turpentine. I pick out three more lures and three spinners and pay with dollars wadded into one of Bill's good hankies. We wish Mr. Turpentine a merry Christmas and out we go, into the slush of the city streets.

"On to Hudson's," Bill says, buttoning my coat up to my chin.

We walk, leaning slightly forward against the wind to where the streetcar—a yellow, square-eyed dragon—stops. I remember to walk on Bill's "good" side.

"What do you have in mind for your mama?" she asks, helping me climb aboard when the streetcar stops to pick us up. Its doors fold shut behind us.

"She likes red nail polish," I say, "and China cups and saucers 'Made in Occupied Japan.'"

Bill nods. "That's true, but she needs a new scarf."

"Do I have enough money for a scarf?" I pull my fist from my coat pocket and open it showing Bill what remains of my hoard of coins and my last dollar bill, now a prized possession. Three coins fall to the muddy streetcar floor. Bill holds the handkerchief while I pick up the coins. A man has to move his foot off my nickel. He frowns down at me.

"I know what I want to ask Santa while we're there," I say as I drop the muddy nickel onto Bill's palm.

Stepping off the streetcar, we hear bells playing Christmas songs and carols. A light snow has started to fall. Through the flakes I see store windows and lampposts all decorated for the holidays. I am so excited I am almost breathless.

We stand in a long line for Santa and when it is finally my turn, he lifts me onto his knee. "Ho, ho, ho. And have you been a good little girl this year?"

I cross my fingers behind my back and nod.

"Well then." When he glances up at Bill I see the string around his ears holding his beard in place, but he is my only hope.

"You just tell old Santa what you want."

"I want a dollhouse," I say, "just like my great grand-mother's house, or the one in the McGregor Library, only smaller. Mine doesn't have to have electric lights, just fur-niture and people. And I want the perfect present for my mama."

Santa nods. "There are some very nice handbags on the second floor," he says to Bill. He smiles at me. "And *you* will find just what you want under the tree on Christmas morning."

"Was he the real Santa?" I asked Bill as we step onto the "Up" escalator.

"He's one of Santa's helpers, I think. Santa's very busy this time of year."

We wander up and down the aisles of hats and hand-bags, gloves and scarves, until—"Look!"—I spy the per-fect scarf, white with yellow, green, and brown designs, all Mama's favorite colors. "Oh look. It will go with her mou-ton coat!"

"I think you're right. She'll like this very much."

Bill helps me pay and collects the change. Outside on the street, she lets me drop the change into a bucket for another one of Santa's helpers. After that, we go across the street to Saunders for hot fudge sundaes.

Back home in our apartment, before Mama comes home from work, Bill pulls the dirty dishes from the oven and piles them on the counter. She fills the sink with hot, soapy water.

"I don't want to wash dishes," I say. "Let's wrap presents."

"Later. Right now I have to do these before your mama gets home."

"Leave them in the oven," I say. "She never looks in there."

"I made meatloaf for supper and I need the oven."

"We could put them under the bed." Once Bill hid the dirty dishes under the bed because the oven was full and we were going to Belle Isle.

"Don't you ever forget anything?" She laughs. "I tell you what. You help me with the dishes now and I'll help you wrap presents later. And if there's time, I'll read more *Rabbit Hill.* Would you like that?"

I nod. Bill knows that's my favorite book. I can almost read it myself, but I like to hear her read it better.

"When we wrap presents," I say, "you can't see the present I got for you."

"And you can't see what I got for you, either." She wrinkles her nose at me.

"What *did* you get me?"

"I am not telling; it would spoil the surprise."

"No it wouldn't." I lie.

"Would you like to peel the carrots for the roast?"

"Do I have to?"

"No. You can run along and play and let me work. I'll be right here."

After supper on Christmas Eve, when it's already dark outside, we turn on the lights on the tree. They reflect in the living room windowpanes, making the room even more beautiful. Just before the distribution begins, one more present for me appears beneath the tree.

I get socks and underwear, a pair of pajamas, and a matching robe from Mama and Daddy. Bill gives me a set of Chinese checkers in a metal box. Hard Christmas candy, a yo-yo, nuts, and an orange are in my stocking.

Daddy holds up the new package. "Why, look at this. Where do you suppose this came from?"

Mama takes a look. "Says 'From SANTA.'" She holds the box next to her ear and gives it a little shake. "Wonder how Santa managed to put it under the tree without anyone noticing?" I wonder the same thing.

"Magic," Daddy and Mama say simultaneously.

Years past, I received, "From SANTA," a red wagon, a complete set of Lincoln Logs, glass wind chimes, and a big stuffed animal. This year I am expecting a dollhouse. But the box is too small. When I open it, I see that it's a Cinderella doll. I like it, but it isn't my dollhouse.

Then I remember what Santa said. My dollhouse would be under the tree on Christmas morning. I will have to wait.

Mama, dressed in her best pink and black taffeta with a full skirt, and Daddy, in his good charcoal suit with a red silk tie, are ready to go to a party. It's snowing again and Mama has on the new scarf I gave her. They leave me with Bill. As soon as they are out the door, I ask Bill about my dollhouse. She says I will have to talk to my parents about that.

The next morning I wake early and run into the living room, positive that Santa will keep his promise, but it isn't there. There is no new, unopened present for me under the tree.

At breakfast, I bring it up again. Mama sighs. "We bought a dollhouse for you months ago and hid it. But when it came time to wrap it, we couldn't find it."

"We've looked in all the places we could think of. It's just gone," Daddy says.

How is that possible?

"Stop pouting," Bill whispers. "You'll make them feel even worse than they already do. They can't afford to buy you another dollhouse."

"Why not? Are we poor?" I ask.

"The dollhouse they got for you was a very nice one," Bill says. "More expensive than the doll."

Later than night, while we're playing with my new Chinese checkers set, I look up at Bill. "I really wanted that dollhouse, and Santa promised." I know I'm whining, but I can't help it.

"I guess he didn't know it would be lost or stolen," she says.

I consider that. "The *real* Santa would have known. Wouldn't he?"

～ 7 ～

Of Lice and Lies

As soon as first grade ends, we move, leaving our apartment above the drugstore forever. My grandfather, who lived in Kentucky, has died, and my dad wants to move there and remodel the old house. Years ago, before Mama and Daddy married, he bought seventeen acres and a house for his parents. After Daddy's mother died, Daddy's sister, Ida, moved in to take care of their father until he died. We visit there most every summer for a week in June, but I have never lived there. The old house is small and has no indoor plumbing.

"Where will Aunt Ida live?" I ask, as we are packing up our new, second-hand, blue panel truck.

"She'll live with us. You and Bill will still share a room," Daddy says. "And Aunt Ida will sleep in the middle bedroom."

"This is going to be fun," Mama says. Something in her tone of voice makes me wonder if she means it.

Daddy's two brothers, John and C.K., live within a mile of the old house. Uncle C.K. has a dog named Rocky. I play with Rocky when we are there. Uncle John is a carpenter and will help Daddy with the remodeling. Uncle C.K. works in the mines.

My daddy can do anything, repair anything, build anything. Daddy and Uncle John plan to dig a basement and move the old house back from the road. They will add

Carole, age 4, with Aunt Ida on the front porch of the old house in Kentucky before Daddy remodeled it.

an indoor bathroom, another bedroom, and enlarge the kitchen. Daddy says when they finish it will be beautiful. He is going to paint the house white with green shutters and put window boxes with red geraniums under the front windows. Maybe now I can get another cat.

I start second grade at Sturgis Elementary, and while I am not unhappy, making friends isn't easy. I'm from the north so to them I talk funny, and although I ride the bus with three or four other girls my age, they do not seem interested in letting me join their group. I miss my friends and my cousins back in Michigan.

One day at school, I make a new friend. We sit beside each other in reading group. Her name is Martha. I am so excited, because Martha invites me to come home with her after school and spend the night. At lunch I call Mama to ask if I can.

Carole, age 7, with Mama, at a time in my life when we looked the most alike.

"What? No! You can't go home to spend the night with some little girl we don't even know. Where are you calling from?"

"The principal's office. Martha is really nice. She says it'll be okay with her parents. You can't call them. They don't have a phone right now, but Martha says they won't mind."

I hear my mother's long-suffering sigh, so I wheedle some more until she asks Daddy what he thinks about letting me go home on a different school bus after school with a child they didn't know. Aunt Ida overhears the conversation.

"Carole Faye could argue paint off the side of a barn," Aunt Ida says. I hear Daddy in the background.

"Who is it she wants go home with?"

Mama tells him and I hear him laugh. "Yeah, I know 'em. Hell, let her go. It'll teach her a damn good lesson."

"Oh, Kenneth," Aunt Ida says. "You can't do that."

To me, these adult cautions are not red flags at all and I am not deterred. "Pleeeease. Let me. I never get to have any fun." Martha is my new "best friend." After all, I reason, grown-ups don't understand about new best friends.

"All right," Mama says, "but don't say we didn't warn you."

Martha and her family live in Henshaw, a small rural community about three miles farther west than the one in which we live. Their house sits very near the road and is reached by a wooden plank over a drainage ditch leading to two concrete-block front steps and an unpainted front door. There is no lawn, no garage (they don't own a car), no driveway, no flowers, no garden, and no shutters on the windows. The siding, which I think had once been painted white, is now mostly raw wood turned gray and splintery.

Inside, the two-roomed house smells of bacon grease and mildew. The living room is also the bedroom, with a kitchen separated by a wall and door across the back. There is no indoor plumbing. An outhouse sits at the end of the backyard by the chicken coop. A pump for bringing water up from a cistern stands ten feet from the back steps.

Martha and I play in the backyard while supper is being prepared.

After supper, which consists of stewed meat, potatoes, and onions, Martha and I play checkers and then get ready for bed. We undress behind a curtain at one end of the kitchen and brush our teeth with baking soda and a cup of water as we hang over the railing on the back porch. Martha and her little brother share a toothbrush. I use my finger. Martha's mother lays out a soft bar of soap and a dishpan of water warmed on the stove for washing our faces and under our arms and then finally our feet. Martha's mother hangs my clothes inside a chifforobe in the living room so they won't be wrinkled for school the next day.

We all sleep on beds in the living room. Her little brother is on a half-bed. Martha and I sleep in one of the two double beds with iron frames. As we snuggle into a pile of old quilts, Martha whispers, "If you hear Mama and Daddy doing something in the dark, don't pay 'em no mind. Just go back to sleep."

During the night, I wake to scratching sounds and raise up on my elbows to see what it is. Martha's parents appear to be sleeping soundly. I am about to lie back down when a rat the size of a football scurries across the floor in front of the fireplace. After that, whenever I doze off, I wake with a jolt, afraid that rats are climbing up the bed frame.

The next afternoon, when I arrive home from school, Mama says, "Get in the bathroom and take off all your clothes and let me check your head. Aunt Ida says those people have lice."

"They do not tell lies," I say. "And how would Aunt Ida know anyway?"

"Not lies, lice," Mama says. "Bugs. In your hair."

"Oh." At the word "bugs" my head begins to itch. "I don't have bugs," I insist, scratching another itchy place.

"And brush your teeth. Then get in the tub. You have to have a bath right now."

Mama washes my hair with a strong shampoo that smells like pine. She makes me bathe with the bar of Lava soap we keep on the sink in the basement, nearly scrubbing me raw, and then she checks my hair.

I was right. I am not infected with lice, but Aunt Ida boils my clothes anyway, just to be on the safe side.

At supper, Daddy says, "How'd you like your night out? Did you have a nice time at your friend's house?"

I peek up at him. "It was okay," I say, halfway between wanting to tell him about it and needing to defend my actions and my friend. "They were very nice," I say, "but I'm glad to be home."

He nods. "Good." I think I see a smile turn up one corner of his mouth.

I want to tell him that how Martha and her family live is not funny. Besides, they *were* very nice to me. They were just people who happened to be literally dirt poor. The experience does, however, make me appreciate my home in ways I had never before considered.

My relationship with my father was always difficult. He was affectionate when I was a baby, but not after I entered school. He thought I ought to be toughened up, that I was too soft. I thought he was unnecessarily cold. That combination made for an unhappy situation.

By winter, the remodel of the house in Kentucky is finished and my father is looking for work. Good paying jobs are scarce and mostly involve mining. Daddy is determined never to be a coal miner, but he is also not the kind of man who can be still even when he is unemployed. He almost always has some kind of project, often more than one, going on at all times. Except for coffee and cigarette breaks throughout the day Daddy is always moving.

That first winter, he decides he wants to make home-made sausage and smoked hams the way they did when he was a boy. He says he wants to see if he can replicate the taste he remembers so fondly. To that end, he builds a smoke house and fences in part of the field on the west side of the house. He buys a pregnant sow who later gives birth to several babies. When they are weened, he sells all but two pink, wiggly, adorable piglets that I name Petal and Pinky.

"Don't let yourself become attached to those pigs," Daddy warns.

"Why not?

"Because we're going to have suckling pigs in the spring, that's why. Your Aunt Ida and I have been planning for this all year."

I didn't understand he meant he was going to kill Petal and Pinky when they were still small. I didn't know most pigs were slaughtered. I also didn't know that pigs are the smartest of the barnyard animals.

Daddy also warns me repeatedly not to wander too close to the fence and that mother sows are notoriously mean. So I watch the piglets play but cannot pet them. I do get to hold them once or twice with Daddy's help. They are squeally and squirmy and very cute. I help feed them most every day all our table scraps and once in a while I get to scratch the little ones behind their ears.

The day Daddy butchers them they are four months old. It is a cold and sunny late fall morning. I am caught off guard and do not realize what is happening, even when I hear the pigs squealing and the mother sow bellowing. Daddy carries each piglet by its feet down into the basement. They struggle and scream; I follow him, tugging and pleading with him not to do it.

"What did you think these pigs were for? I told you they were not pets."

"Nooo. You can't kill them."

"Carole, stop it. Just shut up." He is furious. "If you don't want to hear this, run down to Uncle John's house."

He hangs the screaming, struggling piglets by the feet and takes out a long butcher knife.

I run. "You're horrible and I hate you," I scream, but not until I am well away from the house where he can no longer hear me and I can no longer hear the screaming of the terrified piglets. Daddy hadn't even shot them so they would die quickly without knowing what was happening.

I could not save Petal and Pinky from my father's butcher knife any more than I could save snowflake from Aunt Bessie. I stay at my Uncle John's house for the rest of the day and later refuse to eat Petal and Pinky.

I didn't understand why my father and I were so

different. I didn't think about the fact that I was a young girl from the city and he was a man who had been raised in the rural south where families ate mostly what they killed themselves. Such facts did not enter into the equation for me then. I thought we were so different because I was adopted. Daddy killed animals with knives and guns. I could never do that. How could he? How could anybody? Instead of wishing he would change, I longed to be his natural child so we'd be more alike and he would like me better. Maybe then my life would be less painful because living with someone who didn't appear to have any sympathy for the suffering of other living creatures was, for me, not very easy.

~ *8* ~

About Cousins

My favorite Michigan cousins are Mona and Beverly on my dad's side of the family, and my favorite cousin on Mama's side is Karen. Mona has black hair and Beverly has light brown hair. But Karen's hair is blond. She's the only blond in the family and I think she is very pretty. I get to see her most summers when Bill and I travel west, which we do during our second summer in Kentucky. That summer we stop in Kansas before going on to Colorado.

We have hardly darkened Great Grandma Johnson's door when I begin pestering Bill. "When is Karen coming? When is Karen coming?"

"Rudy said they'll arrive next week."

"When next week?"

An hour later, I ask again. Finally, Bill says, "Asking over and over won't make her get here any sooner. If it would, she'd already be here."

I give up and wait in silence.

Karen is Aunt Bessie's step granddaughter. Aunt Bessie has one child, a son named Rudy. He and his wife, who is Karen's mother, live in Alamogordo, New Mexico. Karen is a year younger than me, but when we are together, either in Kansas or New Mexico, we have the best time.

Rudy and his family arrive late on a Sunday evening. Early the next morning Great Grandma Johnson asks to see us. After she has held our hands and touched our faces, she asks Karen, "How do you like school? What's your favorite subject?" Karen likes school and her favorite subjects are history and English. I suspect she is good at all of it. Great Grandma Johnson asks me the same things. I like reading and art. After a brief visit, she sends us off to play.

"It's too bad you didn't come last week," I tell Karen. "You could have come with me to vacation Bible school."

That year I make a wooden puppet with strings. I think it's ugly, but Karen says she likes it.

"Let's walk down to the church," she says. "Lunch won't be ready for a long time." So that's what we do while we are waiting for the aunts to make lunch. The day is very warm, but the tree-shaded street keeps us cool all the way. We stay outside or in the attic as much as possible.

That night, Karen sleeps on a pallet in the room with Bill and me. The next morning, after we brush our teeth and dress, we hear Great Grandma Johnson crying. We go to her bedroom door to see what's wrong. She is alone and sitting up, looking as fragile and dry as a mummy. She sniffles.

"What's the matter?" Karen asks. We hurry to her bedside and pat her hands and arms. "What's wrong?" we ask. "Don't cry."

"Eva wants me to take my medicine and I don't want to," she says. "It tastes bad and I don't like it."

We pat her some more and kiss the paper-thin skin that covers her bony cheek. "You don't have to take your medicine if you don't want to," I say.

"Not if you don't like it," Karen says. We want her to stop crying and she does, which pleases us greatly. Convinced we have been a big help, we are about to go off to play when Aunt Eva comes in carrying a tray with the medicine on it. Great Grandma Johnson turns her face away. "The girls say I don't have to take my medicine."

Carole, age 6, with cousin Karen, age 5, and Aunt Eva, Karen's mother Mae, and Bill on the farm in Kansas.

"What girls?" Aunt Eva asks, frowning. She and Aunt Effie are always referred to as "the girls."

"Karen and Carole Faye," our great grandmother says.

Aunt Eva gives us a look that could stop traffic. "Mama, they're just children. They don't know what they're talking about. You have to take your medicine." A struggle ensues, during which Karen and I sneak out of the room and up to the attic, which is where Aunt Eva finds us some time later. She is spitting mad.

"Don't you ever contradict anything I tell my mother," she fumes, wagging her finger in our faces. "Especially not about her medications. She's very sick and has to have her medicine. Do you hear me? How dare you interfere with things that are none of your business? It better never happen again, I can tell you that."

She stomps away down the stairs, leaving us in stunned silence. When the door at the foot of the steps slams shut, we erupt into uncontrollable laughter, doubling over and clutching our stomachs. For the rest of the day, we only have to look at each other to ignite a gush of giggles. Whenever we are alone, we egg each other on with Aunt Eva imitations, complete with sputtered threats delivered through protruding teeth. And though we have great fun at Aunt Eva's expense, we do also worry that we might have actually hurt our great grandmother.

While we are together, Karen and I spend much of our time playing princess in the castle. We drape dusty lace curtains around our shoulders, wear discarded hats when we can find them, and fence with unused curtain rods. Karen is precocious, and at seven, is the one who creates most of the dialogue. In all our time together, we never break anything in the attic, and we never again tell our great grandmother she doesn't have to take her medicine.

The reason we came to Kansas first this summer is that this is the week of Great Grandma Johnson's ninety-fifth birthday. With the birth of Rudy's son, Jared, a few months earlier, there are now five generations of my great grandmother's family present—Great Grandma Johnson herself, my grandmother Amanda, Aunt Bessie, her son Rudy, and finally Rudy's new baby. They gather on the front porch for photographs. A woman from the *Topeka Capital-Journal* has come to take their picture for the newspaper.

"You girls stay over there out of the way," Aunt Eva says, standing Karen and me out in the yard where we will not impede the flow of traffic on the porch. We scratch mosquito bites on our bare legs and watch the proceedings. Karen says we are excluded because it's a photograph of the five generations of my grandmother's family.

"They don't want us because we're not blood related," I tell Karen. "I'm adopted and you're not Rudy's real daughter." I am such a helpful child.

"That's not true," Karen says. "We aren't part of the five generations. That's all."

I don't argue, but I bet if she were Rudy's real daughter, she *would* be on that porch—and I *never would* be.

We watch Grandma Johnson holding baby Jared. "Do you like having a little brother?" I ask Karen.

"Not really," Karen says. "He can't even talk. But Mom and Rudy like me best." Karen always seems fiercely self-assured.

"How do you know that?" I ask.

"Because after they had him, they said they didn't want any more babies."

"Sometimes I wish my parents had adopted another baby," I say. "I want someone to play with, and someone else who will get into trouble once in a while."

"If you had a brother or sister you'd have to share everything," Karen says. "You're lucky."

I mull that over. Maybe being an only child isn't so bad after all. It's lonely and very quiet, but I don't have to share anything with anyone, not my toys or my space or my mama. And I don't have to share Bill. The more I think about it, the more I decide Karen is probably right.

After the photographer leaves, several other cameras emerge. This time everyone poses for pictures. "You girls sit in front," Bill says. "We need you to brighten up this group." You can't fool me. I know what's happening. Bill is being nice to make up for having to exclude us from the important picture.

That same summer, after Aunt Eva accuses us of trying to kill our great grandmother, we all go to visit Bill's brothers in Marysville. We walk across the farm, climb fences, and jump creeks, listen to the call of the western meadowlark, and admire the cattle. In the evening, everyone gathers in the old farmhouse to eat and talk. Over coffee and dessert at the kitchen table, we pore through tattered black-paged photo albums sandwiched between the cold fireplace and the hot stove.

Uncle Will is mostly quiet, but Uncle Sid holds forth with family stories and tall tales mixed in, after which Karen and I pepper him with questions.

"Tell us about your daddy, and how he went to the Civil War when he was a boy," I say.

"His name was Hutchison Johnson," Uncle Sid says. "He enlisted when he was seventeen. Walked with the Iowa Volunteers all the way to north Georgia, leaving his sweetheart Amanda (for whom Bill was later named) behind. He was gone from Ottumwa, Iowa, for nearly four years. During his absence, Amanda created a hair wreath woven into the shapes of flowers and leaves from strands of her own long dark hair. She laid the wreath around a drawing of her face and framed it under glass. While she worked, she prayed for Hutch's safe return. When the war ended, he came home uninjured. They soon married and for a year or more were very happy. But Amanda died giving birth to their first child, who also died. They say Dad was inconsolable. He burned down the cabin he'd built for Amanda, saving only her hair wreath and one quilt she'd made with scraps of his clothes."

Uncle Sid pauses to drink his coffee while it's still hot. He takes a bite or two of blackberry cobbler and glances over at me and then Karen. We are sitting across from him, leaning forward, our eyes wide as he continues the story.

"Hutch worked the family farm with his father and lived alone for twenty more years before he met and married Laura Francis, your great grandmother. She was nineteen years old, with fair hair that hung nearly to the floor. They were an unlikely looking pair, don't you think?" He holds up a photograph of them. "See how young and sweet she looks, and how he looks like Moses÷"

The old man in the picture had a huge full beard, a hard mouth, and cold eyes. I wouldn't want to be his little girl, that's for sure.

"Hutch Johnson and Laura Francis were married for more than thirty years and had nine children. They came into northeastern Kansas in a Studebaker covered wagon when your grandmother Amanda was three years old. They homesteaded, built the farmhouse, and had eight more children. Did you girls know your great grandmother finished raising the younger kids and kept the family farm going after Hutch died? That wasn't easy. She's quite a woman."

My cousin Gerald, Uncle Will's only son, leans over and whispers, "Why do you like all those family stories so much? It's not even your family."

I pull back. Everyone else is eating or talking or looking at pictures. "Sure it is." I set my jaw. "It's my family as much as yours."

He frowns. "No it isn't. You were adopted. We aren't redheads. You don't look like any of us."

With a couple of thoughtless remarks, cousin Gerald had tried to obliterate my entire family history. I thought he was as mean as a sidewinder on hot sand, descended for sure from old Hutchison Johnson.

The morning before Bill and I are scheduled to board the train for Grand Junction, the day after Karen leaves with her family to return to New Mexico, Bill says she has something to show me. I follow her into the foyer where she opens a drawer in a small side table. I stand beside her and watch as she extracts a huge old family Bible. The Bible is beautiful with a heavy hand-tooled leather cover and thin, gold-edged leaves. I run my finger around the pattern on the top.

"This Bible has been in the family for more than a hundred years," Bill says as she opens it. In the front, is the family tree listing all the members of her family going back several generations—Bill's mother and father and her grandparents and great grandparents names are there, as well as her brothers and sisters and their wives, husbands, and children. There is my grandmother's name, Amanda Laura Johnson, and next to it is Edgar Williams, and beneath their names are my mom and dad's names, Mona Venda and Kenneth Kirchner, and below that is written, "Carole Faye, adopted daughter." Next to those names are the names of Aunt Bessie and her first husband, Rudolph, and their son Rudy, and his son Jared. But Karen's name isn't there at all.

Bill thought she was being helpful. She'd heard what Gerald Johnson said to me about them not being my family. But if being adopted didn't matter, why record my name that way and leave Karen's off altogether? There was only one explanation. They did it that way because it did matter—to them—just like I'd always known it did.

~ *9* ~

Siblings for Six Weeks

After eighteen months in Kentucky, Daddy and Mama are out of money. Daddy can't find a good job, except for coal mining, and he still vows he will never do that. So we rent the house to a couple from eastern Kentucky and return to Michigan. It's almost February and there are no vacant apartments to be had, so we move in with Daddy's niece Jenna Lou and her family, which includes my cousin Mona, just until we find our own place.

Daddy looks in the paper every day but so far has not been able to find housing we can afford. I register for school where my cousins attend and we settle in for a longer stay. Mona is in fourth grade and her younger brother Bubby is in first. Mona and I are nine and eight respectively, so we get along much better than when we were little. In other words, she has stopped biting me and I have stopped scratching her.

Jenna Lou's house is very small, only three bedrooms and one bath. So Bill moves in temporarily with a friend from our old church in Highland Park. It gives her a break from looking after me, Mama says. I see Bill every weekend. She looks cheerful and rested and says she is enjoying herself.

Jenna Lou's house is located on a side street just off a major thoroughfare about two miles from our old apartment on Hamilton. The house is covered in yellowish-brown shingles with a detached single-car garage at the end of a narrow fenced-in backyard. An alley runs behind that. Inside, the house has a nice kitchen with a dining area set up at one end of a long living room. I share Mona's room, and Mom and Dad sleep in Bubby's room, while he is relegated to temporary sleeping quarters on a cot under the stairs in the basement, which he immediately turns into a fort-like affair that Mona and I are not allowed to enter on penalty of death.

For an only child, staying with my cousins and their family is wonderful. We play games every night and some nights Mona and I talk for hours. The three of us kids never argue, and that's not even the best part. The best part is there's more energy in a house with several children in it. The school is only three blocks away and we three walk there and back together.

Daddy has returned to his old job of bartending at the country club. He leaves for work at two o'clock and works until the bar closes after the last customer leaves sometime after midnight, so he wants his main meal at mid-day. One Saturday, two or three weeks after we move in, Jenna Lou calls us to the table at noon. Daddy sits down, spreads his napkin on his lap, and looks at his plate. "What's this supposed to be?"

"It's Chop Suey with rice," she says. "Chicken and vegetables. I thought it might be a nice change."

My father takes two bites and shoves his plate away. "I look forward to a decent meal once a day before I have to go work. You know I'm a meat and potatoes man. This stuff isn't fit to eat." Jenna Lou's face falls and her cheeks splotch a hot pink. She stares at the table. Mona and Bubby remain silent. Unfortunately, I don't have sense enough to do the same.

"I don't like it, either," I say. Mama tries staring me into silence. "Well I don't. It's stringy."

Carole, age 4 , with cousin Mona, age 5, in Detroit.

"Oh, hush." Mama kicks at me under the table.

Mona giggles.

"Well shit-fire!" Jenna Lou bursts into tears, slams her fork down, and leaves the table.

Mama shoots me another dirty look.

"I can't help it if I'm a meat and potatoes man, too," I say.

"If you open your mouth again, I'm going to spank you. Just be quiet."

I sulk and stare at my plate, which is swimming in some kind of gray gravy with stringy pieces of cooked celery and long white fibers of what is supposed to be chicken. What kid wants to eat shredded chicken and cooked celery for lunch? Plus, my father does not take my side. That isn't fair.

That next morning, I overhear Mama and Daddy talking. "Jenna Lou was just trying to cut expenses with the Chop Suey. I'm sure it's difficult to have three more people underfoot and at the table," Mama says.

"I'll give her some more money," Daddy says. He doesn't say he'll apologize, however.

Jenna Lou is very particular about her house. Each room has been painted a carefully selected color. Most of the furniture is second hand or hand-me-down, but she has made all the drapes and the slipcovers and rag rugs to go with the walls. She starches and irons all the curtains, starches and irons all the sheets, and starches and irons every pillowcase we use. She makes each bed every morning with those perfectly ironed, snow-white sheets and spreads and fancy quilts. She never leaves the house with an unmade bed in it and threatens to beat any child who dares look at one of her beds, much less sit on it, unless they are bathed and ready to get into it. Her own bedroom and bed are all white with lace on the pillows and dust ruffle. She also has a schedule for cleaning: dust Monday, mop Tuesday, vacuum Wednesday, shop and put away Thursday, laundry Friday, iron Saturday, cook and rest on Sunday. Mama helps make the beds and do the cleaning, cooking, and laundry. Mona and I do the dishes most days.

Among Jenna Lou's most prized possessions is a beige and red wool area rug in the living room. Those crisp clean beds, meticulously crafted curtains, and fine wool rug must hold significance for her beyond their dollar value. Perhaps they connect to her sense of self-worth and the soundness of the choices she had made. Mama tells me repeatedly to be careful not to damage in any way the walls, furniture, linen, drapes, or rugs in the house. I try to be careful but it makes me nervous.

After Daddy brings home a large hunk of prime rib from one of the cooks at the country club, there is a thaw in relations between my dad and Jenna Lou. That pleases everyone and soon she and her husband Gordon and my folks are talking and laughing again as though there never had been a tense moment or unkind word among them.

Winter drags on. Every day Mona, Bubby, and I bundle up and trudge to school and back without incident. When a heavy wet snow falls, blanketing cars, streets, yards, and trees while we are in school, we meet at the end of the playground to walk home together. Fortunately, we are all wearing our boots. As we leave the schoolyard, three boys from Mona's class taunt her and call her names. Fatso, they shout, and pig-face. Two are bigger than she is. The smallest boy calls me ugly and four eyes. Bubby comes to our defense, calling them stupid and pushing the smallest boy down in the snow. Bubby is large for his age. As the downed boy gets up, Bubby yells, "Run!" So we run, with the three older boys chasing us. I can hear them yelling and screaming and calling us names, but we are half a block ahead and determined to maintain our lead.

We beat them to our house, get safely inside, lock the back door, pull off our wet coats, hang them up, and leave our galoshes on newspapers as instructed. Then we hurry to the living room windows to see if the bullies are out there.

To our dismay, they are, all three of them standing in the front yard screaming names at us and hurling other insults. The boys, dressed in jackets and dark knit caps, look very cold. Why don't they go away, now that we are in the house?

"What did you do to them?" I ask Mona.

"Nothing." She snorts. "I beat them in a math game and it made them mad. They said I cheated and I said they were stupid and they said they were going to get me."

In addition to fatso and four-eyes, we hear various combinations of stupid, dumb, ugly, and you stink. We yell back, "No, you stink," and "You're the dumbbells."

Still, the bullies refuse to leave. Clearly, more drastic measures are called for. Bubby opens one of the living room windows—to make sure they can hear us clearly. Since Mona and I are taller, we help push the shining clean window up as far as it will go, adding to what we blithely take to be our home-court advantage. There are no screens on the windows, the screens having been removed the previous fall and stored in the basement, and there are no storm windows, either. Splendid. We hang out the window and scream in unison something like, "Go away, you stupid morons!" We stick out our tongues and taunt them for being dumb enough to stand outside in the cold and wet while we are warm and dry inside. Surely that will do the trick, I think.

With a look of maniacal glee, one boy grabs a handful of snow, smashes it into a large ball, and tosses it through the open window. The snowball hits the edge of one drape and lands on Jenna Lou's wool rug. Splat! Two more hard-packed, dirty snowballs follow; one hits the opposite wall. Until that moment, I have been screaming and yelling and participating mindlessly, caught up in the excitement. Now, I am starting to be afraid. What if we can't stop them? What if they come in the house?

We scoop up what we can of the snow and toss it back outside. Then we reach up to close the window. The window we had worked so hard to open as wide as possible is now stuck—and so are we. No matter how hard we pull and tug, it will not budge. As the bullies close in, we panic. They fling half a dozen snowballs into the house while we try to block them and scoop the snow up to throw it back. One icy gray snowball after another comes flying into the open window while we desperately try to block the opening with our bodies, the drapes, and the back of one upholstered chair, the one Mona's father likes to sit in while he listens to the radio and reads the paper.

We are screaming now. "No!" and "Stop!"

The boys, red-nosed, snow-soaked, and grimly determined, continue throwing snowball after snowball as fast as they can make them.

Plop! Splush! Thwack! Soon we are soaked, as is much of the living room floor, furniture, rug, and drapes. While I scoop up slush and dump it out the window, Mona screams at the boys to stop. Bubby slips and slides on the filthy muck that now gives off a sour stink and steps on one corner of the sagging drapes. Both panels and the rod all fall to the floor to be trampled in the slush.

Frantic to end the carnage, Mona goes out the front door, and Bubby gets a butcher knife and goes out the back door. The situation is so desperate I pray for an adult to come home now. As Mona screams at Bubby to get back in the house and put the knife away and I scream at them both to come back inside, my prayers are answered. My parents arrive. They are only fifteen minutes late.

The bullies flee, but Mom and Dad do not go after them. Instead, they come in the back door. My father fills the doorway between the kitchen and the living room. Mama gasps at the wreckage and sinks onto a dining room chair, her hand covering her mouth. Before she can speak, Jenna Lou and Gordon pull into the driveway.

As all four adults survey the damage, Mona tries giving our side of the story.

"Those bullies…"

"Be quiet. I don't want to hear it," her mom says.

I take a stab at it. "It wasn't our…"

"Don't open your mouth," my dad says.

"What were you thinking?" Mom says.

"We didn't start…"

"I don't care who started it. How could you?" Mama says.

Bubby pipes up. "But those guys…"

"I said shut up," Jenna Lou says.

We go to bed without supper. Both mothers sob well into the night, each in their separate rooms. My parents have to be wondering not only how they can help pay for the damages, but how fast we can move out.

We move the following weekend to a furnished upstairs flat on Dexter Avenue and I change schools one more time to finish third grade. I don't even remember the name of the school. We never lived with Mona and her family again, and saw them less and less as the years went by.

My parents must have been thinking that anyone who had kids on purpose was a fool. Though the snowball fiasco wasn't my fault, I had participated. And as Jenna Lou pointed out, "We've lived in this house for years without anything like this happening—until now."

This was a disaster of unprecedented proportions, and one my parents could hardly afford. It damaged my father's relationship with his favorite niece and her family and for that I was extremely sorry.

Like some of the aunts on Mama's side of the family, neither my aunt Ida nor her daughter Jenna Lou seemed very fond of me. Years later, another cousin told me they said no one they knew ever adopted a stranger's child and they never thought it was good idea. In addition, they blamed Mama for Daddy not having children of his own, though it was never clear whose fault their childlessness actually was.

We settle into our furnished flat and wait for school to be out. Mama and Daddy want to send Bill and me west for the summer, but can't really afford it. We don't go to Kentucky that June, either, because Daddy has no vacation time yet. Besides, my father is barely talking to me. After several weeks of the silent treatment, Mama intervenes and Daddy agrees to take me fishing in Marine City.

When we go fishing, it's always to the same place where Daddy rents a boat and buys bait. We always bring the same lunch, so one trip blends into all the others—except for this one. We are trolling along the American side of the river. I am relieved Daddy's speaking to me again even though he is not much of a talker at the best of times. Especially when he is fishing, he wants to be quiet.

"Where's that big boat from?" I ask.

"Look at the back when it passes," he says, softly. "Its origin is on the stern."

"What's it hauling?"

"Different cargo." He pulls his hat down a little lower on his head and turns away.

"Where do you think it's going?"

"Chicago maybe, or Duluth," he says, without turning back.

"How do the big boats get their names?"

"Whatever the owner wants, I guess." He hunches his shoulders.

"Did that one come all the way across the ocean?"

He sighs. "Can't you be quiet for five minutes? You're scaring away the fish."

I watch the big boats and wonder about them. Mama knew a stowaway once. He got arrested, but then he married an American lady before they could deport him permanently, and now he is back in the country working. Maybe there's a stowaway on that big boat right now watching us, wondering who we are and how many fish we've caught and what we have to eat in our little boat.

"Will it scare the fish if we eat lunch now?" I ask.

We have fried egg and sausage sandwiches and iced-down bottles of soda pop, homemade cookies in waxed paper, a bag of potato chips, and paper napkins. Around two in the afternoon, we head back to the dock to return the boat, clean the fish we've caught, and load up the car for the trip home. Before he goes inside to pay for the boat rental, he gives me a warning.

"Don't go back down to the dock. The river is unusually low for this time of year and the planks in front where we pulled the boat up are covered in slippery green slime."

Daddy at his favorite fishing camp on the St. Clair River.

If he hadn't mentioned it, especially the part about the green slime, I wouldn't even want to go back to the dock. I'm tired of fishing. But now I want to see that green slime. What does it look like? How green is it? Is it shiny? How slippery is it? To my mind, I am not disobeying; I am merely checking it out for myself.

As it turns out, the moss is very green and *very* slippery. I put my foot on it and press down ever so slightly. My foot shoots out from under me and I pitch backwards, hitting my head with a thwack and plunging me into the icy water of the wide and swiftly flowing St. Claire River. I go under the water and under the dock.

Daddy, who could not have seen me fall, hears me hit the water and knows instantly what I've done. He runs to the far side of the pier where he lies down so he can reach me when I come out from under the dock. When I do, he grabs my shirt collar and hauls me out of the water. Had he not thought and acted quickly, I really might have drowned.

He sits me sopping wet in the back seat on newspapers and we ride all the way back home in total silence, an act of great restraint on his part, he says. Later, as he is explaining to my mother and grandmother how I happened to come home drenched, he says he was so mad he was afraid he might kill me if he ever got started so he just kept quiet and drove. "She was just determined to disobey me," he says. At least in telling them the story, he laughs. I take that as a good sign.

Looking back, I think my father was afraid I might actually be stupid rather than merely willful. He did not seem to think it possible that curiosity had overridden his command to stay put, and I suppose it shouldn't have. As soon as Mom and Dad saved the money, they packed my grandmother and me off to the west again for the remainder of the summer.

∼ *10* ∼

Crisis of Faith

Every Sunday, no matter where we are, in Highland Park, Topeka, or Grand Junction, Bill takes me to church. From Aunt Bessie's house we walk down the dusty road along the canal to the little Baptist church on the highway. Aunt Bessie is already there. She opens up and turns on the lights.

"Were you ever baptized?" I ask Bill as we walk and I drag the toes of my shoes in the dirt. "You know, like your whole body underwater—head and all?"

"Yes I was," she says. "The preacher came from another county in January to baptize several of us. They had to break through the ice to perform the ceremony. We all thought we'd freeze to death."

"Why didn't you just wait until summer?" I ask. "You could have caught pneumonia!"

"What if we didn't survive the winter?" she says. "Lots of folks didn't back then. I wanted to be ready to meet my maker. I was thirteen, and that meant I wasn't a child anymore."

I wonder if Bill will think I'm all grown up when I'm thirteen. I doubt it. I wonder if my biological parents are Baptists or something else. I wonder if it matters.

One Wednesday evening, Bill takes me with her down the road to hear a missionary from the other side of the world.

It is a special program to raise money for his work, Bill says.

In the church basement, we sit in a semi-circle, me next to Bill, with several other ladies around us including Aunt Bessie. I am the only child. After sharing photographs, and telling us about his school and clinic and church, the speaker peers over the lectern and asks the audience what happens to the unbeliever if "they never hear the good news, never learn of God's grace through his son, Jesus Christ?"

When no one answers, my hand goes up. Bill tugs at my sleeve. "Shush." She pinches me.

"Ouch," I say. Several people laugh. That hurts my feelings. Getting pinched by your grandmother is not funny.

The speaker points at me.

"They are condemned to hell," I say. Bill elbows me sharply. She really wants me to be quiet and I would if someone else had volunteered to answer.

The speaker's expression is serious but kindly. He shakes his head.

"We might easily think so, but no. They are considered in a child-like state and therefore are not subject to the everlasting fires of hell."

Heads around us bob up and down, arms fold across ample chests that heave in solidarity with the speaker's point.

"They cannot be held accountable," he continues, "for what they have never heard. But *we* are required, in scripture, to bring them the message of salvation so that they might have a more abundant life. And in doing so we lay up riches in heaven for ourselves for every soul we save. Amen. Hallelujah."

The audience is all smiles. Heads nod even more vigorously.

I am stunned. Acquiring riches is part of this deal? My hand pops up. Bill begins to fidget and her eyebrows levitate. "Hush," she hisses.

I shirk her off. "So what about after they've heard *The Word*?" I ask. "What happens to their souls then, if they don't believe?"

"That's different, isn't it?" The speaker sighs dramatically. "You have reached the heart of the matter. They must believe or face eternal damnation. And we must help them." He spreads his hands, palms up, in front of him. "This is our calling, our sacred trust."

Okay, now I am seriously concerned about the heathen. By this man's account, they are perfectly fine just the way they are; they don't need us. Aren't we all created in God's image? Hearing the story of the Gospel puts their immortal souls in peril. He just said so. Did I miss something? This is not fair. I mean, how likely is it any heathen is going to believe the story of Jesus unless, like us, they'd grown up with it. What could be worse than telling the heathen about Jesus and having them disbelieve? Their eternal damnation would be our fault. And my grandmother and I have been supporting foreign missions for years. I am horrified. Of course I could not articulate my concerns that clearly at the time, but I had them nevertheless. I did not say, "Let me get this straight," but I must have been thinking something along those lines because I raise my hand and ask another question. Bill pinches me hard on the leg, but I persist.

"They go to heaven if they've never heard about Jesus, but may go to hell after we show up and tell them? Is that right?"

"Well, in a manner of speaking," he says, "but…"

"Then shouldn't we stay home and not tell them?" I say.

A lively discussion ensues. Bill is furious. She says I just don't understand. I ask her to explain it to me. "I can't explain it now," she says. "It's an old argument. But you are a child and you should not be talking about things you don't understand. When we get back to Highland Park, you can ask Rev. Hughes about it. For now, just be quite. You've said quite enough."

Well that was totally unhelpful. How can I learn about things I don't understand if I can't talk about them and ask questions? Do people just automatically know more when they turn thirteen, or eighteen, or fifty? Do they? Somehow, I didn't think so.

After the service, as we wait outside the church for Bill, Aunt Bessie fusses at me some more. "You embarrassed me in front of my friends and neighbors. Why can't you just be quiet like other children?"

The missionary is at the door saying good-bye to people and thanking them for their contributions. He walks up behind my aunt and lays a hand on her shoulder. "Don't be angry with the child," he says. "She's a natural leader. Other children will follow her lead, look to her for direction and guidance. Therefore," he glares down at me, "she has to be mindful of what she says and you must help her see that."

Now I'm doubly horrified. I don't want anyone following me. I don't even know who I am, and I certainly don't know where I'm going. I'm not a leader. As usual, Bill is right. I should have kept my big mouth shut.

That summer when we leave Grand Junction, we take the train to Alamogordo, New Mexico, to visit Rudy and his family since they will not be traveling to Topeka. Bill is his grandmother, too, of course, and helped raise him the same way she is helping keep me. She adores Rudy and is anxious to see him.

They live on top of a mountain at a place called Sun Spot. It's where the National Solar Observatory has been established and Rudy works there taking pictures of the sun for the scientists who study solar flares. While we are at Sun Spot, we watch a three-stage rocket blast off from

Carole and Karen in front, with little Jared, and more of Bill's family in Kansas.

the missile range at White Sands. Everyone is very excited about that, but all I see is a long white tail in the sky.

Karen and I pick wild flowers, especially Indian paintbrushes, explore the woods around the compound, and play make-believe among the trees. We catch horned toads and play caveman with them. Horned toads look like little dinosaurs, but are generally gentle and eat leaves, although one bit my finger once and I screamed. That made Karen fall down laughing. I must have looked pretty funny with a toad hanging off my finger while I ran around crying and jumping up and down. It didn't hurt. It just scared me.

I wish Karen and I were real cousins. Maybe then I'd get to see her more. She always makes me laugh, and apparently I serve the same purpose for her.

One evening, during supper, Rudy says he has been listening on the shortwave. "They're talking about war in Korea," he says.

Korea is a long way away. The missionary we heard in Grand Junction works in Korea. Why is America involved in a war way over there? I hope the war isn't because of our missionaries.

~ *II* ~

Piano Lessons Plus

After spending a week in New Mexico and two in Kansas, Bill and I return to Detroit to a new apartment. While we were away, Mama and Daddy moved from the furnished flat back into Highland Park to an apartment building directly behind Ferris School. Though I have been away for two years, I hope some of the kids I knew in kindergarten and first grade will still be there. Maybe they'll remember me, but even if they don't, I am very happy to be living back in Highland Park. Our new apartment is also less than a block from Woodward Avenue and the McGregor Public Library.

Our apartment building is u-shaped around a center courtyard with benches and flowers and trees. Because ours is in the very front, on the third floor, we have more windows than the interior units. I still share a bedroom with Bill, but the living room is large enough to hold a sofa, two chairs, end tables and lamps, and a brand new floor-model television. Mama has gone back to her old job at the restaurant downtown, so now we have more money.

On Labor Day, Daddy takes us all to a new beach on Lake St. Claire. The water is warm and the air even warmer with a hazy silver sun overhead. We unpack the car and carry our picnic basket, a small red cooler filled with ice and soft drinks, and an old army blanket to a level, grassy spot where we spread out to enjoy the view. An ocean-going ship makes its way across the lake.

The beach is filling up with people like us who have come out of the city to enjoy the last warm day of sunshine and semi-fresh air. Mama refolds the towels we brought and Daddy opens a bottle of ginger ale for himself and a Coke for Mama. Bill sits on the canvas folding-chair we brought for her and shades her eyes under the brim of her straw hat.

A rope stretches from a large white sign to a post several yards out into the water. It divides the beach in half. The sign on our side says, "For Gentiles Only."

I turn to Bill. "What's a Gentile?" I've heard the word in church, but I don't really know what it means.

"White people," my grandmother whispers.

There is so much noise crowded around us that I don't understand. "What people?"

Bill sighs like a puff adder and rolls her eyes. "White people," she repeats carefully and quietly, "rather than Jews and Negroes."

"Oh." I look at the sign and the rope and the water. "I don't get it."

Mama, who usually is at work when I ask Bill hard questions, intervenes, evidently thinking she can explain the situation better than my grandmother. "This side of the beach is for Gentiles," Mama say, "and the other side is for everyone else, everyone who isn't considered a Gentile."

The best picnic tables are on our side of the rope. We have the widest part of the beach, too. We even have some grass and playground equipment. Sand is pretty much all the other side has.

I frown. "Why?"

Mama throws her hands up. "I don't know. I didn't make the rules. Can't we just enjoy the day?"

I turn back to Bill. "So are we Gentiles?"

"Yes," Bill says. "Of course we are."

Why did she say *of course?* And how does she know for sure I'm a Gentile since I'm adopted?

"I thought we were German-American and Irish on Daddy's side and English on your side. I never heard anything about us being Gentiles. Where do they come from?"

"Gentiles are everyone who is not Jewish," Mama says in a hushed, but emphatic tone. "Or a Negro. Now stop asking."

"What about Spanish people or Koreans? Are they Gentiles?"

"No. They are all non-Gentiles, as far as I know." She rubs a spot between her eyes. "I don't know any more than that. Just hush. For goodness sake."

I am confused. "Are Negroes Jewish?"

Mama gives me one of her long-suffering sighs and leans close. "Neither. This beach is restricted. It means all non-whites swim over there." She grits her teeth. "We'll talk about it later."

I'd heard that promise before. Usually, there is no later. I scratch my arm and gnaw a hangnail.

Nope. There is no way to make this all right. A vague, uneasy feeling has come over me. I can't name it, but it means, I don't like being a Gentile if that's the way we treat other people. I consider this situation for a few moments.

"That sign is the stupidest thing I ever saw," I say, loud enough for several nearby families to overhear. One lady, standing a few feet away on a blanket, has stop shoving her blond hair under her white swim cap and is obviously listening.

"If we're not supposed to swim together," I say, "what good does a rope do? The water doesn't know the difference."

During this entire exchange, my father has been staring off in the opposite direction, swigging down his cold drink, hoping no doubt that I will shut the hell up.

"If you think it's so stupid," he says, softly, "the next time we come here, you can stay home."

"Okay, I will," I say. "That rope is not fair."

My father has a pained expression on his face, as though if he hears me say the word *fair* one more time his head might explode. "They could have made the whole beach for Gentiles Only," he says, setting his empty bottle in the sand.

I had not considered this even worse scenario. "Nobody would do that," I say.

"All right," Mama say. "That's enough. Good Lord. The sun is shining. It's a beautiful day. Be quiet and enjoy yourself."

My dad gets up and stalks off into the water. Mama follows, laughing and splashing, trying to cajole him back into a better mood. I hunch over my ginger ale. Going to the beach isn't as much fun as I'd thought it would be.

My grandmother scoots forward to speak to me privately. "You did the same thing in Chattanooga when you were six," she says. She isn't smiling, but her face has softened.

"What did I do in Chattanooga? I don't remember that. There's no beach in Chattanooga, is there?"

"I don't mean exactly the same thing. It was the summer we first lived in Kentucky." She takes off her glasses and wipes the lenses on her skirt. "I wanted to see where my papa fought during the Civil War—especially the battles of Lookout Mountain and Chickamauga Creek. So one weekend the three of us drove down into Tennessee. You weren't seven yet."

"Was that the time we saw Rock City?"

"Yes. That's also where you saw your first 'Colored Only' signs on the drinking fountains and restrooms. You kept asking what that meant. Your mother tried to explain, but the more she said the more upset you got. You went on and on about how awful that was, how it wasn't nice to treat people that way. Caused quite a commotion." Bill laughs. "Your mother was afraid the police would come and arrest us, or fine us, or something. She kept trying to shut you up and get you back in the car."

"I probably just wanted to be the center of attention," I say.

"No. You rarely want to be the center of attention. You really didn't like those signs."

"Was Mama very mad at me?"

"I wouldn't say she was mad exactly. She just didn't want any trouble." Bill rubs her chin. "Life is hard. Most things aren't always so black and white."

"What does that mean?" I say.

She sits back in her chair and closes her eyes, letting the sun warm her face. Our discussion is over.

I don't know why I am so different from my parents. But I know one thing. I would never create a public beach and then try to separate people and make half of them feel bad, like they were unwanted. Daddy says I just don't understand. But he's wrong about that.

On the Tuesday after Labor Day, I start fourth grade and meet several old friends, Susan, Sandra, Doreen, Agnes, and Janet, but almost from the first moment, my best friend is someone I didn't already know, Mickey (Marion) Locke. Mickey lives with her mom and little brother in a house on Tuxedo Street. The house has a picture window in front and a white sectional sofa in a turquoise living room with pink accents. It is the most beautiful room I've ever seen and I want one just like it when I grow up.

Mickey and I plow through fourth, fifth, and sixth grades together. We make each other laugh and by sixth grade are even skipping school from time to time. About the only things we don't do together are church and my Saturday piano lessons.

For Christmas that first year, Mama and Daddy buy me a small, second-hand, upright piano. It fits perfectly in one corner of the living room. After that, every Saturday, I ride the streetcar or the bus downtown to take lessons in the Maccabees Building near where Mama works.

After each lesson, I want to tell Mama she's wasting her money. Whatever gifts I might have, if any, musical talent is not among them. But she is determined, so I keep taking lessons. I think she is hoping for a miracle. Bill wants me to practice at times when it won't disturb the neighbors. That would have to be when no one is in the building. At least I'm not screeching into a trumpet or strangling a clarinet.

After each lesson I usually have time to kill before meeting Mama, so I walk over to the Museum of History or the Detroit Public Library next door. Sometimes I cross Woodward and go to the Detroit Institute of Art. I like looking at all the paintings in the art institute and reading the newspaper in the library, but my favorite part of Saturday, after my piano lessons, is going into the basement of the Museum of History. Down there is a street of dioramas that begins with depicting life when Detroit was a fort on the river. Each showcase moves forward in time by twenty-five to fifty years, from the late 1600s to the present 1950s. I could look at each scene for hours.

When I get hungry, I walk a block to the restaurant where Mama is working. We have a late lunch and then I sit in the back corner reading or coloring and wait for her to get off work so we can go home together or out shopping. Her restaurant only serves breakfast and lunch so it closes at four when all the nearby office workers and Wayne State University employees and students go home. Once, I talk Mickey into coming downtown with me, but she doesn't like it as much as I do.

During fourth grade, between air raid drills in the event of atomic war and searching the sky for enemy aircraft and UFOs, which we are told is our patriotic duty, Mickey and I manage to make reasonable grades. Miss Tibbits is the best teacher I ever had. She teaches us about art and reads aloud from the classics like *Huckleberry Finn* and *David Copperfield*. She plays classical music for us on her phonograph. I never knew there was such beautiful music in the world. It makes me want to stop taking piano lessons even more because I know I will never come close to being able to play music like that.

Miss Tibbits is also the only teacher I ever had who took her class home. She lives with her mother, who serves us tea and cookies and shows us her dark house filled with books and little figurines she and her daughter have collected from around the country and the world. Some of the students laugh at Miss Tibbits behind her back. Mickey says that's because she's too old to be a teacher.

"How can she be too old," I say, "if her mother is still alive? Maybe she just looks old because she never got married."

"Maybe," Mickey says, "but I can't wait for fifth grade. We're gonna get Miss Mack."

Miss Mack is young, not long out of college, and likes sports. Miss Mack is short and stocky and teaches us basketball and volleyball, which is great. During fifth grade, we spend a lot of time in the gym. Unfortunately, Miss Mack also loves spelling bees, which is not so great. I am what Mama calls a creative speller. In spelling, my arch nemesis is Patricia. No matter how many words I manage to memorize, Patricia knows more. To make Patricia jealous, I kiss Johnny Kozak by the schoolyard fence. Patricia likes Johnny, who has black hair and blue eyes and is the cutest boy I have ever seen—a Tony Curtis look-alike. Johnny knows how cute he is, too.

When we kiss, he tries to hold me while our lips touch, but I push him away, though not too far.

"Why do you always do that?" he asks one day.

"Do what?" I say.

"Push me away. Do you want me to kiss you or not?"

"I don't know. I guess I want you to kiss me. Don't you like being pushed away even a little?"

"Not really."

I think about that and what I'm doing. I often instigate kissing and then push the boy away, even Johnny. I can't seem to do it any other way.

"If you keep pushing me," he says, "I'm gonna kiss somebody else." And he does. He kisses Patricia. I hate her and spelling.

I don't know why I feel compelled to kiss the boys and simultaneously push them away. What am I trying to accomplish? Maybe I push Johnny away so I can be kissed without feeling guilty. Or maybe I am driven to see what it feels like to be wanted but not available. I'm not sure, but I'm fairly clear about one thing: whatever I'm doing, it doesn't have much to do with the actual kissing part.

Our sixth grade teacher is Mr. Granger. He is very nice looking, but he can't control the class. His room is chaos and I don't like that. But I don't do anything to make it better. In fact, I take advantage of his lack of control to skip school, kiss the boys in the cloakroom during class, pass notes, and sneak snacks and comic books into my desk. I am not sure what I'm learning, but I know Mr. Granger is not my favorite teacher and I am certainly not his favorite student.

Fortunately for me, my kissing days on the playground and in the cloak closet soon come to an abrupt end when I get braces on my teeth. In one long dental appointment, enough metal is installed in my mouth that, if magnetized, would make my face point north. According to Bill, my teeth were as crooked as a dog's hind leg. So although braces are outrageously expensive, I get them. I am one of the few children in school wearing braces and I compulsively cover my mouth now when I smile because my teeth are so ugly. Also, I don't want to cut anyone's lip by kissing them, and I don't want to cut my own, so no more kissing. My grades begin to improve. My parents think it's because I finally have a male teacher who won't put up with any nonsense.

In the spring of 1955, the apartment across the hall becomes vacant and is leased by a Mr. and Mrs. Fink. Prior to moving in, Mr. Fink comes to clean the apartment and repaint. His wife is not well, he says, but she works and he is between jobs. My parents sympathize and welcome him to the building. Apartments don't change hands often in our building, so my parents are curious about our new neighbors.

For several days, Mr. Fink arrives at the empty apartment with paint cans and brushes, drop cloths and wallpaper, mops and other cleaning paraphernalia. Mom and Dad invite him over for coffee twice. A short man, only about half a head taller than Bill, and balding, but Mama says he's very nice. He is especially polite to Bill, who gives him lunch one day when he forgets to bring his own and knocks on our door to ask if we have some cheese and crackers or an apple he might eat to tide him over until he gets home.

One day, when Daddy goes to the track before work and my mom is already at work, Bill sits down on the couch to listen to her favorite soap opera and is soon snoring. It is unseasonably warm out and all our windows and doors are open so any breeze can waft through and cool us off. Across the hall, Mr. Fink is painting the woodwork around his front door. All his doors and windows are open, too.

I take a bath and wash my hair so I can go outside later and meet Mickey on the playground. We are going to the library. To get from the bathroom to my bedroom, I have to pass the front door in my bathrobe. I don't think anything of Mr. Fink seeing me in my belted bathrobe, with my hair in a towel. My dad and our other neighbors sometimes take the trash down the hall to the garbage chute in their bathrobes and I am not even out in the hall. When Mr. Fink sees me, he gives me a cheerful hello and motions for me to come over. I don't hesitate. He says he has something he wants to show me.

"What?" I say, glancing around the empty apartment. At a time when most apartment walls are painted some shade of white or wallpapered with flowers, Mr. Fink has painted his living room walls a deep rosy pink trimmed in white, which I think is beautiful.

He sets his paintbrush down on the paint can lid and closes the door behind me.

"You're getting to be a pretty big girl, aren't you?" he says. "How old are you, now?" "Eleven," I say. That's a lie. I won't be eleven until August.

"That's such a nice age." His eyes dart back and forth, looking at nothing. "You know, we could have a lot of fun together," he whispers. "You like fun, don't you?" I nod cautiously. I am standing with my back to the closed door. "We could have fun, you and me, if you don't tell anybody," he says. "You wouldn't tell on Mr. Fink would you, just for having a little fun?"

I am more curious than alarmed, but I do think it's strange that he is referring to himself by his name. "What kind of fun?" I ask.

"It will be a surprise, but only if you promise not to tell."

"Okay," I say.

"I love little girls. They're all so pretty. Can I have a look? Just a peek." He pulls the belt on my robe and the robe falls open. I am wearing bright red cotton underpants and a white tee shirt that I got for Christmas last year. My tummy pooches out and I am embarrassed. Between my poochy stomach and my braces, I think I'm pretty ugly. I pull my robe back around me. "I have to go," I say.

"Don't go." He sounds breathless. "Do you like candy?"

"What kind of candy? I'm not supposed to eat candy with my braces."

"Chocolate won't hurt your teeth," he says. "I don't have any chocolate with me, but I'll bring some tomorrow. How about money?" He shoves his hands into his pants pockets. "I bet you just love silver dollars." He pulls out one silver dollar and licks his lips. "I have lots of silver dollars. I'll give you more if you play a little game with me." He reaches for my robe again. I step back against the door. He whispers, "You know Mr. Fink wouldn't hurt you. I just want us to play, have a little fun. No harm in a little fun now, is there? You like playing games, don't you?"

Why does he keep saying that? I like playing games with my friends, but not with an old neighbor. I find the doorknob and open the door behind me. He does not try to stop me. I back through the doorway. Mr. Fink's knobby knuckled fingers hook the belt of my bathrobe again. What he's doing is not nice. I know that, but I can't seem to react very fast. I am supposed to be polite and respectful of older people and never make a fuss. I wonder what kind of fun I could have with him. On the other hand, what he's doing is naughty. Still, I wonder what he'll do next. Suddenly, he is rubbing the front of his pants like he has an itch.

"I think I hear my grandma," I say. Our apartment door, across the hall, is still standing wide open just the way I left it.

Mr. Fink lets me go. "You come back tomorrow," he whispers, "and I'll have chocolate for you and more money, lots of money. You can do anything you want with it, but only if you keep our game a secret. Remember, it's just a little harmless fun. Okay?"

"Okay," I say.

Before I close our apartment door, Mr. Fink glances up and down the hall and whispers, "We are going to have lots of fun, you and me."

I smile and nod and shut the door. I flip the lock in case he tries to follow me. Letting Mr. Fink see me naked, which is what he wants to do, I think, isn't my idea of fun. That's why I didn't take his old dollar or actually *promise* not to tell. I had not crossed my heart and hoped to die or made a pinky swear because Mr. Fink isn't a very nice man.

He thinks we are going to play his game and that I won't tell, but what he doesn't know is that I plan to tell Bill almost everything.

Still, I hesitate. I do not want to talk to Mr. Fink again, but I can't decide what to do. I hate to wake Bill up. And if I tell her what happened, she won't like it or she might not believe me because she likes Mr. Fink. But if I don't tell, he might think I want to play his nasty game. I could wait until Mama comes home from work and tell her, but I don't want to upset her after a hard day's work. Maybe I shouldn't tell at all. If I do tell, I wonder if I'll get Mr. Fink in trouble. I never got a grownup in trouble before.

"Bill. Bill. Wake up. Guess what just happened."

Her eyes flap open. She sits up. "What?"

After I finish telling her, she stumbles to the phone and calls my mother at work. I hear some of what she says, though her voice is low. A brief silence follows.

"I was asleep on the couch," she says. Her face is red and she looks like she's about to cry. "The door was open," she says, her hand fluttering up to her throat. When she hangs up, she says my mom is going to call my dad, who is at work by now. Mom will be here as soon as she can.

"Why is she leaving work? Nothing bad is going to happen now."

I ask if I can call Mickey to tell her I can't meet her at the playground. Bill says yes, but to make it quick. When I get Mickey on the phone, I don't explain, but say I will tell her all about it later.

Then Bill tells me to go to my room and get dressed and not to come out until she says it's all right. I think she must be mad at me for talking to Mr. Fink in the first place, but how was I supposed to know he isn't a nice man?

Bill is acting so strange, I am getting nervous. After I dress, I sit on my bed gnawing my nails and spitting out the pieces. I peer out the window onto the courtyard and street below, waiting for Mama.

Within a few minutes, a police car pulls up and parks in front of our building, and then Daddy is there, too. I thought he was at work. He parks, speaks to one of the officers, and enters the building by the side door. I hear him running up the stairs. Mama is not home yet. The two policemen remain sitting in their squad car, facing forward. Next, I hear thumping and banging and yelling. Suddenly, Daddy shoves Mr. Fink out the side door and into the courtyard. Mr. Fink hits the ground. His nose is bleeding and he stumbles trying to get up as Daddy hits and kicks him. By then, I am screaming and sobbing and banging on the window, terrified my father will get hurt and be arrested. What have I done? I should never have told. I am so scared. This is all my fault.

The policemen get out of their car and shove Mr. Fink onto the back seat. They slam the door, say something to Daddy, and then drive away. Daddy is rubbing his knuckles as he walks back to the building.

By then, Mama has arrived. She comes to my room to

check on me. She assures me this is not my fault. But the blood was real. Mr. Fink was hurt and so was Daddy. How is this not my fault? Both Bill and Mama insist I did exactly the right thing. Still, I am not convinced. Daddy cleans up and goes back to work without even coming to my room to tell me he's all right.

Mama sits with me while I cry. She strokes my hair and tells me everything is going to be all right. Bill says she feels terrible. If she had not fallen asleep none of this would have happened. She should have known he was up to no good. Mama says if he was going to try something, better now than after they moved in.

"According to the police, Mr. Fink is a known child molester and pedophile," Bill tells me later. I ask her what a pedophile is. She says that is a person who's crazy and likes to hurt children, which really scares me. Why had he picked on me? It never occurred to me that he had rented the apartment precisely because a young girl was living just across the hall. Nor did I realize he had been nice to my parents and grandmother to put them off their guard. And, since he had been jailed before on molestation and attempted rape charges, his wife knew perfectly well that he should not be around children. She knew I was in danger and did nothing.

When my parents realize I will have to testify in open court against him, they drop the charges Daddy had filed against Mr. Fink. At the time I did not consider that a court might have ruled my grandmother unable to care for me adequately, but I imagine my parents thought about that issue, among others.

For the remainder of the school year, Mickey and I decide it's our duty to be on the lookout for Mr. Fink, since, according to my grandmother, he's neither in jail nor in the hospital. To protect other girls, Mickey and I hide in doorways and peer up and down streets and alleys playing detective. If we see a man, any man, who fits Mr. Fink's general description, we run headlong in the opposite direction, excited to the point of shrieking by our own terrified imaginings, weaving in and out around parked cars and garbage bins, circling the block until we reach the safety of Mr. Myoski's Corner Grocery, where we collapse in excited giggling fits.

Now I become aware of older girls in school talking about s-e-x. Clearly, I need more information. There are things I do not understand about where babies come from that maybe I need or want to know. I decide there are only three ways to accomplish such a mission. I can ask the older girls, I can go to the library and try to find a book on the subject, or I can ask Bill.

The beautiful McGregor Library is a huge tan stone building facing Woodward Avenue. I enter through its tall metal double doors that look like angel wings to me. I bypass the big dollhouse I usually stop to admire, and walk directly to the head librarian's desk.

"Excuse me. I want to read about sex," I say in a normal voice. Then I whisper, "You know, where babies come from. Can you help me?" The librarian's jaw actually drops, then snaps shut again. She eyes me suspiciously. I try not to blink first. She has a long sloping nose the exact same shape as her face. I've never seen anyone with a nose quite like it, except for Bob Hope.

She cocks her head. "How old are you?"

So age is an issue. Hmm. Bill said thirteen was almost grownup. "Almost thirteen." I say. I figure almost thirteen is better than almost eleven.

She glares at me while she makes up her mind. Finally, she opens a drawer in her desk and takes out a set of keys. "Come with me."

She leads me across the marble foyer to a small door near the front of the building, pulls the keys from the pocket of her smock, and unlocks it. The door opens onto a small, windowless, closet-like room with floor to ceiling shelves filled with thick, old, darkly bound books.

"Sit here." She points to a table with leather-padded seats on the chairs. My feet don't even touch the floor. I tuck one leg under me and prop my elbows on the table. "You can only read these in this room." She sets two large books before me. "You may not check them out or leave the room unattended. When you finish, come back to my desk and tell me. Do you understand?"

I nod and open the first book. Here are some serious books. I don't think I can read much of the text, but the illustrations are good—dozens of pages of drawings and information, in more detail than I want. This is not dirty. It's scientific. I flip through page after page for nearly an hour, mostly new information, although there have been hints along the way, remembering Mrs. Peacock and baby Leonard and what the older girls whisper about in the girls' bathrooms.

I don't connect what I see in the pages of these books, the acts between men and women that lead to babies, to what Mr. Fink wanted to do. But I do decide why my mom and dad have no children of their own. That's because they don't do s-e-x. My "real" mother did, I guess, but my mama and daddy don't. Of that, I am convinced.

The following Monday, before school, I tell Mickey what I learned about why I think my parents have no children of their own. She practically falls over laughing.

"Of course your mom and dad 'do it.' All grown-ups 'do it,'" she says.

"No they don't. It's not nice,"

"Okay," Mickey says after she stops guffawing. "Ask your grandma. I dare you."

I have no intention of asking Bill any such thing.

After school, Mickey tells one of the older girls what I said.

"You are such a baby," the older girl says.

"I am not."

"Yes you are. I bet you never even said it."

"Said what?"

"Fuck. I bet you never even said it once in your whole life."

"I have so, lots of times." Of course, she's right. I have never uttered that word—although from time to time I have heard my daddy say it, especially when he's really mad or when he's hurt himself. He also says, hot damn, son of a bitch, and, of course, bastard.

"Oh yeah. Let's hear it, then," the older girl says. "My mommy and daddy fuck. Go ahead, say it. I dare you! I double dog dare you!"

I don't know why she is so insistent—but a double dog dare simply cannot be ignored. Nevertheless, after I say it, I feel guilty. God hears everything, right? Besides, no matter what Mickey and the older girls say, I still don't believe my mama and daddy you-know-what.

The minute school is out for the summer my parents send Bill and me packing again. No doubt they want me as far away from the city and Mr. Fink, who is still out there somewhere, as possible.

As soon as we arrive in Grand Junction, I walk down the road to the next farm to find my friend Charlotte. I tell her what I've found out about sex and where babies come from. She says she's known about all that for years. "Can't live on a farm and not know where babies come from," she says.

"Do you think all grown-ups do that?" I ask her.

"Sure," she says, "but mostly when they first get married, I think."

Maybe Mickey was right after all.

I envy Charlotte's life around animals. When you live in a third-floor apartment in a big city, you miss out on all sorts of things, like pets and other animals and vegetable gardens and tree houses and the smell of freshly mowed hay and grass and flowers in bloom and clean air.

The giant weeping willow tree whose branches sweep the ground is still our playhouse and refuge. Beneath its draping limbs, inside its swinging green walls, where no grass grows around the trunk and no one on the outside can see us, we live pretend stories and tell each other our secret longings. We have set up a table and chairs and collected broken cup and saucer pieces from Charlotte's and my aunt's houses. We name our sanctuary Weeping Willow Playhouse. I confide to Charlotte that I am going to be a famous actress when I grow up. She says she is going to win prizes with her horses and maybe become a veterinarian.

One day, I tell her about Mr. Fink and that Daddy called the police and Bill said he liked to hurt children.

Charlotte tells me about a time when her mom and dad thought she had been killed.

"What happened?" I ask.

"They got a phone call from the police saying I'd been in a car accident and that they needed to come to the hospital right away."

"Were you hurt? I never heard anything about you being in a car wreck," I say. If that had happened, Aunt Bessie would have told me.

"No," Charlotte says, "It wasn't me, but it was still terrible. That other Charlotte Jenkins died and my parents thought it was me until they went to identify the body and saw her face. I was at a friend's house and didn't know anything about it." Charlotte sighs. "Mama says I can't imagine how hard that was." Charlotte crinkles up one side of her face. "Then the hospital had to find the real parents." I am so glad my friend Charlotte hadn't died in that car wreck.

For the month we are in Grand Junction, I go to church every Sunday and after church I go to Charlotte's to play for part of the afternoon. I have my first hayride with Charlotte and her family. In one of their pastures, Mr. Jenkins shows me how to feed a calf from a bucket. The little calf butts the bucket so hard he knocks me down. We laugh and laugh. Mr. Jenkins dips our hands in milk and lets us feel the rough tongue of one calf who tries to suck our fingers off. It's not a new sensation for Charlotte, but I have never felt anything like it. I shriek and giggle until I'm so weak I'm on my knees. I wrap my arms around the little calf's sweet smelling neck. He seems to like being hugged and nuzzles against me.

I will miss the farm and the animals and Charlotte when I return to Detroit. But this year, because we are older, Charlotte and I promise to write until we see each other again next summer.

$\backsim$ *12* $\backsim$

Another Moving Experience

While Bill and I were in Kansas and Colorado, Daddy and Mama moved again. Daddy took a new job at a country club west of the city, and rented us a house on a hill overlooking a small lake. Both the lake and the house are beautiful, and I am glad to be there, but once again I didn't get to say good-bye. I never thanked Miss Tibbits for being my favorite teacher, and I never said good-bye to all my friends, not even Mickey.

My parents moved in the summer while Bill and I were out of town because it was easier for them to sell our belongings, pack up, and drive away when we were not there. But it is not easier for me, and I doubt if it's easier for my grandmother. Each time we move, she loses all her friends and the church she loves. It does not occur to my father that either of us might want or need to say good-bye. At least Bill can write to some of her friends explaining what has happened and where she's living. I could write to Mickey, too. I know her address, but it seems pointless. I also know I will never see her again.

Though our new house is no more than thirty miles west of Highland Park, it might as well be a thousand. Instead of two- and three-story houses and four- or five-story apartment buildings with small shops tucked here and there,

*House at
the lake.*

the surrounding landscape is all rolling hills thick with trees and a lake in every valley. The houses have manicured lawns with flowers blooming in every one. There is even wildlife—squirrels, rabbits, frogs, and water birds. The people who live around here have more money than people back in the city. The girls I go to school with have closets and drawers full of pretty blouses, skirts, jackets, and sweaters. Cadillac convertibles sit in driveways all around the lakes. Every house on the water has a dock and a speedboat. Our house is not on the water, but for the first time in my life I have a room of my very own. I think living at the lake means we are coming up in the world.

Daddy's new job sounds important. He has gone from being a bartender at a large urban country club to being the manager of a small rural country club with a nine-hole golf course, a restaurant and bar in the clubhouse, a swimming pool, and two tennis courts. Twin Beach Country Club just opened and Daddy is now its manager. He works long hours and commandeers both my mom and my grandmother to help out. Mom has quit her job at the restaurant in downtown Detroit because it is too far away. She plays hostess, greeting and seating people in the restaurant. Bill bakes cakes and pies in the kitchen. The first Thanksgiving Daddy is in charge of the little country club, even Jenna Lou comes to lend a hand. They supplement what the official cook produces and feed more than two hundred people that day.

I do not see this family effort as the bad sign it actually is. It never occurs to me that Daddy, with his eighth-grade education and limited managerial experience, took a risk attempting this new job, or that he did it mostly to get me out of the city. Until Mom finds another job, we actually have less money than before. I have just turned twelve and am largely oblivious to everything that does not revolve specifically around me.

I am enrolled at Walled Lake Junior High and think it is the best school I've ever gone to because we have block classes with social studies and English together and another class that combines math and science. Students here do projects, so there is less sitting and listening and more hands-on learning.

Mama buys me a few new clothes and lets me stop getting my hair cut short. I start shaving my legs and wearing nylons because all the other girls do. More is changing than just my address.

Along with physical maturation, I begin to perspire copiously, a condition called hyper-hydration. My body seems to be permanently damp no matter what I do. Mama takes me to the doctor, convinced that I'm seriously sick.

"She rings her wool sweaters under her arms the size of dinner plates," Mama tells the doctor. "What's wrong with her?"

"Oh, I don't think anything is wrong. It's probably an inherited condition, stimulated by puberty." He examines my gnawed fingernails. "Are you nervous?"

I curl my hands into fists. "Sometimes. I guess."

He turns to Mama. "Do either you or your husband have this problem?" Being adopted comes up at the most unexpected times.

Mama explains our situation. "Of course. I see," the doctor says.

He prescribes liquid aluminum chlorohydrate to be applied sparingly with a cotton ball to my underarms when needed. "Which ought to handle the excessive perspiration," he says.

Mama is not satisfied. She worries that this liquid aluminum stuff, applied to sensitive areas of the body, however sparingly, cannot possibly be good for me. She only lets me use the liquid aluminum on special occasions, which do not occur often. These are the years when "Better Living through Chemistry" is the leading slogan on TV and cigarettes are said to be good for us, recommended by doctors, guaranteed to help people relax. I wonder if smoking would help me stop biting my fingernails. Mama says boys don't like girls with raggedy, chewed-off fingernails. She also says boys don't like girls who smoke.

One of my new friends, Ginny, who lives nearby, uses Mitchum antiperspirant. She says it's the best product of its kind on the market. It's a little more expensive than the others and isn't carried in every drugstore, but I decide I have to use that or nothing.

Ginny has red hair and is very pretty and very popular and I want to be like her, mostly because she is a year older. But my best friend is Betty Swan. Betty and I are in the same class. We decide that when we graduate from high school, we are going to college together at the University of Michigan, although I have no idea yet how my family could afford that or what I might want to study. I like reading and writing, science, theater, history and movies—not necessarily in that order.

For the first time in years, Bill and I do not go west that summer. My parents probably couldn't afford to send us, but I am just as happy not traveling. Instead, I spend time with my new friends swimming, playing ball, and water skiing while Bill helps out with the cooking for the country club. I write Charlotte Jenkins in Colorado and tell her I hope to see her in another year. I tell her about our house at the lake and my new school.

Walled Lake also has an amusement park situated on its north shore less than a mile from the school. The amusement park boasts the largest wooden roller coaster in the midwest. Twice that summer, I meet several of my friends there and we spend the day.

The following winter, someone scrapes a smooth square on nearly every lake in the area. These patches of smoothed ice are for ice-skating. All the lakes freeze over thick enough to drive a car or truck on. And there are hills for sledding, as well as parties, sleepovers, and school dances. I have never had so much fun.

Also, shortly after we move to the lake, I get the puppy I always wanted. He is so small I can hold him in the palm of one hand. I name him Pee Wee. He grows to be knee-high, with short, wiry, reddish-brown fur and a black muzzle. At Christmas, I write to Charlotte and tell her all about my dog. She writes telling me about her new horse and all the snow they are getting.

Pee Wee carries rocks and bricks around in his mouth all summer and rolls in piles of fall leaves. As soon as he is allowed outside on his own, he meets me at the mailbox by the road when I get off the school bus. He has a doghouse, but he sleeps in my room if he's had a bath. In the very worst of the winter weather, Mama lets him sleep inside no matter how bad he smells. Though technically he is my dog, I suspect he loves my father best. He follows Daddy around the yard as he mows or plants shrubs along the front of the house or paves the driveway. Daddy is always working and Pee Wee wants to help.

Pee Wee likes me, too. A large wooden dock floats about a hundred yards off the lily-pad-choked section of our lake. On warm days, I swim out to the dock and sun bathe or practice diving. Pee Wee stands on the shore whining and barking until he finally works up enough courage to swim after me. When he reaches the dock, I haul him onto the platform where we sit in the sun together.

One Saturday after we've lived at the lake house for nearly a year, my parents leave me home alone, probably for the first time in my entire life. Bill is visiting a sick neighbor. My dad went to work early and Mom went with him to help out. It's also raining. I'm supposed to stay inside and do my homework. But the minute the car pulls out of the driveway, I am in their bedroom searching for my adoption papers, birth records, whatever I can find about who I "really" am.

I don't know when it occurs to me to look. I seem to be hunting among their things before I have time to reconsider. I listen for sounds that mean someone's coming, although I should be alone for a couple of hours—unless something happens. I dig through boxes on the closet floor and upper shelf. I pull open drawer after drawer feeling under the clothes for any papers that might be hidden there.

Rain beating on the roof muffles sounds—a car in the driveway—a key in the front door. I stop, hold my breath and listen again. Nothing. More than once, I stop what I'm doing and go into the kitchen to peer out the window. From there I can see the driveway and down the road in both directions. If my mom comes home and catches me snooping in her things, she will never trust me again. I only hope what I'm looking for isn't stored in the attic. I really don't want to go up there.

Finally, in the bottom drawer of their chest-of-drawers, under an orange and brown knitted afghan, I find a flat white box. I sit on the floor with the box on my lap and remove the lid. My whole body is damp. Where is that bottle of aluminum chloro-whatever when I need it?

Inside the box is a pink watermark-satin-covered baby book, which I had not seen in years, and under the book are my adoption papers. I am identified as Baby Girl Pugh, mother Ann Elizabeth Pugh, father unknown. What kind of name is Pugh? Why did it say father unknown? He wasn't unknown. She knew who he was. But the dates were right, and the state of Michigan seal and signatures made it official.

I stare at the document for a long time, then lay the papers back under the baby book and carefully put the book back in the box. I return the box to the bottom of the drawer just the way I found it and hope I won't get caught.

Ann Elizabeth is a nice name. And Pugh, I learn later, is Welsh. So my biological mother's father's people were from Wales. That's a start. I read about Wales, an ancient place, full of shepherds and explorers, poets, coal and copper mines, castles, ghosts, and wild mountains—a proud and romantic people, the Welsh. The poet Dylan Thomas was from Wales, and Richard Burton, the actor. Half my biological roots come from Wales. I study a map of Wales and struggle to pronounce place names like Caernarfon and Gwynedd. There are cities by the sea in Wales. Geologically speaking, it was probably once connected to Ireland. Someday, I will go there to see it for myself.

A few days later, Bill and I are alone in the house, in the kitchen washing dishes. I am drying and putting them away. Something has been bothering me ever since I saw my adoption paper. My biological mother and father never married and I want to know why not. Did they decide they didn't love each other? Finally, I work up the nerve to ask my grandmother.

"I knew you'd get around to that one of these days," she says with a sigh. She continues washing and does not look at me. "I guess you're old enough to know. It's because he was already married and the father of a four- or five-year-old little boy when you were born."

I am surprised, maybe even shocked. I don't quite know what to say. Then I realize that means I have a half-brother somewhere who is at least four years older than me. It's sad to have a brother you don't know. I want to meet him, find out who he is and whether we are similar in some ways. Maybe if we knew each other, he would like me.

Of course, I probably have lots of biological relatives who will remain hidden and unknown. But knowing for sure I have an older half-brother is somehow different. He's a child like me. No, he's seventeen now, at least. At that age he probably wouldn't want to have anything to do with me.

Bill tells me my natural parents are from Tennessee, from Knoxville, she thinks, or maybe it is Memphis. She can't remember. My biological father's name is Jimmy, but she doesn't know his last name, she says.

Here is something else I want to know now: Why do my adoption papers say *father unknown*? Surely she knew who he was. That doesn't make sense. But of course I can't ask that since I'm not supposed to have seen them.

According to Bill, Ann Elizabeth stayed in Detroit and worked in a defense plant until the end of the war. She married and had two boys. Bill doesn't know what happened to Jimmy except that some of his family disowned him over his relationship with Ann Elizabeth and what it did to his wife and son. Bill said she thought his wife's name was Gladys.

So I might have *three* half-brothers somewhere. Oh, that is so unfair. For an only child, such information is actually painful. Do I look like any of them? Where are they? What are they doing right now? What are they like? Will I ever meet any of them? Do they know about me? If I do ever meet them, what will I say to them? What will they say to me? Will they like having a half-sister?

"How do you know Jimmy's family disowned him?" I ask, suddenly realizing she might know even more than she has told me.

"Jenna Lou told me," Bill says. "Your mother, Elizabeth, stayed down the street from Jenna Lou when she was expecting you. Jenna Lou knows the people Elizabeth lived with. That's how your parents knew you were going to be put up for adoption. The woman is one of Jimmy's older sisters, I think."

"What was her name?'

"Virginia, maybe. I'm not sure."

"But…"

"All I know is what I've been told," Bill says, lifting her shoulders.

"Did Jimmy love Elizabeth? Did he want a divorce from Gladys? My real mother must have loved him. Right?"

"Oh, honey. I don't know about all of that. The way I heard it, he went back to Tennessee to his wife and little boy and left Ann Elizabeth in Detroit two months before you were born. I think his wife came up and got him."

Bill moves to sit down on the metal step stool we keep at the end of the counter. She wipes her hands on her apron. "Jenna Lou said Gladys threatened that if Jimmy didn't quit all his nonsense and come home, he'd never see his son again—or something along those lines. Anyway, he went back to Tennessee. What happened to him after that, I couldn't tell you."

"How old was Jimmy when I was born?"

"Old enough to know better—older than Ann Elizabeth by more than a decade. Did I tell you that she picked your parents from several other couples that wanted you?"

"Yes, Bill. You did."

"Did I tell you she said your mom and dad were a lot like her own family?"

"Yes, you told me that, too. What else do you know about them?"

"They were just hard-working, God-fearing people.

So they weren't rich or famous then, not movie-stars, or royalty. Too bad. I never really thought they would be.

"Now if you want to know about your daddy, Kenneth's, people," Bill says, "I can tell you a lot about them. His grandparents immigrated to Pittsburgh from Bavaria when his father was a boy, back in the 1870s. Your great grandfather was a cobbler in Germany." She went on for some time telling me what she knew about Daddy's side of the family, but if she thought I didn't know she had intentionally changed the subject, she was mistaken.

"Bill?"

"What, honey?"

"Last week I found my adoption papers, in that little white box in the bottom drawer of Mama's dresser."

"Oh Lord." Bright pink circles have popped out on her cheeks as though she'd just put on too much rouge. "Don't you know better than to go nosing around in other people's things? Shame on you."

"I wanted to see my adoption papers and my birth certificate," I say.

"That's no excuse."

"If that isn't an excuse, I don't know what is. They should have shown me years ago. They knew her name all along. I bet they know Jimmy's last name too."

"Maybe they do, but I don't."

"But if his sister lived down the street from Jenna Lou, how could they not know his name?

"I don't know. But I'll tell you something, your mama was plenty worried about Ann Elizabeth not being quite nineteen. She had to be nineteen to sign the adoption papers by law, without her parents. If you'd been born before her nineteenth birthday, she couldn't legally sign the adoption papers. Apparently there was some possibility you would have become a ward of the court, or the state, in that event. But that didn't happen."

"How do you suppose they met, if he was so much older and already married?"

Bill twists her mouth and narrows her eyes. She heaves a big sigh, so I know she is going to tell me, whether she really wants to or not. "We always surmised she was Jimmy's little boy's babysitter."

That makes sense. "So they picked Detroit because Jimmy had relatives here?"

"Yes. Jimmy brought your mother up here. As I understand it, Virginia told Jenna Lou and Jenna Lou told your mom and dad. Elizabeth said she didn't want her people, especially her daddy back in Tennessee, to know anything about you. I guess he was very religious."

So I was a secret? If no one in her family knew about me and someday I found her, how would she feel about that? She probably wouldn't like it much. After all, she had traveled six hundred miles from where her parents lived to have me. "Was that the reason she didn't want to keep me, because she didn't want her parents to know she'd had an affair with a married man?"

"That was more than enough back then, and also she was so young. How was she going to take care of you?"

"Why did Mama and Daddy name me Carole Faye? Why wasn't I named after anyone on either side of the family? They could have named me Laura after you and Grandma Johnson, or Lucinda after Daddy's mother." Laura Lucinda might have been a bit much. "Where did they come up with my name?"

"Your mother named you after her favorite actresses,

*Daddy with his mother,
Lucinda Mayberry Kirchner,
circa 1940.*

Carole Lombard and Fay Wray," Bill says.

"Did Mama like the movies *that* much?" I knew she and Daddy went to the movies when they were dating, before I was born, but if they were going to name me after a movie star, it's a wonder Daddy didn't want to name me Shirley after his favorite child star, Shirley Temple."

"They thought about naming you Cindy Lou, a twist on Lucinda."

"Yeah, Daddy told me once." Everyone called his mother Cindy, and he thought Cindy Lou would be cute, but Mama didn't like it. "My grandmother Lucinda died before I was born, didn't she?"

"That's right," Bill says. "But they decided they liked the way Carole Kirchner sounded. Why, don't you?"

"I like it okay." I shrugged. "I was just curious." Carole Faye was definitely better than Cindy Lou. Talk about a close call. I wouldn't have minded Laura or Lucy or Lucinda or even Amanda or Temple, but not Shirley. As for the rest of the closest relatives' names, Francis, Ida, Annie, Effie, Eva, Velma, Bessie, or Pearl, I hated them all equally. I wouldn't have minded Anne, but not Annie. I liked Anna Beth. That would have been a nice name. My favorite biblical name was Rebecca, but no one on either side was named Rebecca. When I was in fifth grade, at about the same time I started dotting my i's with little hearts, I decided I would have liked being named Lucinda Eleanor, after my paternal grandmother and Eleanor Roosevelt. Now there was a seriously dignified name.

I didn't know what difference it would have made being Carole Faye or something else, but I was convinced it would have made some difference. I tried on dozens of possibilities—Cindy Lou, Anna Beth, Temple Pearl, Rebecca Anne, Lucinda Eleanor—but none seemed to fit me any better than the name I had. Did Elizabeth even know my name? She had to remember my mom and dad's last name, but she wouldn't necessarily have known my given names, especially if she never even saw me. What would she have named me, I wonder, if she hadn't given me away? How important was a person's name, anyway? When I was thirteen, it seemed vital.

"What was Elizabeth like?" I ask. "Was she pretty?"

"I never saw her close up," Bill says, "but your mama and daddy did, and they said she was very pretty. They hoped you'd look like her, that you'd have her coloring, and you do."

I knew I had her coloring, but now I wondered how much I looked like her and I wanted to see her more than ever. I love my mom and dad and Bill, and always will no matter what. They are my parents, my family. But I want to see my biological mother—just to meet her and talk to her. Is that too much to ask?

For the first time in my life, I had seen concrete evidence that I was indeed the child of someone else. Before, I had been merely told. Seeing it in black and white made a difference somehow—made it less easy to dismiss as inconsequential. This was also the first time I had seen my biological mother's full name in print, first, middle, and last. That day, as I was staring at it, I suddenly knew, the way people sometimes just know things, that I would have to remember it, Ann Elizabeth Pugh, for a long time. And I was right. I would not see her name again in print on anything official for thirty-four more years.

~ *13* ~

Reassurance

A few weeks after I find my adoption papers, Mama and I are driving back from a shopping trip to town when out of the blue she says, "Sometimes I worry that one day, when you get older, you'll go off and look for your biological family and leave us." She keeps her eyes on the road.

"No, I won't," I say. "I would never do that. You're my mama for always and ever. You know that."

She never mentions such a fear again, but I get the message. Bill has told her what I did and that I am asking more and more questions. So, curiosity is fine as long as it doesn't go too far.

There was another subtler message in what my mother had said, though I'm sure she did not intend for me to hear that way. Hadn't she inadvertently admitted that the bond between us was not as strong as the bond between natural parents and their children? It was my worst fear— as well as hers. That was our bond, one of fear, I suppose. I had to reassure us both that our connection was deep, unbreakable, and permanent. Mama was my mother and Daddy was my father. Their families were my family; that was all there was to it. If I asked about my natural family, it was out of curiosity, not longing.

Most of the time I didn't think about being adopted. I didn't like knowing I was the child of another couple, not related by blood to all the people I loved. So I tried not to think about it, but there were so many dissimilarities between my adoptive family and me. I was fair with freckles and had reddish hair and blue eyes. Both Mama and Daddy were darker skinned than me, with brownish black hair. Mama was outgoing. I was more introverted. They were both slender with straight teeth. I was not overweight, but I was not stick-thin like they had both been as children. I didn't have any eyebrows and had to draw them on with an eyebrow pencil—and they never looked right. Mama had beautiful, arching eyebrows. And my permanent teeth came in looking like a split-rail fence. Mama's teeth were perfect. Then there was my tendency to sweat too much and the fact that I gnawed my fingernails. Mother was cool and her hands were lovely. In truth, no two people looked less alike than my mother and me and I knew it.

I thought such differences only applied to adopted kids. I didn't know that parents and their natural children could look vastly different from one another and that siblings could differ widely, sometimes exhibiting almost no similar physical or personality characteristic at all. For these reasons, I tried to be like them in as many other ways as I could.

Mama liked to dance. So did I. Mama did not like women who smoked, especially in public. I vowed never to be a smoker. Mama's favorite color was green. Therefore, it was my favorite color, too. Daddy and I both had blue eyes. He liked baseball, fishing, and horse racing, so I did, too. Daddy was stubborn. That was where I got it, being stubborn, willful, and headstrong—from my daddy.

Neither of my parents went to college. Mama finished high school, while Daddy quit after the eighth grade to work and help his family. I knew that, but I never connected such information with who *I* was as an eighth grader. He had only been thirteen at the time he stopped his formal education. It must have been very hard. I didn't even know if he had wanted to stay in school, but Mama definitely had wanted to go to college. So I wanted to go to college, too.

She made straight A's in math, and having lived in south Texas, she learned to speak Spanish like a native. She wanted to be a teacher, but her parents couldn't afford to send her to college, and Grandma Johnson, who had sent her sons' daughters to college, refused to help send my mom and Aunt Bessie on the grounds that, because they were pretty, they would just get married and never work and the money would be wasted. Mama resented the insult for the rest of her life. By the time I was thirteen, I realized my parents were self-conscious about their lack of formal education. Sometimes I used it against them.

I have homework to finish before bed. Mama tells me to turn off the TV and get to work.

"But Mom! You don't understand. I shouldn't have to stop watching in the middle of *Wuthering Heights*. This is one of the best pieces of literature ever written. They study it in school. Don't you want me to be exposed to the classics? You've read it, right?"

She hesitates, so like any good salesperson with her foot in the door, I press my advantage. "Please. This is really important. It will help me in English class when we read *Wuthering Heights* next year."

She stares at me as though she can discern whether I am telling the truth with her super x-ray vision. She purses her lips. "What time does it end?"

"Ten, but I don't have much homework. I can finish it when this is over and still be in bed by ten-thirty."

Her jaw clenches. "I suppose it will be all right. Just this once."

She and Bill go off to bed, leaving me alone in the living room with the TV on. When the spirits of Cathy and

Heathcliff wander off across the moors, I turn "Playhouse 90" off and go to bed without giving homework, or how I had made my mother feel, a second thought. I felt strongly about fairness and kindness, until they interfered with something I wanted.

In the spring of my eighth-grade year, we become a two-dog family. I'm thrilled. A friend of Daddy's from work has to give his dog away because of where he lives. The dog, a golden cocker spaniel named Dennis, is beautiful. He might not be the smartest dog in the world, but he is the sweetest. He's five years old when he comes to live at our house, and we all love Dennis, especially Pee Wee. They become instant best buddies. Dennis follows Pee Wee and Pee Wee follows my dad, around the yard and the neighborhood, down to the lake and back, in the car for a ride. They make quite a troupe.

When I am out on the lake ice-skating in the winter, both Pee Wee and Dennis sit side-by-side on the bank like little sentinels. They whine and bark until I stop skating and return to land. Apparently they do not like me being on ice, even though it's probably thick enough to support the weight of ten 1955 Cadillacs.

We have Dennis for more than a year and everything seems fine, but then one day he suddenly stops eating. Mom takes him to the vet only to discover that Dennis has never had any shots. So the vet needs to keep him to run some tests. The next day, the vet calls. Dennis has hepatitis. There is no cure and he's suffering. He will have to be put down. He never comes home again. Dad goes to be with him at the end.

When he comes back home he is furious. "Carl told me Dennis had had all his shots. How was I supposed to know? We could have saved him if he had just told me the goddamn truth." Daddy loved Dennis as much as I did. "It's not like Carl didn't have the money." Daddy stalks off to grieve in private. He sits on a picnic table down the hill by the water's edge for over an hour, shoulders hunched, smoking and gazing out at the lake.

The next day, I am home alone. I've been crying off and on and my nose is stuffy, my ears are plugged up, and my eyes are red and puffy. When the phone rings, I answer, but can barely hear. It's Aunt Bessie from Colorado. She almost never calls, except at Christmas, and it is definitely not Christmas.

"Charlotte Jenkins is dead," she says.

"What?" I say. "Who?"

"Charlotte Jenkins—she's had a bad accident."

"No," I say. My head feels like it's the size of a watermelon and I can't breathe through my nose. "That's a mistake. That was a different Charlotte."

"Not this time." My aunt sounds like she's been crying, too. "Charlotte was thrown from a horse yesterday, one her daddy had told her repeatedly not to ride. She hit her head on the pavement. She's gone. She was not quite a year older than you are."

Gone? Dead? But I just got a letter from her at Christmas. It can't be true.

"Tell your Grandma," my aunt says. "She'll want to know."

Five minutes after we hang up, the phone rings again. It's the vet calling about the bill we owe for Dennis. I am shocked. We have to pay him for killing our dog? It's too much. When my parents come home, I tell them about the vet, but I don't tell them about Charlotte. I'm not sure I believed my aunt. I certainly don't want to believe her.

That evening, Aunt Bessie calls again and when she finds out I have not told my grandmother about Charlotte she is really angry. How could I have forgotten? Because it seems impossible for Charlotte to be dead, that's how, and I tend to ignore things that seem impossible. If I ignore something hard enough, won't it just go away?

The last summer I saw Charlotte, we whispered and giggled over her cute older brother and his friends. We planned our futures, if not our weddings. Now, we would never do that, or anything else, again. I will never see her again. She will never grow up, never get married and have children, never become a vet and work with horses. I am stopped in my tracks. Why did that happen? Charlotte never hurt anybody.

Why do some babies come into the world unwanted, and some well-loved children and good dogs die too soon? Does God decide who gets to live and who has to die? Had God tried to kill Charlotte once before and missed, striking down another Charlotte Jenkins by mistake? But God doesn't make mistakes. Maybe He just doesn't like kids named Charlotte Jenkins.

After Charlotte dies, I tell Bill I don't want to go to church any more. She says as long as she's living, I will go to church and like it. "As the twig is bent, so grows the tree."

I picture the wind-swept, gnarled, and twisted trees I've seen, clinging to the edges of cliffs in the mountains. I'm pretty sure that's the way I am shaping up inside, all twisted and stunted, willful, hardheaded, stubborn, and doubting. Had she lived, Charlotte would probably have become a better person than I will be. Why is the world the way it is? Nothing seems to make sense to me these days. Where do I go for reassurance?

14

Adolescent Humiliations

Toward the end of eighth grade, my English class takes a field trip to the Fisher Theater in downtown Detroit to see Kathryn Hepburn and Howard Keel in *Much Ado About Nothing*. I don't understand all the lines, but I think Shakespeare got the title right. This is my first taste of professional theater, though, and I love it. Acting involves wearing beautiful costumes and being generally adored and famous. That's for me. Actors get to be all sorts of people. I like that idea, too.

In school the following Monday, the drama teacher hands out fliers about a summer stock theater program for high school students in our area. Scholarships will be awarded on a competitive basis. The experience provided by the workshop covers everything an aspiring young actress could want: acting lessons, of course, a chance to be in two semi-professional plays over the summer, horseback riding lessons, fencing lessons, set and costume design, and more. I really want to win that scholarship.

I am so excited I'm breathless. The playhouse, created by a former Broadway actress, offers ten scholarships, one for a boy and one for a girl at each grade level from ninth through graduation from high school. Since I will be entering ninth grade in the fall, I qualify.

The actress-turned-director founded her theater complex on the farm her parents left her. There's a stable with several horses, a small studio for dancing and fencing lessons, and a workshop for set and costume design and fabrication. The theater itself is in the barn. The whole place reminds me of the set of the 1940s movie *Holiday Inn.*

Along with a school friend from drama club, I develop an audition piece and on the specified day, his mother drives us to the theater. Our drama teacher has already warned us that the owner of the theater does not like timid, hesitant auditions. She is looking for self-assurance and personality, so I try to act like I have both. And we win, in our age division, against perhaps a dozen other rising ninth graders. This is one of the best days of my life.

Even though I cleared the audition with my parents, when I come home and tell them I won, they are not happy. They didn't expect me to win and now say I can't accept. Surely they aren't serious. After they think about it for a day, they'll change their minds. That night I can't sleep. At breakfast the next morning, I try again to persuade them. The answer is still no.

"But why?"

"We work six days a week and can't take you or pick you up and your grandmother doesn't drive. That theater is more than ten miles away."

"Mrs. McMillan, Terry's mom, says she'll be happy to take me. She has to drive him anyway."

"Yes, but she'd expect to car pool and we can't help. We can't accept a favor we can't return. They're members of the country club. It just wouldn't look right."

"But you don't understand. This is a once-in-a-lifetime opportunity."

Mom sets her coffee cup down. "It's not that great. It's just a way for them to get free help for the summer."

I am appalled and indignant. "No it isn't. It's real theater. No one cares about what *I* want. This is really important. You're going to ruin my life."

Mama rolls her eyes and inhales deeply. She blows out a long-suffering breath through puffed cheeks. "Don't be ridiculous. That is too melodramatic even for you."

"That's because I'm a natural actress."

I pace the living room and turn on Mama. "You could have been a movie star. You told me so, when you were out in California, but you chose not to do that. Why don't I get to choose? It's not fair." They remain adamant and Daddy says he does not want to hear any more about it.

Later, after he leaves for work, I bring it up again. "You just don't want me to be happy!"

"Carole, this discussion is over. You can't do it and that's that."

Having to refuse the scholarship is hard. I call the number on the acceptance form and tell the girl who answers the phone that I will not be coming on Monday. I go to my room and cry.

To make matters worse, starting the very next week, my friend Terry tells me all about the wonderful workshop I'm missing, in glowing detail, on a daily basis. He does say the ninth grade girl who was the director's second choice is not as good as I would have been, but that is small consolation.

I decide to concentrate on boys. I have been aware that boys are starting to notice me for some time. Lately, I have spent time with Jack, who lives down the road. His parents own a beautiful Chris Craft speedboat and Jack is teaching me to water ski.

I also spend time with Wayne. Wayne is teaching me to drive his stick-shift, pickup truck. In Michigan, kids can get a learner's permit at fourteen.

When Bob invites me to a dance at the country club, I really want to go. This will be my first formal dance. Bob and I have known each other for a year, and since his parents will be driving, I am certain my father will let me go. After all, Bob's parents will be there the whole time. Both of my best friends, Betty and Ginny, are going and we want to all go shopping for dresses.

We are in the living room when I ask Daddy for permission. He is about to leave for work and I need an answer so I can talk to Mama about a dress. I catch Daddy at the door and tell him about the invitation.

"Absolutely not." He frowns down at me. "You're too young. Don't be silly."

I'm not too young to go to a nice dance, but I am too young to give up without a fight. In addition to Jack, Wayne, and Bob, there is Ray, who wants to take me to Detroit's equivalent of "American Bandstand," and Tim, who asks me to the movies, and Dan, who likes science and wants to build his own rocket and will let me help. Dan and I look for UFOs together.

My father says no, no, no.

"But Daaaady," I wail. " I just want to…"

"Well you can't. You're too young."

"If his parents drive us? All my friends are going. Plus, there's a dress in…"

"No."

"But why? That's not fair. If I can't go he'll take someone else and…"

"I said no and that's final. Stop asking." And then, almost as an afterthought, he adds, "We have to be so careful with you."

I smile in spite of myself, thinking he's going to say something like, "What would we do if anything bad happened to you?" Or maybe, "We couldn't stand it if something bad were to happen to you. It's our job to protect you." But that is not what he says. Not even close.

"We have to be so careful with you," he says, "because

we don't know if you are going to turn out to be bad like your mother. Bad blood. It happens."

What? His words hit me like a jolt from a cattle prod. I can't speak. I tell myself they're just words, that words can't hurt us if we don't let them. Right? What I'm feeling must show to some extent on my face, because when Daddy looks at me, he starts to say something else, but changes his mind.

He leaves for work, and Bill comes into the living room. She's been in the kitchen, listening. "He didn't really mean that," she says.

"What did he mean?"

"Sometimes, your father has a hard time choosing exactly the right words."

"Was my real mother a bad person?" I ask.

"No. I don't think so." Bill wrinkles up her forehead and takes her glasses off. She breathes on them and wipes the lenses off with the hem of her dress. "Did I tell you she interviewed several couples who all wanted to adopt you? But she liked your mom and dad best."

"Yes," I say. "Several times." Of course, that made *them* handpicked. Not me.

It occurred to me then, at that moment, that if Ann Elizabeth interviewed my mom and dad, she probably sat across a table and talked to them. She knew their names, where they lived, what they looked like. She could have found me any time she wanted. She probably walked away and never looked back.

"Ann Elizabeth wanted a family for you that was as much like her own as she could find," Bill says. "One she thought would be good to you. Pretty smart for a girl barely turned nineteen, don't you think?"

"Pretty smart for a 'bad' girl, don't you mean?"

"Are you sassing me?" Bill says.

"Well, I'm mad."

"I think you better go to your room until you get un-mad," Bill says. "I'm trying to help you. I don't need your sassy mouth." My grandmother never did appreciate sarcasm. "And shut the door!" she calls behind me.

I stalk off and slam the door to my room behind me. What was it Daddy had said, bad blood? Like blood poisoning—like Mama had when she was little—only mine would be inherited from my "real" mother? Is that what Daddy thinks? That I am going to be a bad person?

Mama would never have said something so mean. What had I done to make my father think that? If he was afraid I'd turn out to be a bad person when they adopted me, why did he agree to do it? Maybe my father never loved me. I curl up on my bed and stay there until supper.

Years later I realized being adopted might not have been such a big deal for me, had it not been such a wrenching ordeal for my father, not to mention some of the other members of the family, on both sides.

In the fall, I enter the ninth grade and join the drama club. If it weren't for school, play practice, and church, I'd never get out of the house. Finally, daddy relents and allows me to go to the movies with Bob, if his parents drive and we come straight home afterward.

At school, Bob and I have lunch together. During assemblies we sit together in the auditorium and hold hands. We hold hands in the hallway when no teachers are watching. He is my first real boyfriend. We talk on the phone daily and sit together on the school bus.

News of Bob's every activity reaches my ears daily, weaving the fabric of our adolescent courtship. His where-abouts when we are not together, who sits by him in class, who he talks to in study hall, which other girls might like him are the subjects endlessly discussed among my friends and me.

"He likes you soooo much."

"He never even looks at another girl."

"Jayne wants to go with him, but he can't stand her."

"Is he a good kisser? He looks like he'd be a really good kisser."

In all likelihood poor Bob was totally oblivious to the furor raging around him created by my dedicated, intelligence-gathering girlfriends. Those were exciting days. I had never had so much fun. Then…

"I don't know if I should tell you this. Are you sure you want me to? Well, yesterday I saw Bob talking to Marcia! She's after him. You better watch out," Pat says.

"Yeah, I think he might be starting to like her," Linda says.

Further sleuthing suggests that Marcia and Bob were seen kissing behind the school. To preserve my pride, I break up with Bob, hoping he will pursue me and tell me he still loves me—which he does not do. Later, I discover that he did not like Marcia after all and had in fact not kissed her behind the school or anywhere else.

I regret my actions as soon as I discover my mistake and decide to win Bob back. That evening I write him a letter telling him I'm sorry, that I hadn't meant it, and that I still love him. The next day I give him the note in which I allow my adolescent romantic proclivities to overtake my better judgment. Among other regrettable sentiments, I wax poetic about missing the way he smells. This does not set well with a fourteen-year-old jock and probably wasn't true anyway. Bob, who has evidently been insulted over being dumped, reads my note aloud to several of his friends. For days, I am the laughing stock of the ninth grade. Lesson learned. Never put it in writing!

Maybe a career in theater will still work out. Though I could not accept the summer stock scholarship, I am in drama club and elected secretary-treasurer. I also win a major role in the school play.

The play is a murder mystery set in New Orleans and involves Voodoo. Great literature, it isn't. We rehearse for an entire month. Mama makes my costume. I even get to wear a wig. Unfortunately, in this particular script, there are two very similar lines, one in Act I, the other in Act III, and my character has to respond to them both. In Act I, the cue is, "What's that sound?" My line then is, "It's thunder. Storm's a-coming." The Act III cue line is, "What was that?" My line is supposed to be, "Voodoo drums. Trouble's brewing."

On opening night, with all the students, parents, and teachers in attendance, I hear the line, "What's that sound?" and I respond, "Voodoo drums. Trouble's brewing." The rest of the cast follows suit and the play ends thirty minutes later, unmasking the killer before the crime has been committed. I have, single handedly destroyed the entire show. Even though we perform the same play flawlessly the next night, I am, once again, humiliated. I was right about what that old missionary said. If people follow me, bad things will happen. I probably should also rethink a career on the stage.

15

Unwilling Transplant

A couple of weeks before I start tenth grade, Bill and I are home watching TV when the newscaster says something about Sturgis, my Dad's hometown in rural western Kentucky. There has been an attempt to integrate the high school there, since the Supreme Court ruled in 1954 that segregation was unconstitutional. Bill and I glance at each other. This will be one of the first segregated public schools to be integrated by court order following the Topeka schools in Kansas, and that mess in Little Rock, Arkansas. The national news shows Sturgis with army tanks and the National Guard escorting a handful of Negro students into the local high school. White residents are making fools of themselves screaming and carrying on in the background. It's embarrassing, and what's even worse is the fact that, if my dad had been there, he probably would have been yelling, too.

In tenth grade, I now go to the senior high. It's a much larger school fed by three nearby junior highs. Betty and I still have several classes together. We talk about college and plan for it right down to the yellow bedspreads we are going to buy for our dorm room. Self-absorbed as I am, it never occurs to me that life might not continue as it has for the last three years. But my dad is struggling at work.

I see how tense he is and I hear the hushed conversations between my parents and the frustration and worry on my mother's face. Still, I blithely assume their problems won't affect me in the least.

Less than two months after the beginning of my sophomore year, my father announces that we are moving back toward the city. I feel like the foundation of my world has just dropped out from under my feet.

Dad has quit his job and returned to his old job as bartender at the country club in Royal Oak. The nightly commute after work out to the lake is long and arduous and too hazardous to risk during bad winter weather. Therefore, we have no choice but to move again. This can't be happening.

"But Daddy, you don't understand. I love it here. All my friends are here. Betty and I are going to go to U of M together in three years. We can't move. It will ruin everything."

"We won't go back to apartment living," he says. "I've found us a nice house to rent. You'll like it." He's confusing his needs with mine. How could he? I don't care what kind of house we have. I desperately do not want to move away from the place where I have been the happiest. Can't he see how bad this is going to be for me?

"Can't you tell them you're sorry," I say. "Take your resignation back. Tell them you didn't mean it. They'll want you. Surely they will. Nobody can manage that club like you can."

"There are too many problems," he says. "You don't understand."

"But I don't want to move." I could more easily have seen an alien spaceship overhead, than I saw this move coming. I feel blindsided. How will I stand it? I want to tell him I'm not going and that he can't make me, but even at my most willful, I do know that's not true.

Looking back, of course, I realize we had no choice. The twenty or so miles out to the lake from Royal Oak and his old job were winding, hilly, narrow, and would often be treacherous if not completely impassible in the winter. Even as a self-centered teenager, I realized the issue for my dad was life and death. So I steeled myself to the idea of moving and began to pack. At least this time I got to say good-bye.

By the end of the following week we are living in an ugly, rented brown brick house with a steep pitched roof and detached garage on a flat street with flat yards and few trees for miles. I enroll in Troy High School on the following Monday and am instantly miserable.

Troy High School is older than the new senior high I had been attending. It is also over-crowded, filled largely with working class families who have moved out of the city looking for houses to buy, small houses with real backyards and basements. Troy is not only flat and largely treeless since the subdivision is new, the houses are not particularly attractive, and there isn't a lake in sight.

I hate it here, as I compulsively tell anyone and everyone who'll listen. I can't believe we've moved here on purpose. I am unrelentingly angry with my father. He has ruined my life twice. But it isn't just that I mope and sulk my way around this new house and my new school. I actually do not fit it in.

The principal puts me in debate and journalism rather than chorus and theater, which are already filled beyond capacity, he says. The debate coach and journalism teacher make it clear they are not pleased with having yet another student in class who doesn't really want to be there. Mama says things will get better over time, but they don't. I feel displaced, disconnected, and unwanted. Self-doubt oozes through the thin skin of my self-confidence and renders me unable, for the first time in my life, to make even one new friend.

The fact that I will not stop talking about my former life might have something to do with my difficulties. I cling to the recent past like a drowning person clings to a buoy. I talk about how good my old school was, compared to Troy, how much there was to do, summer and winter, compared to Troy. Every chance I get, I make sure everyone knows I had a life there and now I don't.

Consequently, no one talks to me more than once. I sit alone on the school bus. I sit alone in class. In the halls, I am bumped and pushed until I hide in the girls' restroom every morning waiting for the final bell. Then I make my way to class not caring if I'm late. After school I hurry out to the bus so I can sit directly behind the driver. As soon as I arrive home I disappear into my room, shut the door, and stay there until supper. After supper dishes, I retreat into my room again and do not willingly re-emerge until morning.

One morning, just after Thanksgiving, I wake unable to breathe. My chest and face are on fire. I am panting like my lungs are filled with concrete. I prop myself up on my elbows and try to catch my breath. My arms and fingers tingle. I'm terrified that I'm dying. I tell myself to count and breathe the way we learned to do in swimming class. Finally, my lungs expand and the sense of suffocation fades, my heart slows, my face cools. I'm going to live.

The next morning, it happens again. Am I losing my mind? I don't know what to do. I only know I can't tell anyone. My parents are upset enough with me as it is.

After a few more such spells, in which I do not die, I figure I'm probably going to be all right. Still, these episodes are frightening and I dread when the next one will occur. Decades later, in therapy, I learned what a panic attack was after suffering with them off and on since the age of fifteen.

In an effort to help me fit adjust, Mama takes me shopping for new clothes. She even lets me pick out the skirts, sweater sets, and saddle oxfords just like all the girls wear. I had let my hair grow long and wear it in a ponytail, with bangs in front. I roll my white bobby socks like all the other girls in Troy do, even though it makes my ankles feel weird, all cold and exposed.

Because I am increasingly depressed, I talk less and less about my former life at the lake, which ironically allows me to make a couple of semi-friends, Francine and Angela, who live down the street. We ride the school bus together and are in the same English and math classes. They let me sit with them at lunch. They have boyfriends, older boys who play football and have a different lunch schedule. They offer to "fix me up" with a friend of Angie's boyfriend, another football player who is between girlfriends at the moment. My dad says no. This time I don't care enough to argue.

Before Christmas, Mama suggests I throw a Christmas party.

"No thanks," I say. "Bad idea. No one would come. Besides, I don't know how to give a party." Mom wants to believe that a couple of new skirts and a dozen cupcakes will solve all my social woes.

"Oh come on," she insists. "It'll be fun. Of course people will come. You can invite Francine and Angie and their boyfriends and all the kids from your debate class and anyone else you like."

Mama does not know what she's talking about. She has no idea what to do with a shy and introverted child like me. I didn't used to be quite so shy and introverted and would love to be more outgoing, but I don't know how, though I'm pretty sure a party in my parent's basement for people who don't really know or like each other, or me, is not the answer. Nevertheless, no amount of protest on my part can talk my mom out of it. She is determined.

The house dad has rented may be ugly on the outside, compared to houses around the lake, but it is the largest house we've ever lived in, on three floors, three bedrooms, two bathrooms, and a finished basement. Mama and Bill decorate the basement with red and green streamers, red and green balloons, and strings of Christmas lights. Dad buys an aluminum tree complete with revolving colored light, which he sets up in one corner. When they finish, the basement looks like the set for Santa meets Buck Rodgers at the Hop.

I invite Fran and Angie and their boyfriends along with the friend they say they want me to date. I also ask all the kids from debate class. Even though I understand the folly of trying to mix these two groups, they are the only people I know. Angie suggests a few other couples from class, so I invite them, too—about twenty kids altogether.

The only other party I've ever given was a Halloween party back in Highland Park in the basement of our apartment building when I was ten. Everyone wore costumes. I went as a gypsy. I suppose Mama is remembering that party because she has planned essentially the same menu: cupcakes, cookies, and punch. But these party goers are not nine-year-olds. I manage to talk Mom into cartons of Cokes and bags of potato chips. I make onion dip and Dad brings home a platter of little hot dogs in barbecue sauce. At the last minute, Mama plans to pop popcorn to put into bowls on the table. I want sandwiches, but real food is too expensive.

I borrow my cousin Mona's portable record player and Angie agrees to bring all her 45s. The party will start at

Carole, age 10, Halloween Party.

seven on Saturday night. I am dreading it and looking forward to it at the same time. After all, it is going to happen so I ought to make the most of it. Maybe it will be fine. A corner of my mind still believes in magic. I might have a good time, maybe meet a boy I like, maybe Angie and Fran will have a good time and we will be better friends afterward.

At 4:30 on Saturday afternoon, the phone rings. It's Angie.

"Um, hi there." She sounds hesitant.

"Hi. What's up?"

"I thought I ought to tell you. No one really wanted to come to your party because all you do is talk about how much you liked living where you used to live and how much you hate living here and we're sick of it. But Fran and I decided it would be too mean, so we talked the guys into coming. But we're only going to stay for a little while, a couple of hours, and then we have to leave. We have another party to go to."

I sit there holding the receiver, unable to react. Time comes to a halt. Next to moving to Troy in the first place, this is the worst thing that has ever happened to me. Apparently I had not stopped talking about my life at the lake quite soon enough.

When I fail to respond, Angie says, "You always act like you're so superior, like you think everybody else is so stupid and we're tired of that, too."

Just like that, they have gotten even for all the complaining I had done. Though that had not been my conscious intention, there is a certain amount of truth in her accusations. I had insulted them and hurt their feelings and they struck back. But Angie was wrong about one thing. I didn't think I was superior to them. If anything, I thought they were more sophisticated than me. How was I going to survive the next few hours?

When the doorbell rings, I answer it. Angie and Fran, three football players, and half a dozen other students are on the porch. I imagine the look on my face gives the girls satisfaction. The debate squad mostly comes together shortly after Fran and Angie arrive.

By nine, most of the food is gone and so are Fran and Angie and their boyfriends, though Angie leaves her records, saying she'll pick them up after school on Monday. The debate kids hang around for a little while, but I can hardly come out of the dark place in which I find myself long enough to even talk to them. They dance and discuss an upcoming debate trip to Kalamazoo. That is all I remember. By ten-thirty they say good-bye, too. Finally, it's over.

"What did you expect, the way you moped around, like you were in a trance?" Mom says as we shove trash into large shopping bags. "I'm sure they thought you didn't even want to be at your own party."

"I tried to tell you I didn't want a party, but you wouldn't listen. I don't think anybody wanted to be here."

"I'm sure they didn't after the way you acted." She knows the party has been a flop; she just doesn't know why. And

I can't tell her. She would never like Fran and Angie again and they may be the only friends here I will ever have. But how will I get through the rest of the school year, much less the next two years after that until I graduate?

Between Christmas and the start of the new semester, I write in my diary: "I am trapped in a flat gray hell, friendless and obscure, an unwilling transplant from the Lake District." I consider myself a budding writer.

Toward the end of January, everything changes again. It's Sunday afternoon, and Daddy receives a phone call. After he hangs up, he and my mom disappear down to the basement where they talk in private for at least an hour. Bill and I stay upstairs cooking dinner. Neither one of us conjectures about the nature of the phone call, but we are curious.

When we sit down to supper, Mama thanks Bill and me for finishing cooking so she and Daddy could talk. She brags about how good everything tastes and how nice the table looks. I am pleased, but leery. Something is definitely up.

Over pie and coffee, Daddy asks me how I'd feel about moving again. I nearly levitate out of my chair. My nightmare is over. We're going home! "Back to the lake?" I ask.

"Um, no. To Kentucky, back to Sturgis," he says.

"To live in our house again," Mama says. "Now that Aunt Ida is living up here with Jenna Lou, it's empty. All we really have to do is clean it up and repaint a little."

"But there are no jobs for Daddy in Sturgis," I say. I glance at my father. "Why do you want to do that?"

"I have a chance to go into business with Buster," he says.

Buster is married to one of my father's nieces. He owns a drive-in restaurant in Sturgis and is opening another one in Morganfield, the county seat, eleven miles to the north.

"That phone call was from Buster. He wanted to know if I would consider coming home to run the new place for him."

"When would we go?" I ask. "Will I have to finish the semester?" I don't know how I feel about leaving Michigan, but if we are going to do it, I want to go now.

"I don't know," Mom says. "We haven't decided. It's only just come up."

"Will Bill come with us?" I ask. Up to that point, Bill has remained silent. She is moving a little slower these days and I wondered if she is willing to be uprooted yet again.

She laughs. "Of course I'll come with you. I like Sturgis."

Dad shrugs. "I'll give two weeks' notice at the club, and then we're free to go."

"Can I stop going to school here until we move?"

Mama and Daddy exchange a quick glance. "I tell you what," Mama says. "We'll split the difference. You stay in school one more week. After that, we'll withdraw you and you can spend the last few days helping me pack. How about that?"

Mom and I check the calendar. If I go to school this coming week and then we take five days to pack, we can rent a U-Haul, load it, and leave here on a Thursday morning, weather permitting, and be in Kentucky early afternoon on Friday. I will have two days to rest and unpack before I have to start school there on Monday.

"Okay," I say. "Deal." I can stand anything for a week. If I can't live at the lake again, moving back to Daddy's hometown in west Kentucky is actually an acceptable alternative. In Kentucky, at least I'll know a few people. I have cousins there and maybe some of my childhood friends still live nearby. Memories of my time there are mostly good. If Walled Lake is two states away, instead of only an hour, maybe I can finally stop thinking about it and missing it so much.

Carole's first dog, PeeWee.

Daddy lights a cigarette and leans back in his chair. He inhales and blows out a thin line of smoke. "I guess that settles it then. We're going home."

We move as a family for the seventh and final time in mid-February 1959. During the two weeks prior to our actual departure, we sell most of our furniture. Mom and Dad say we'll buy more when we get there. Even so, we fill a small U-Haul that Dad's new car will pull. We also fill the trunks of both cars and every spare space in the rear seats. Mom will drive the Buick with Bill and me. Pee Wee will ride in the Pontiac with my dad.

At the time, I don't realize that my parents have been trying to figure out what to do because they know I am not adjusting. I didn't think they cared or even noticed. Years later, Mom said they had been considering a move to Las Vegas, where they knew Daddy could make good money tending bar. But they decided Vegas was no place to take a fifteen-year-old girl who was already distressed. Daddy sought another course.

At the time, I didn't understand how precarious our financial situation really was, how poor we actually were.

We were totally dependent on my father and were always one or two paychecks from disaster. But my parents shielded me from such realities. They worked hard to make me feel that everything would be fine, and for the most part they succeeded. I had complete confidence in my father's ability to take care of us all.

Saying good-bye to Michigan was harder than I expected, even though there were no people I cared about leaving except my cousins. As it turned out, I wouldn't see Detroit or my cousin Mona again for nearly a decade.

I wondered if I was also leaving Ann Elizabeth and my two half-brothers. Were they still living somewhere in or around Detroit? Would she know where we'd gone? Was anyone keeping in touch with her? There was no way for me to know and no one to ask.

We pull into the driveway in front of the house in Kentucky late on a Friday afternoon, tired but expectant. Pee Wee is sitting in the passenger seat next to my dad, looking around like a little person. The February sky is overcast and threatening some kind of precipitation, but it's twenty degrees warmer than what we left behind up north. Dad opens the car door and Pee Wee leaps out, races around the house and yard a dozen times, then collapses on the front porch to watch us unload. Clearly, the dog is home. Actually, we all are.

PART 2

Moving On

$\sim$ *16* $\sim$

Culture Shock

According to the sign at the city limits, Sturgis has a population of 2,300. The town was built back in the late 1800s on a railroad line near a narrow river that empties into the Ohio. Small, neat houses with well-tended lawns line fewer than fifty cross-streets. In summer, flower and vegetable gardens fill unfenced backyards. With a church on almost every corner, Sturgis is like most small towns in the mid-south, drab in winter, blooming in spring, sultry or parched by the end of summer, and ablaze with color every fall.

There are two grocery stores, two gas stations, one car dealership, a small post office, a hardware store, a farm and feed store, and a factory that makes men's trousers. A silver-colored water tower hovers in the sky with the name of the town painted on it in big black letters. Two long blocks with shops and offices on either side of the street make up the "downtown." The men in town are mostly merchants, miners, or farmers. There are two doctors' offices, one dental office, one bank, and a couple of law offices. Women either do not work outside the home or they work as secretaries, receptionists, teachers, and seamstresses at the factory. Boys graduate from high school and follow their fathers into farming, mining, or business, or they leave town never to return. Girls graduate from high school, if they're lucky, and marry or leave town as well. The economy and the fabric of American life is changing and small towns like Sturgis will soon begin to perish, but in 1959, we didn't know that—we didn't know a lot of things. Who could've predicted the changes that were just around the corner.

From the top of the ladder on Sturgis's water tower, one could see the edges of town in all directions. Nevertheless, for most of its inhabitants, Sturgis and the surrounding county form the boundary of their whole world. While I am in high school there, it becomes the focus of my world, too. I start school on the third Monday in February in the middle of my sophomore year. I remember that first day like it was yesterday.

It's a few minutes before eight in the morning when Mom and I pull up to the front of the building, which sits on a side street two blocks west of Main. I take a deep breath and walk to the front door. Mama follows. Snow surrounds the base of the flagpole in front of the columned porch. Inside, the floors and all the glass in the doors, windows, and cabinets shine. The principal's office is the first door to our right. We enter and are asked to wait. After Mr. Evans makes his morning announcements over the intercom, he invites us into his inner office. Mama introduces us, gives him my school records from Michigan, says goodbye, and leaves me there.

"I'm sure you'll fit in nicely here," Mr. Evans says after examining my material. With his hand he smooths his narrow yellow knit tie and tucks it into his brown suit coat. "There are seventy-seven students in the sophomore class," he says. "You'll make seventy-eight."

"My last school had over two thousand students," I say.

"There's a lot to be said for small schools," he says.

Like what, I wonder.

He doesn't elaborate. "Most of our students have known each other all their lives."

Gee, thanks, that makes me feel so much better.

I follow him out of his office and into the foyer where he pauses in front of a wall-sized trophy case across from the main entrance. "Sturgis may be small," he says, "but we have championship football and basketball teams nearly every year in our division." He points to the case. Photographs of groups of boys in football and basketball uniforms are on display. Dozens of gold and silver trophies and ribbons line the shelves. At the top are photos of the marching band, the majorettes, and all the cheerleaders.

"Do you like sports?"

I nod.

"Then you know about Kentucky basketball."

I don't, but I nod again anyway.

"You might consider going out for cheerleader."

My right eye begins to twitch. "I'm not the cheerleader type," I say.

"What about the marching band? Do you play an instrument?"

"Piano, but my parents sold it before we moved."

He snorts and clears his throat. "Well. Perhaps you twirl?"

Did he really just say that? I swipe my sweaty palms on the sides of my skirt and follow him down the hall. He stops at the last locker on the right and I hang up my coat. The lockers are scratched and dented, but otherwise, the school is clean and neat.

My first class is biology. When we enter the room, heads snap up. "Class, Mr. McCormick, this is Carole Faye Kirchner, recently from Troy, Michigan. She and her parents have just moved back here, to DeKoven, actually."

DeKoven is the name of the even smaller community in which my Dad's house is located. It lies six miles southwest of the Sturgis city limits.

Mr. McCormick holds out his hand to see my blue schedule card. He looks at it, then at me. "So, Troy, is that anywhere near Dee-troit?"

I cringe at his accent, but his smile is nice and I tell him, yes, it's at the edge of the city.

"What brings you and your family all the way down here?"

I clutch my old three-ring binder to my chest like a shield. "This is where my dad was born. We have a house here and relatives."

He glances at my name again. "I bet you're related to Buster Timmons. He owns the Dairy Maid."

"Yes. His wife is my dad's niece. We lived here when I was in second grade. I went to school here for a year and a half."

"Well, that practically makes you a native. Welcome home." It's the nicest thing anyone could have said and I start to relax.

I take the empty desk Mr. McCormick indicates while he adds my name to the roll and finishes roll call.

Principal Evans is still there, hovering over me like a big brown vulture. "May I leave you now?" he says.

"Yes," I say. "Thank you."

"Yes, thank you, what?" he says.

I'm at a loss. What does he want from me? "Yes, thank you very much?"

"Yes, thank you very much, WHAT?" he barks.

My face is on fire. Is he trying to humiliate me?

From my right, I hear, "Say sir."

Several students snicker. Some laugh out loud. Mr. McCormick raps on the board with a piece of chalk to re-store order.

"Yes, thank you very much, sir," I say.

"That's better," he says and leaves the room muttering something about the lack of good manners in some young people. What about the lack of good manners in some old people? Doesn't he know that where I come from saying sir is considered a smart-aleck remark?

Mr. McCormick resumes class.

I have just begun to breathe a little easier, when the boy seated directly behind me leans forward and whispers something totally unintelligible into my left ear.

"What?" I turn part way round.

"Whar'ju sigh you's from? I jes cain't staund the why you tawk. It mikes me sick."

"Oh, shut up. Nobody can stand the way you talk, either." It's the girl seated to my right again.

"Hi," she says, leaning across the aisle and whispering. "I'm Sheila. We moved here from Pennsylvania four years ago. I got the same crap about *my* accent," she waves her hand dismissively. "Don't pay 'em any attention."

"Right," I say. "Thanks."

She hunches her shoulders. "Anytime. Us Yankees got to stick together." Her grin widens, exposing a small gap between her two front teeth. Having had my braces taken off only a few weeks ago, I notice people's teeth. "Don't let Skinhead give you a bad time," she adds.

"Who?"

"Old man Evans." She nods in the direction of the classroom door and wrinkles her nose, which bobs up and down as she talks.

"Yankees still aren't very popular down here, you know."

After class, as we collect our things and head down the hall to second period English, I ask Sheila, "So, how do you like living in Sturgis?"

"I love it here," she says. "It's great. I miss my friends and my cousin back in Pennsylvania, but I really like it here." She grins and the corners of her eyes crinkle. "You will, too. You'll see."

I follow her to second period English.

"Guess what, Miss Evans. We got a new student today," Sheila says, by way of introduction.

"Have a new student, dear," Miss Evans says, leveling a gaze at me from behind thick glasses. Miss Evans is a rather large woman with a stern face and short, wavy, white hair. I wonder if she's related to Principal Evans, but I don't ask.

While she checks my name on my schedule card and adds it to her roll book, I look around. There's a bookcase in back with real books in it, not just textbooks, and some framed travel posters on the wall above the chalkboard. There are even curtains at the windows.

She fixes me with a penetrating gaze. "Do you read, young lady?"

Is she asking if I *like* to read or if I *can* read? Either way, yes is the right answer. "Yes, ma'am." Do they have many students here who can't read?

"And what have you read for pleasure lately?"

"Pleasure? Um, lately? Um, *Frankenstein?*" I make it sound like a question. I'd read *Frankenstein* over a year ago, along with *Dracula* and *Dr. Jekyll and Mr. Hyde.* But after we moved to Troy I mostly read movie magazines and some stuff for debate.

"Do you remember who wrote it?"

"Wrote what?" I've lost the thread of the conversation.

She gives me that disgusted teacher look. "*Frank-en-stein,*" she says.

"Oh. Some woman, um, Shelley? Mary Shelley, I think?"

"Excellent! In that case, I'll expect good work from you, Miss Kirchner." She waves me away as if fanning an annoying gnat. Miss Evans's class is probably going to be about as interesting as watching a dead ant farm, but her room is pretty.

"What was that all about?" Sheila asks, as I slip into the

seat she is saving for me behind her.

I shrug. "Beats me."

"Way to go. Brown-nosing already. You're gonna do just fine."

When class starts, students take turns standing and reading aloud from the textbook. I haven't been in a class where that happened since third grade. After that, the remainder of the period is to be spent working on questions at the end of the chapter. I was right about the dead ants.

Sheila and I hide behind the book and our binders and whisper about life up north, our previous schools, our friends and families, favorite cousins, favorite music and singers, old boyfriends, and the terrible plane crash a couple of weeks earlier that killed Buddy Holly, Ritchie Valens, and The Big Bopper. Then we're back to boys.

"There was this guy, Joe. Looked just like Fabian. I think he was starting to like me when we had to move." That wasn't exactly true. The truth was I thought maybe I might like him. He was in my journalism class and had been nice to me once. Otherwise, he probably didn't know I existed.

"I left my boyfriend, too, when we moved here," Sheila says. "Ever watch 'American Bandstand'?"

"Sure, but we can't get it down here yet. Daddy hasn't put up the roof antenna, so we only get one channel."

"We get all three. You'll have to come over to my house and watch. My old boyfriend is on once in a while. I'll point him out."

In addition to being from the north and liking the same music, movies, and movie stars, we discover we were born four months apart, to the day, have the same taste in clothes, and we've each lost best friends, cousins, places, and things we loved. From day one, we are sisters of the heart.

After English we flounce down the stairs to third period.

"So what's there to do around here?" I ask.

Sheila rolls her eyes. "Nothing! Oh, you know, there are games most every Friday night. Football's over, but basketball's started. We're number one so far. There's the Broadview Drive-In Theater near Morganfield. It opens in April and goes through Thanksgiving. Oh, and there's a Teen Canteen in Morganfield where we go to dance once in a while. Sometimes someone has a party. We have dances here at school for stuff like homecoming." She shrugs. "You know."

At the foot of the stairs, she grabs a boy by the arm. "Here he is. This is my boyfriend, Fred. His father's the chief of police."

Fred slips his arm around Sheila's waist. "I heard there was a new girl in school," he says. Fred also has black hair and dark eyes, but where Sheila's face is oval, his is square. I bet if he became a boxer, they'd say he has a jaw of granite. His teeth are straight and white, too.

Sheila ambles down the hall to home ec. Her long dark hair, held back with a pair of barrettes the same color red as her sweater, bounces around her shoulders as she walks. I follow Fred into math class.

By the end of the first week, I am fairly entrenched. I've made a few other friends, Patsy, Marsha, Sondra, Bobbie Jo, and Judy. Even so, I follow Sheila around like we're joined at the hip. She doesn't seem to mind. I am grateful to have her as my friend. She knows everyone and everyone seems to like her.

Math class is the worst. At the beginning of each class, the teacher, Mr. Holt, calls for the day's homework to be passed forward. And every day, as papers move up each row of desks, some clown, one of the white boys, acts like he doesn't want to touch the papers from any of the black students sitting behind him. And when he does finally take the papers, he holds them out at arm's length with his thumb and forefinger while holding his nose at the same time. Several white students snicker. At first, I think maybe they are doing this for my benefit. I expect them to do the same to me, since I'm a Yankee, so I pretend I don't see them and they leave me alone. At the time, it seemed my only option.

Sheila and I meet for lunch across the street from the school at a small grocery store where we line up to buy sandwiches and pop. While we're waiting, I complain about algebra. "All Mr. Holt does period is talk about basketball. What a dip-shit!"

"Shush." Most of the students who don't go home or bring their lunch are in line with us since the school has no cafeteria. Sheila whispers in my ear, "He may be a dip, but he's a local good ole boy with a winning record. The whole town loves him. Everyone calls him coach. You like bologna?"

"I guess." Actually, I prefer pastrami on rye with a thin slice of red onion and a little brown mustard, but I don't think now's the time to mention that.

Sheila smiles at the old man behind the counter. "Give us two bolognas on light bread with mayo and Velveeta."

"Comin' right up." The man reaches into the long, glassed-in meat case for a ring of bologna. "I'll make 'em extra thick, just for you." Sheila could charm the fur off a polar bear in winter.

She opens the big red icebox at the end of the counter and pulls out an icy bottle of Fanta, holding up the lid for me. I grab a Grape Nehi. She picks up a package of Hostess Sno Balls off a rack. "Want to split?"

"Sure," I say.

I pay for my part and I pocket the change. At these prices I won't have to ask my grandmother for more money the rest of this week. I hate taking money from my grand-mother, but I have no choice. The only income we have right now is her old-age pension. Fortunately, the restaurant in Morganfield that he is to manage for Buster is just about to open.

Sheila and I take our lunches outside to one of the two picnic tables in front of the market. In the sunshine we can eat in relative comfort. In the shade, our breath fogs the air and we shiver. Several students speak to Sheila as they file past. One really cute boy, with hazel eyes and dimples, nearly bumps into the door frame gawking at us.

"Who was that?" I ask after he goes inside.

Sheila lifts her eyebrows. "That's Nicky. Big, bad senior."

"He's cute," I say.

"And available."

"Really?"

"His brother Johnny is in our class. He's even cuter, I think, but I bet you'd like Nicky better."

I'm licking marshmallow and pink coconut off my fingers when Sheila's boyfriend Fred joins us. He goes home for lunch.

"How do you like it here so far?" he asks, taking the last of Sheila's chips.

"Sturgis is small, but it's a nice town."

He grins. "I thought you'd like it."

Sheila only has on a light jacket and is shivering. Fred takes off his heavy, black and gold varsity jacket and drapes it around her shoulders. She snuggles into the warm, over-sized coat. "There's a home game Friday," Fred says, rolling down the sleeves of his white shirt and buttoning the cuffs. "You should come into town and go with Sheila. I have to be at school by six, but the game doesn't start until seven."

"Yeah," Sheila says. "You could come home with me on the bus after school. My mom can drive us in and Fred can take us home. We'll watch 'Bandstand' and go to Morganfield on Saturday if you can spend the night."

"Okay," I say. "I mean, I'll have to ask when I get home and let you know. Are you sure it will be all right with your parents?"

Sheila grins. "Absolutely. The more the merrier at my house."

When I told Fred I liked Sturgis, I wasn't kidding. Compared to how life was for me in Troy, I am happy for the first time in months. I have friends; I fit in. The only drawback is the lack of all the things I loved about living at the lake: swimming, boating, and water skiing in summer and ice skating and sledding in the winter.

My parents are so glad I'm not depressed and all weird with this latest move that they are willing to let me do most anything within reason. Mother insists on speaking with Sheila's mother, but after that, I can go to her house pretty much whenever I'm invited.

At the basketball game that first Friday night, Nicky joins us in the stands. The next week, he asks me to go to the movies with him. Daddy says yes as long as it's a double date and I am home before eleven. I am almost shocked. At least, he doesn't lecture me about maybe having bad blood. But I wonder if he still thinks it.

On our very first date, we double with Sheila and Fred and go to the only movie theater within a twenty-mile radius, just off the courthouse square in Morganfield, the county seat eleven miles north of Sturgis. While we wait for the guys to buy the tickets and popcorn, I suggest we sit in the balcony. I can see that it's open.

"We can't go up there," Sheila whispers.

"Why not?"

"The balcony is where the colored kids sit."

"What? School is integrated, but the movies aren't? How come?"

"How should I know? They just aren't and neither is much of anything else in town."

"Like what?"

"Like all the stores. Colored people have to go to the back door and tell whoever waits on them what they want."

I can't believe it. "No they don't. That's crazy."

She nods. "Maybe so, but that's the way it is."

"How do people down here get away with that?"

Sheila peers up the red-carpeted steps and shrugs. "Who's gonna stop 'em? It's always been like that down here. Nobody thinks anything about it. Actually, everybody *likes* it that way."

"I doubt if *everybody* likes it," I say.

"You know what I mean. My daddy says there's something in the Bible about how we're supposed to keep the races separate. That's why things are the way they are." She jabs her finger at me. "Oh, and colored people don't go to the front of the Dairy Maid, either. They phone their orders in and pick 'em up at the back door."

"They do not!"

"They most certainly do. Ask Mr. Timmons if you don't believe me. I dare you."

"Okay, I will." But I didn't have to ask him. The more I thought about it the more I knew she was right. I couldn't remember ever seeing a Negro man, woman, or child at the Dairy Maid, or the drugstore, or the IGA, or anywhere else, for that matter. I had lived near Sturgis for more than a year when I was younger and never realized it was segregated. Now the absence of black people is staggeringly obvious.

On Monday, I'm still thinking about it when we go to lunch. I am eating with Sheila and another friend, Patsy. "None of the theaters back in Michigan are segregated," I say. "And Kentucky is north of the Mason-Dixon line. So how come everything down here is?"

Patsy glances around to see who might be listening. She shrugs. "It's the law and folks want to keep it that way."

"But it's not right, it's not fair," I say. "Maybe Negroes here have their own stores like Italians or Polish people back in Detroit."

"Maybe," Sheila says, "but I've never seen any. Where would they be?"

"Y'all are kidding, right?" Patsy shakes her head.

"It's possible," I say.

"It *is* possible." Sheila says.

Patsy snorts. "No, it isn't. You two need to think white and get serious!"

That's an expression I'd never heard before. I start to ask what that's supposed to mean, but Sheila kicks me under the table. Later, in between classes, Sheila says, "If you're smart, you'll drop it. That kind of talk will get you in serious trouble down here."

So I drop it. What has happened to that feisty little kid I used to be? That kid protested against segregated bathrooms and drinking fountains and restricted beaches simply because they weren't right, because they hurt people. What good is having a conscience if I won't use it? Am I so desperate to fit in that I will no longer risk voicing even the smallest objection to injustice? The answer seems to be yes, and I don't much like knowing that about myself.

Daddy does not seem to like being a manager. He says no one works hard enough or pays attention to what they're doing. But Daddy and Buster have hatched another plan. With a man named Charles Durrett, a businessman from near Kentucky Lake, they are seeking capital for a new venture. Mr. Durrett wants to build a small factory to make modular, pre-fab houses—like trailers, but without the wheels and with a variety of optional floor plans, L shaped, U shaped, and so on. It's supposed to be housing for poor people that will be better quality, look better, and last longer than traditional mobile homes.

I have never seen my father so excited. Buster sells the Dairy Maid in Morganfield to help raise some of the cash. Still, financing and FHA approval are slow to materialize. The possibility that he and Buster might bring jobs to their hometown has lifted Daddy's spirits to the point where he is laughing again and has a twinkle in his eye the way he did when I was little.

One Sunday evening, while negotiations for financing and securing the land on which to build their factory are still incomplete, the phone rings. It's Maxine, Daddy's niece and Buster's wife. Buster has had a heart attack. Mom and Dad should come right away.

I stay home with Bill waiting for news. Bill says life has a way of turning on a dime and doesn't seem to care much about the plans and hopes we puny humans have.

It's nearly midnight when my parents return home. Buster died sitting on the sofa in his living room before they arrived. He was only forty-nine years old.

He leaves a wife and two young sons. His untimely death devastates his children, and ends my father's reasons for moving back to Kentucky. My dad is crushed.

Over the few months we've been here, Daddy and Buster had become very close. Now Daddy has to cope with the loss of his nephew, his plans for making a decent living, and finding another job. He tries to be a surrogate father to Buster's two boys, but the demands of a job search are heavy. There are still no jobs locally except mining underground. Daddy's hopes for creating a better future for us have slipped away once again.

By month's end, he has taken a job as a bartender at a supper club in downtown Evansville, over fifty miles away.

The drive there and back takes more than an hour in good weather. Coming home at three in the morning after the bar closes on winding two-lane roads is dangerous even in the summer. In winter it will be treacherous. Most of the people out driving in the middle of the night are drunk. But Mama is adamant.

"We're not moving again until after Carole graduates from high school. You'll just have to make the drive. It's only two more years. Then we can do something else."

This is a difficult time for my father. He likes living in Kentucky, in the country, near his family and old friends. We have a huge yard and garden and a bigger house than we had even in Troy, and this is *his* house. But he did not move here merely to find himself in another dead-end bartending job with a long and arduous commute. As far as I know, he does it without complaint.

At the time, what it takes for my father to earn a living, to feed and clothes us all, is barely a blip on my radar. I am still adjusting to life in the south, out in the country. I have friends. I'm making decent grades. I have a real boyfriend. At school I join the drama club and the staff of the school newspaper, such as it is. Life is good; it may not be as much fun as living at the lake, but it's definitely good.

At the end of my sophomore year, Nicky graduates and immediately goes to work with his father in the only independent auto repair shop in town. We are fairly serious from the very beginning. My mother is certain I am so in love I will marry him and trap myself in Sturgis forever. My father is afraid I will *have* to marry Nicky. I am fairly confident I will do neither.

One day, while Dad is showing me how to wield a spade and weed the garden, he says, "I don't like it that you are going steady with that Holeman boy."

"Everybody goes steady, Daddy," I say. "It's no big deal."

He stops working and leans on the long-handled tool. "Maybe not, but just remember, girls who are 'hot-to-trot' mess their lives up." My father can be artless and hurtful without even trying. "Look at what happened to your real mother," he says. He tilts his head and raises his eyebrows. "If you do that, I'll wash my hands of you. You'll be on your own."

I am mortified, not to mention furious. My father and I can barely discuss horse racing, fishing, or baseball. We never talk politics. He usually sticks to safe topics like the weather and what Mama and Bill are making for dinner. Suddenly he feels free to bring up that bad-blood crap up again? I can't believe it.

He shoves the spade into my hands. "I'm going for a smoke. You finish up, like I showed you."

That summer, Mama and Bill and I take a three-week road trip to Grand Junction and come back through Kansas. Mama hasn't seen her sister, Bessie, or her aunts in Topeka for several years. I don't want to go. I won't get to see Karen since her family is living in California now and don't come to Colorado or Kansas anymore, and Charlotte Jenkins is gone. I will be reminded of her all the time we're in Grand Junction and I will hate that. Besides, I don't want to leave Nicky. I complain loudly, but have no choice in the matter. I'm going whether I like it or not.

In Grand Junction, while Mama is horseback riding with Uncle Reggie and Aunt Bessie is working a summer job at a nearby fruit-packing plant, Bill and I clean up the house. We have also been charged with making supper most evenings. One afternoon, while we work, Bill says, "Did I ever tell you about when you were born?"

"Of course," I say.

"No, I mean the actual birth. That old doctor who delivered you nearly killed Elizabeth. Did you know that?"

"What?"

"He bragged to your mother about teaching Elizabeth a lesson." Bill stops working and looks at me.

I do not want to hear this story, but Bill has decided to tell it and when she starts telling a story, there is no stopping her.

"He withheld pain medicine during labor and delivery. He said he didn't think she'd be so quick to spread her legs next time."

"Oh my God. You've got to be kidding! That's horrible." Here was one story about my natural mother I have never heard before and never want to hear again. "Wasn't I a big baby?"

"Yes, nine pounds, ten and one-half ounces, and watch your language," Bill says. "You were a very big baby, so Elizabeth paid the price in more ways than one. Young girls have to be so careful."

I did not want to think about what Elizabeth must have gone through giving birth to a baby she didn't even want. I know why my grandmother told me that cautionary tale.

For a time, my father's threats and my grandmother's horror story had the desired effect. They slowed down my headlong rush into adulthood. I worried about turning out to be a "bad" girl, and tried to do what my parents expected. But biology trumps sociology every time.

After returning home from Colorado, I spent as much time with Nicky as my parents would allow. We engaged in furtive, heated groping and deep passionate kisses—he was a wonderful kisser. One particularly beautiful, wind-swept hill west of town was my personal favorite parking spot. The view was magnificent, if immaterial, since we fogged up the windows in no time regardless of where we were.

During the summer between my junior and senior years, I get my first part-time job. There is a new fast-food restaurant opening at the edge of town. Sheila and I apply together and both get hired. I learn to fry French fries, flip burgers, make shakes, and swirl soft-serve ice cream into cones, then dip them in a waxy liquid chocolate. I am sixteen, almost seventeen now. I have dated Nicky for more than a year. Mom wants me to stay home more, to work in the house and garden. She wants to teach me to sew, and worries that I exhibit no interest whatever in domesticity.

"Nice boys don't want to marry girls who don't know how to do anything. You need to know how to cook and put out a nice laundry and keep a clean house, at least."

Surely actresses don't do their own laundry and housework.

The day before the Fourth of July, slate-colored clouds blanket the sky, trapping in all the heat and humidity. Clearly, a storm is brewing. If it rains, we won't have as much business as usual and I'll get off early since it's my turn. I'm praying for a downpour. Working in a fast-food joint is hot and greasy, but not boring, only because I am working with my friends. On the best days, we steal corn from the nearby cornfield and boil it and eat it with fried chicken, but only when the owners aren't there.

This particular Sunday starts like all the rest. I am in the front of the restaurant filling several tall glass straw dispensers and watching for early customers when a shiny blue Chrysler with Illinois plates pulls up in front. A man, woman, and two children climb out and come inside. I get my note pad to take their order, but when Patsy, my other co-worker, sees them she grabs my arm so hard I fling straws all across the floor.

"Oh my God!" She whispers and points to the eat-in area. "Colored people can't eat inside."

I peek through the door. The children are looking at the jukebox, while the man and woman study the menu on the wall.

"The owners will raise holy-you-know-what if they show up and find those people eating in their restaurant," Sheila says. "We'll all get fired."

"You gotta do something!" Patsy says.

"Me?" I scoop up the straws and throw them in the trash. "What can I do?"

"Go out there and tell 'em they gotta eat in their car."

"I am not going out there and tell them we'll take their money, but they can't sit down and eat with their kids same as anybody else. That's not right and I'm not doing it!"

"Well, if you put it that way..." Patsy glances at Sheila.

"I don't care one way or the other," Sheila says, "but we better do something quick 'cause if anybody sees 'em we'll all be up a creek without a paddle."

Patsy shakes her head vigorously. "*I* can't wait on 'em. My daddy would skin me alive."

"I don't want any trouble," I say, aware of how much I just sounded like my mother. I am also aware that there are children to consider. I really don't want anyone to threaten these people and their children. What I should have done was explain the situation and give the adults the choice. What I do is take their order and hope no one comes inside and sees them.

They eat in peace while the jukebox plays, but are barely out the front door before two pickups slide to a halt in the gravel parking lot. Several boys jump out and stomp toward the Chrysler. I am standing, hiding really, behind the ice cream machine with my hand on the wall phone ready to call the police in case of serious trouble. The boys toe gravel like extras in a bad TV Western.

"Hey there, y'all." Patsy leans out the front window. At the sound of her voice, every one of the boys turn toward her, stopped in their tracks. I am pretty sure they are all staring at her cleavage, which gives the father time to shepherd his family into the waiting car and start the engine.

"You all get better lookin' every time I see you," Patsy drawls.

"Hey girl," one of the boys said. "I reckon that's cause you got good taste."

"That's a pretty shirt you got on. You been to church?"

"Nah. We're just out rumbling. You still dating that four-eyed freak from Morganfield?" the first boy asks.

"Maybe. What's it to ya?"

"You know you ought to be going out with me."

The Chrysler pulls out of the parking area, turns left, and heads slowly north. The boys seem torn between looking at Patsy and glaring at the departing car. Patsy wins.

As soon as the car is out of sight, she backs out of the

window, straightens up, and smooths her apron. "So, what can I do y'all for?" The expression on some of their faces reminds me of my dad whenever he lets a really big fish get away. One of the boys says, "You let them niggers eat inside?" He waves his hand at the front door. "You better not have, you know what's good for you."

"Don't be silly. And don't you be threatening me," Patsy says. "Or I'll tell your mama." Small towns are great like that. Threaten to call a boy's mama or daddy and you have them, usually right where you want them.

Later, after all our customers are fed and gone, and we are finally alone, Patsy says, "You don't understand how it is down here. You're fixin' to get somebody hurt. My daddy says it's the communists who are pushing integration. You want to be accused of being a nigger-lover and a communist, you just keep it up." She scoots onto the big ice chest and sips a Coke.

Sheila nods. "I bet you thought the police would be on your side, but they wouldn't. I can tell you that."

When Nicky picks me up that evening to drive me home, I almost tell him about the blue Chrysler. I'm not sure why I don't. I suppose it's because I don't want to hear what he might say. For that same reason, I don't tell my parents or my grandmother, either.

Nothing exciting happened again at the restaurant, at least not that I know of. Eventually, Patsy was fired for giving her boyfriend quarters out of the cash drawer to play the jukebox. "What's the diff?" she said to me. "The owners get it all anyway." Evidently, the owners didn't agree.

~ 17 ~

Other Shocks that Flesh Is Heir to

Over the year and a half we date, Nicky grows increasingly possessive. Sheila says it's because he's out of school and working and is ready to get married. Since I'm not, just before the start of my senior year, we break up for good. He has a date the following week.

I miss the freedom that having a steady boyfriend with a vehicle provides. Without him, I am once again trapped at home, six miles from town, unless someone with a car comes to get me. I miss our Sunday afternoon rides out into the country. I miss seeing his mother and his grandparents. I miss kissing him and the careful, furtive sex in which we engaged. But getting married right out of high school is the last thing I want to do.

Three weeks into September and my senior year, it is still unbearably hot. On Saturday morning, I play softball with a group from church. After that, I clean up and get ready to walk down the road to the house of my nearest girlfriend. She has asked me over to spend the night. Mama and Bill are going to visit an old friend in the hospital in Evansville and will pick my dad up when he gets off work so they can all drive home together. The fact that I will be with Janice at her house, relieves their worries about leaving me alone so long.

When I arrive, Janice tells me a boy she has dated off and on is now back home from the army and is coming down to see her that evening. Joe is bringing his best friend, who has also just gotten out of the Army. I have on a yellow sundress and a little white cotton sweater for the cool night air. We can play cards, she says, or maybe drive into town with them for a Coke at the Dairy Maid. I think I look all right and I agree.

The boys arrive around seven in Joe's car, a black and white '57 Chevy. Janice's boyfriend is very good looking, so good looking in fact that I am surprised he is interested in her, though I can see instantly why she likes him. I had hoped I would like his friend Bobby Joe, but I don't, not at all. After an hour of playing cards, they invite us to go into town for a Coke. Her mother says it's all right. I don't really want to go, but I think I have no choice. Besides, it's only a ride into town, for an hour.

I sit in back with Bobby Joe, a crude, ruddy-faced, beefy guy with blondish hair and a big mouth. As soon as we are in the car, he starts talking about his army days, about drinking binges and all the women he's fucked. He's loud and distasteful and I am embarrassed and very uncomfortable. I realize I have made a mistake. He is worse than I thought, but I keep telling myself I will go with them to town, and then have them take me home. I will be fine by myself until my parents get home.

When Bobby Joe tells me he's twenty-three, my misgivings increase. I should ask them to take me home. Now. I could tell them I don't feel well, but I don't want to make Janice mad and I don't want to make a fuss. The consequences of making a fuss seem huge compared to spending an uncomfortable hour with this crude, rude, and obnoxious man.

After buying soft drinks at the Dairy Maid, Bobby Joe pours bourbon into everyone's cup, including mine. I don't want it. With my dad being a bartender, I have tasted all kinds of mixed drinks and liquors and don't really like any of them. My dad would have several objections, starting with the fact that I'm too young to be drinking. In addition, he doesn't like bourbon. He prefers blended whiskeys, and he doesn't like most sweet drinks, especially bourbon and Coke. He says people who drink that don't know what a good mixed drink is. I take a sip and almost spit it out. No wonder my dad makes fun of people who drink this. I tell them I don't like bourbon and Coke, trying to act and sound more sophisticated than I am. "We got beer in the trunk," Bobby Joe says.

"I don't like beer either," I say. He drinks my Coke when he finishes his.

On the way back, Joe turns off the main road and heads for the Ohio River. Though this is the long way around, I know we can get to my house and Janice's from here. The moon is out and the night is soft and warm. Joe parks along a flat stretch of sand bar near a bend in the river. We exit the car and walk to the water's edge. In addition to beer, they have quilts and blankets in the trunk. Soon we are all sitting on the wide sand and rock-strewn bank.

The surrounding hills are black against the moonlit sky. The reflection trails a broken silver zigzag across the swiftly moving river. I like the way my skirt flares out on the patchwork quilt.

While Bobby Joe goes back to the car for more beer, Joe and Janice say they are going to take a walk along the water. I get up to go with them, but Bobby Joe says he thinks they want to be alone. They disappear beyond a stand of trees, leaving me with a man who is now on his third beer following the bourbon, and that is just the drinking I'm aware of. I do not want to be here. I want to call Janice back, but I don't. I just stand there.

"Come on," he says. "Sit down." He pats the space beside him. I feel like a fool standing there, so I sit down again.

"There's a cemetery on top of the hill behind us," I tell him. "My grandparents on my father's side are buried up there."

"Yeah. So?"

"There's a really great view. You can see the river for a long way in both directions. We should drive up there."

"I ain't here for the view."

"I think I'll go find Janice and Joe." I start to get up, but he pulls me back down.

He laughs. "Why? You like to watch? Maybe you like to *be* watched?"

My whole body tenses. Should I run or go after my friend? I can't seem to decide what to do. If I don't budge, maybe I won't attract his attention and he'll leave me alone. So I remain motionless while this hulking, grown man finishes off his beer and flips the bottle by the neck into the river. It sinks immediately. Why can't he disappear like that, too?

All at once he is on me, pushing me down. I try to get up. I try to push him away. I tell him to stop. After a brief struggle, he hits me in the jaw so hard I see stars in one eye. I can't open my mouth or close it without pain. He reaches up my skirt. I grab his arm to stop him.

"Don't. Please don't," I try to push him away. He slams me back and holds me down with one forearm across my throat. He says if I make another sound he'll beat me to death. I freeze. Instead of fighting him, I shut my eyes. I don't think I can stop him. He outweighs me by seventy pounds at least, and he's been drinking.

I tell myself if I don't react, none of what is happening will affect me.

"Don't just lay there," he says. "If you don't move, I'll hit you again."

I remain frozen, praying no one can see us, screaming inside, hoping to get it over with as fast as possible, wishing he was dead, hoping no one will ever find out.

Afterward, I get to my feet. He pays no attention now. I pull my underwear back on and tug my dress back in place. I walk back to the car while he smokes a cigarette. Quietly, I pull the car keys out of the ignition and fling them into the tall weeds nearby. Then I run.

Moonlight shines on the gravel road well enough for me to find my way, but where the trees block the light, every step feels like I might be stepping into a deep hole. All I can think about is getting as far away from them as possible. How could I have been so stupid? I'm more like a deer in the headlights than a person. I had caved in at the first blow. Why was I such a coward? What was wrong with me?

Behind me I can hear Bobby Joe and Joe cursing and yelling when they discover their car keys missing. They don't know they're looking for them in poison ivy.

Twenty minutes later, I am still walking when I hear an approaching car. I don't know how they found the keys so fast. Maybe he had a second set.

Still, I know it's them because Janice is hanging out the passenger-side window calling my name. I have hidden in the bushes along the side of the road and slide farther down the wet embankment as the car goes by. Stiff weeds scratch my legs; something sharp cuts my knee. I don't even consider the possibility of poisonous snakes. Minutes later, they come by again from the other direction. This time, I see the lights in time to hide behind a tree on the dark, up-hill side of the road. My heart is hammering so hard I can barely hold my breath until they pass. They do not pass again.

No one is home yet at my house, but the door isn't locked, so I am able to quietly slip inside and lock the door behind me. I had walked at least three miles in my sandals, raising blisters on the bottoms of both feet. I undress and shove my underwear under the trash bin for burning. My dress goes to the bottom of the dirty clothes basket.

I shower for a long time and am sick for weeks with a jaw that feels swollen and won't quite open and close right. My stomach is constantly upset, I can't seem to sleep through the night, and I have poison ivy from ankle to thigh. Within twenty-four hours, my legs are covered in long rows of oozing blisters. The sores itch and drain and look as terrible as I feel. They last for weeks. I tell everyone, including my parents, I fell into poison ivy shagging fly balls in the weeds at the edge of the ball field.

Memory of what happened hangs in my mind like a carcass swinging on a meat hook. Every morning when I first wake up, I am treated to the image of Bobby Joe's red sneering face in front of me. I hide the bruises on my throat and cheek with makeup and lie about what happened. Janice and I talk about it once. She says she had no idea he would do that. What I didn't realize, until it was too late, was that Janice was having sex with Joe and therefore Bobby Joe felt entitled.

Just before the month is out, when I can't stand it any longer, I tell Miss Pat, the school's new speech and theater teacher. She is young and sponsors the drama club and I like her very much. I am convinced I must be pregnant and really need someone to talk to. She says if I am pregnant, she'll help me take care of it. No one will ever know. There's a doctor in Louisville. She says this is not my fault. I don't believe her, but I'm glad she says it. She's only a few years out of college, so I think she understands.

"I don't know why I didn't try to fight him," I tell her. "What is wrong with me?"

"Nothing is wrong with you," she says. "You are a shy, private person. And you couldn't have fought him off anyway. Sounds like he outweighed you by sixty or seventy pounds at least."

As it turns out, I was not pregnant, but Miss Pat saved my life anyway. Because of her, I was able to sleep again. Still, *if* I had fought him, *if* we had stayed in Michigan, *if* I'd known about Janice and her so-called boyfriend, *if*...

I was almost more shocked at my own silent paralysis than by what Bobby Joe had done. I had blocked much of it. He was a criminal. There was no doubt about that, and I could not have fought him off no matter what I'd done, but if I'd put up a fight he might have stopped. Since I didn't, I could not press charges against him. Back then there wasn't much a girl in my situation could do. I had not been smart enough to refuse to go with them before it was too late. I knew I didn't want to be there, although I had not the slightest idea that such a thing as rape could happen. But I was smart enough to know that a rape charge against him would never stick—unless of course he'd done it before, which was a distinct possibility. But finding someone credible to come forward would have been a million-to-one shot. So it was simple. I had not fought him off. I had no broken bones or serious injuries. He had no marks on him at all. I could never tell. Never. Not even my grandmother could help me this time. My father would blame me if he found out. I was sure of that. If either of my parents found out, they would not be on my side. Daddy might use it as an excuse to move again, to Evansville or Las Vegas.

For weeks, I bit my nails until they bled. I had nightmares and migraines. When the pressure built, I would tell the teacher I felt sick or faint or weak. Then I'd go to the school nurse. I liked being taken care of. The nurse let me lie down for a few minutes and gave me cold water.

She took my temperature, which was often elevated, felt my cold and clammy hands, checked my rapid pulse, and talked to me quietly until I calmed down. Then she'd send me back to class. No one ever mentioned these bouts. My parents acted as if they didn't know, though they must have. Someone from school surely must have called them. I could have had a brain tumor or a previously undetected heart condition or something else equally dreadful. Apparently everyone decided I was "high strung" and they simply ignored my aberrant behavior.

I withdrew from most things social and my grades suffered. By spring of my senior year, I am better. I still can't focus on school, but I win a part in the spring play. Without a boyfriend to act as chauffeur, I am in need of transportation for after-school play practice. A neighbor and friend, who is also in the cast, agrees to drive me home so my mom doesn't have to come to town to pick me up four days a week. Bruce is distantly related to my dad, third cousin once removed, I think. One evening, on the way home after rehearsal, Bruce suggests we park. He and I have never even been out together. I say no. He seems surprised. He is very popular, with beautiful blue eyes and a wicked smile. All the girls like him, including me, but that doesn't mean I am interested in him that way and I tell him so.

He grumbles, but drives on. Before we reach my house, he says, "How can anyone with such a weak chin have such a strong character?"

I am stunned. What weak chin? I try to see myself in the side window. Never having seen my own profile, I didn't know I had a weak chin. No one ever told me I did. What does having a weak chin mean about a person anyway? Who in my biological family had a weak chin? No one in my adopted family had a weak chin. They all had strong jaws and good profiles. Why couldn't I have a nice profile like one of them? How many things can be wrong with one person? In my preoccupation with the criticism, I lost the compliment completely.

Why is human nature such that we tend to remember the bad events of life in rich detail, and forget the good things almost as soon as they happen? For years, I believed the rape was my fault. Much later, when I finally accepted the fact that it wasn't, those memories and feelings remained nearly impossible to alter.

$$\sim 18 \sim$$

Chicken, Chicken! Pluck, Pluck, Pluck

With graduation ten days off, and no boyfriend to date, I spend Friday night at Sheila's house. She and Fred have no money and can't go out, so she invites me over to play Monopoly with her, her family, and Fred. Sheila's dad sits at the head of the table with a bottle of Heaven Hill open beside him. We play until he passes out and Sheila and Fred put him to bed. When everyone else is asleep, the three of us go to her room to listen to music and talk. Her room is an add-on to the rest of the house, which is actually a converted barn. Since her room is off the main house, we can make a little noise and not wake her family up. There are two iron twin beds with pink chenille spreads, a small nightstand in between with a lamp, and a pink and brown oval rag rug on the floor. In the daytime, two windows look out on the side yard into a line of evergreen trees.

Final exams begin the following Wednesday and Sheila is upset. She put off taking algebra until her senior year and is in danger of failing.

"I learned more about football and basketball than I did about math," she says. "A lot more."

"What are you going to do?" I ask.

She shrugs. "Probably flunk."

"I'm not doing all that great, either," I tell her. My grades at this point are mostly B's and C's. But I want to go to college and she doesn't.

"Would you help me study?" she asks.

"Fred's better at math than I am," I say.

"Yeah, but you're a better explainer," she says.

"Not about algebra."

Fred lifts the record player's arm to exchange the stack of 45s that has finished playing.

Sheila wrinkles her nose. "Crap. All I want is a damn C."

"You *must* be upset," I say. "You never swear."

"You'd swear too if you had my grades." She wraps her arms around her legs and rests her chin on her knees. Her dark hair falls forward obscuring her face. "I feel like such a dumb bunny. If it wasn't for Jake letting me copy his homework, I wouldn't have a prayer. As it is, I barely got a D average. I'd have to make an A on the final to get a C."

"Too bad we can't get into the school," Fred says. "If we could, we could steal the test. I got a key to the office." He looks over at Sheila and nods. "You'd get a C for sure."

"What office?" I say.

"Skinhead's office. But we can't get in the building." Fred rolls over onto his back, laces his fingers behind his head and gazes at the ceiling. "Too bad, too. Miss Lillian was running off mimeographed exam copies this afternoon. They're stacked on a shelf in the closet behind her desk just begging to be lifted." He grins.

"How come *you* have a key to the principal's office?"

Sheila stares at me like I'm an idiot. "That's where they keep the money before they take it to the bank." She rolls her eyes. "Fred *is* vice president of the senior class."

"They trust me because of my dad," he says. "But over the weekend all the doors are chained and the windows locked."

"Not all the windows," I say.

"What do you mean?"

"The window on the landing above the band room isn't locked. It isn't even shut all the way. At least it wasn't this afternoon. It was open, not very far, just three or four inches. Maybe the janitor didn't see it."

Fred is on his feet in a flash. "Are you sure?"

I sit up. "I kid you not. I noticed it when I was coming downstairs after last period. This enormous red wasp was crawling in underneath it. I hate wasps."

Sheila is on her feet now, too. "If that window is still open even a little, we can get in."

"Wait a minute," I say. "We'd have to climb up onto the band room roof first without being seen. Won't a ladder be just a tad conspicuous?"

"Oh, we don't need a ladder." Fred looks like a fox that just found a chink in the hen house wall. He is practically salivating. He stands behind Sheila with his arms around her waist and his head hanging over her shoulder. He grins at me. "When the band room was added on to the end of the main building three years ago, the construction company got fancy so every third layer of bricks sticks out two bricks deep. Makes a great ladder. We can climb up the back corner easy. I've done it lots of times."

Sheila looks hopeful.

"You guys really want to do this?" I say.

"Is the Pope Catholic?" Fred says.

"It's too risky. *If* the window is open, *if* the exams are there, *if* we aren't caught."

"You worry too much," Sheila says.

"It'll take two of us," Fred says. "Those old windows are really heavy." He raises his eyebrows at me. You'll have to hold the window up and keep a lookout while I go inside." He turns her around. "Actually, it'll take all three of us."

"Yeah," Sheila says. "Somebody has to drive the getaway car." She gives him a quick kiss on the cheek.

"We can't very well leave it parked behind the school while we do it," Fred says.

"That white oxford cloth you're wearing." She points

at me. "That isn't going to cut it. Better put on my long-sleeved navy blouse."

"We're doing it now, tonight? I don't know about…."

Fred nudges my foot. "You aren't chicken, are you?"

"I am *not* chicken," I say, on my feet now, too.

"Oh yeah?" He makes chicken wing arms and high-steps around the room like a chicken pecking in a barnyard. "Chicken, chicken. Pluck, pluck, pluck."

I am about to hit him when Sheila steps between us. "Shut up, both of you. This is serious." She looks me squarely in the eyes. "You're my best friend. You have to help. Please. Pretty please. Pretty please with sugar on it."

She's right. As her best friend, I should help. She helped me when I first arrived in town. Besides, this is my one chance to do something brave—if I have the guts. I take a deep breath. "Okay, okay. I'll do it."

"All righty then." Fred claps his hands together with a pop.

Sheila squeals and jumps up and down. "I knew you would."

"Shush. You'll wake the whole house." I look around. What have I gotten my fool self into?

Sheila hunts for her navy blouse for me, then she goes to the kitchen for the flashlight. While she's gone, I rationalize. Breaking into the school makes sense. Sheila needs help, her teacher is a joke, most of the teachers and the school board are all racists. They are not serious educators. They made us move the prom to a hotel in Evansville so the Negro students couldn't go. No one even tried to stop them. They don't deserve respect, except for Miss Pat and a couple of the others. I vaguely recognize that rationalizations are coming way too easily.

"We ready?" Fred claps his hands together again and that startles me. My heart feels like it's about to leap out of my chest.

"What will happen if we get caught?" I ask.

He shrugs. "Nothing much—just somewhere between getting expelled and facing a firing squad. But it won't matter. My dad will kill me anyway."

Just thinking about what my father would do makes me want to puke.

Dressed in Sheila's dark blue, long-sleeved blouse and my Madras plaid Bermuda shorts, with my hair slicked back in a ponytail, I look like a cat burglar's apprentice. We pile in the front seat of Fred's car. Sheila drives. On the way he fiddles with the radio. The school is less than three miles away. I check my watch. Twenty minutes after one.

Fifteen minutes later, I am wedged in the window above the band room like a broomstick, holding it up with my shoulder. Sitting here, exposed in the half-moonlight, I have plenty of time to better assess the reality of the situation, which worsens by the minute. We had climbed up the side of the building with no trouble, just like Fred said we could. We tugged the window up far enough for him to sit on the sill, swing his legs over, and jump down onto the stairwell, landing inside the main building. I suppose I could argue that this isn't breaking and entering—just entering! And technically I haven't entered so it doesn't count, right? Still, if we get caught, Fred will lose his football scholarship and I'll never see the inside of college anywhere as long as I live. We might not even graduate from high school. This is crazy. What am I doing? It's a good thing I went to the bathroom before we left Sheila's.

Time ticks by like Big Ben in slow motion. The pungent aroma of roofing tar stings my nose. My shoulder aches under the weight of the heavy sash. My butt is numb. Down below, Sheila drives past at least three times. That's bad. If someone sees her and recognizes Fred's car they are going to wonder where he is. The moon disappears behind more clouds. That's good. In the moonlight I could be seen plain as day sitting in this window, if anyone thinks to look up. My only hope is for the clouds to stay put for the next few minutes. All the nearby houses remain dark. Still, if someone peeks out… What is taking Fred so long?

I am about to risk turning around so I can shift the weight of the window to my other shoulder, when a car materializes out of the darkness. It's heading down the side street toward the back of the school. Who could be driving around this time of night? Sheila just went by in the opposite direction. Did she turn around? I squint. Sweat trickles down my ribs. That isn't Fred's car. What the…? Oh no.

It's the deputy sheriff. Without making any sudden moves, I shrink into the opening, trying to disappear as much as possible. Thank heaven for this dark blouse and for the clouds that still hide the fattest half-moon that ever shined on crooks in the night.

The squad car slows then stops at the end of the building where I can no longer see it. Has the cop spotted me? The car door opens. I hold my breath and pray. Under the circumstances, calling on divine intervention is not appropriate, I know, but I do it anyway. *Dear Lord, please… I promise I will….. If you just….*

What if the deputy comes over the rim of the roof? What will I say? *Thank heavens, officer. I've been stuck here since Friday afternoon. Why? Um, would you believe I was killing a wasp and the window fell on me? No? How about…*

That's when I hear Fred running down the first floor hallway. Each footfall sounds like thunder. He bounds up the stairs and skids to a halt when he sees me waving at him to stop. He switches off the flashlight and we wait. Though there are two walls and no eye-level window between Fred and the deputy, he may have heard something.

I hold my breath. Why doesn't he just get back in his car and move on? What is he doing? Smoking a cigarette, eating a Twinkie, taking a leak? *Good grief. Go away.*

He jiggles the band room door. It's locked tight. In a few seconds, I hear a car door close and the squad car motor start up. As it pulls quietly away, I breathe a silent *Thank you, Lord!* Seconds later, Sheila is there when Fred and I scramble off the roof. We jump in the car and drive away, not knowing if we've been seen and will be expelled on Monday. That made for a very long and unpleasant weekend.

~ *19* ~

My Worst Fear

We did not get caught and expelled. We passed every subject and graduated. So little fanfare for such a major life change. A week later, I return to my part-time summer job feeling depressed.

With high school behind me, it's time to figure out what to do next. My options are to get a full-time job, get married, or go to college. Since I don't have a boyfriend, and hate the very idea of marriage at this point in my life, I am once again contemplating college.

I want to get a full-time job and save my money, but I barely passed typing, and I hate sewing. As I assess my abilities, it occurs to me that I don't really know anything, and I am not good at much of anything, except maybe lying. Therefore, college really does seem like my best option. When I approach my father about it, he says he doesn't want to discuss it.

Before graduation, I took the SAT. My scores were high enough that the University of Kentucky offers me one-fourth off tuition. Mama says that's nice but it isn't nearly enough. I write to Berea College for an application, but when the envelope arrives, I tear it up without opening it. I have decided that by the end of the summer, if I don't have any better job, I will talk to the owners of the Family Drive-In to see if they will hire me full time. Maybe in a year I will be able to go to college and then we'll see.

In the meantime, perhaps I can take a class or two at that community college in Henderson. It's still just one building out in the middle of a field, but that would be better than nothing.

Sheila has to work, too, and by the end of June, while I am flipping burgers, she has landed a job as a receptionist for the local dentist. We are going our separate ways already.

One Saturday evening, a couple of weeks before my eighteenth birthday, I have a date. One of Sheila's boyfriends before Fred has asked me out. His nickname is DeCon because at a school fundraiser he sold more rat poison than the next three students combined. He invites me to the movies and I say yes. He graduated the year before and is now working at one of the two gas stations in town. He's taller than me, with short, light brown hair and a contagious smile. I have always liked his easy humor and open, honest face, but we are just friends.

I see him in town from time to time. We've talked briefly about what we were going to do with the rest of our lives now that we are out school. Like me, DeCon doesn't have the money for college, but admits, "Working at a filling station is a real drag."

I tell him about the school in the eastern mountains. He says he's heard of it but doesn't seem interested in applying.

The evening of our date, on the way to the drive-in movie, we drop by the VFW where my parents are attending a dance. Daddy has asked us to stop by and DeCon says he doesn't mind.

The room is smoke-filled and crowded. A live band is playing some tasteless country-swing hybrid. At the age of seventeen, I am a music snob, so of course I want to leave as soon as we arrive. Daddy tells DeCon to sit down, that he wants me to dance with one of his friends. Daddy shoves me at a man I don't know. "Here," he says. "Give an old man a thrill."

I am shocked. Behind my father's back, mild shock registers on DeCon's face, too. Neither of us knows what to say. My father is acting so weird. He's red-faced and talking too loudly. Evidently, he's been drinking. Where's Mom? I look around and see her dancing with another of their friends.

Dad doesn't usually drink much, so I have no experience with him in this condition, but I also have no intention of dancing with some strange old man, no matter what my father wants. It's creepy.

I mumble something along the lines of, "Gee, sorry. Can't dance. Gotta go. Running late. Don't want to miss the first part of the movie. Just stopped in to say hi. Bye."

The man says, "Of course. I understand. You two have to run along." He may be embarrassed, too.

My father glowers at me, but doesn't say anything. Did Daddy really expect me to dance with some old man I don't even know? All I want is to get out of there. I grab DeCon's hand and we head for the door. Once outside, I don't give my father a second thought.

After the movie, we stop by the Dairy Maid in Sturgis to see who is hanging around, so it's nearly midnight when we arrive at my house. Every light seems on, which is highly unusual. My first thought is that something has happened to Bill. She is eighty-three, with worsening eyesight and arthritis. I jump out of the car and run inside.

Bill is fine and in bed, Mom says. But my father is not. He is sitting at the kitchen table and Mom's pouring him a cup of black coffee. His hair has fallen onto his forehead; his eyes are half-shut. The glass ashtray on the table is overflowing with cigarette butts. Daddy's mouth droops to one side and spit dribbles onto his forearm. When he sees me, his face twists into an angry mask.

"There she is. Little Miss Goody-Goody. Can't spend five minutes doing one thing I ask." He sucks in a breath and swallows. He is slurring his words, but I understand him perfectly. "I clothe and feed you. What do you do around here? Nothing."

How do you handle an angry drunk? I look at Mama, but she's watching Daddy. What should I say? I must have that deer-in-the-headlights expression on my face, because when my dad looks up he yells at me.

"What are you looking at? Embarrass me in front my friends. I don't know who you think you are."

I want to say I don't know who he thinks he is, either. Who asks his seventeen-year-old daughter to give an old man a thrill?

"All you are is boy crazy," he says.

How can I be boy crazy? I don't even have a boyfriend.

"Think you're so damn smart." His head droops and I think his tirade is over, but then he tries to stand up, loses his balance, and flops back down. His face is dark and his shirt hangs cockeyed on his body. One hand looks scraped, like he fell down, probably on the sidewalk leading up to the front porch.

Mama moves his cup out of his reach. She pats his hand and pours more coffee. "Here, drink this," she says, sliding the cup next to his hand. "I warmed it up."

I should slip away now, while he's preoccupied. I could go to my room and shut the door, but I'm curious, as well as angry. I am also afraid he might follow me and then I'd be cornered. I've never seen him like this. His head snaps up.

"Ought to send you back to Michigan, you like it so damn much up there. If you can't do one thing I ask, you can just pack up and get out!"

I want to scream at him. I want to move back to Michigan, to live at the lake. I open my mouth to speak and get a wide-eyed, withering glance from my mother. The message is clear. "Shut up!" Her expression softens into a half eye-roll, which means don't pay any attention to your father—he's drunk.

"Money, money, money," Daddy growls. "Take, take, take. That's all you know how to do. Ungrateful… You got a part-time job. You ever even bring home even a loaf of bread? Hell, no. Now I'm supposed to pay for college?"

"Ken, this not Carole's fault," Mama says. "She's just a kid."

"Yeah, but she ain't *my* kid. I'd give her back if I could. Wish we'd never adopted her." Whap! Daddy's open palm smacks the tabletop like a crack of thunder.

The next thing I know I'm in the bathroom, the only room in the house with a door that locks, sitting on the floor shivering. I wrap the bathmat around my shoulders and hug my knees.

"I'll tell you one thing. If she goes, I go too," Mama yells. "You just remember that, Ken Kirchner!" It's the first and only argument I ever overheard them having and my mother was defending me against my father, something I never thought she'd do.

There's a roaring in my ears like I'm standing near a waterfall. I can't make out what else they say, their voices are too muffled, but I know it's mostly Mama talking. When I think they've gone to their room, I open the bathroom door and tiptoe into my room. I sit on the edge of the bed in the dark. Before long, Mama comes in.

"Everything's going to be all right," she whispers. "You're not going anywhere. Daddy didn't mean it. He's had too much to drink. He can't hold his liquor, never could—that's why he doesn't do it very often. You go on to sleep, now. Everything will be fine in the morning."

I crawl into bed. Maybe Daddy agreed to adopt me because Mama wanted a baby and he wanted Mama. Maybe she threatened to leave him if he would not agree to adopt. Maybe he never wanted me in the first place. I try to keep it together, but my head feels like my brain is a bowl of wet noodles without the bowl. My father had never forgotten I was not his flesh and blood. It *did* make a difference. It always had.

The next morning, I get up early. No one else is up yet so I go to the bathroom and start getting ready for church. My father doesn't want me. He doesn't want to be my father any more. What am I going to do? I seem to feel numb all over.

Outside, the day is bright and clear. I know it will be hot later, but now a soft breeze is wafting in through my open windows. Everything beyond my bedroom windows looks so normal, so healthy, so green and growing. Something in me hurts, but I can't seem to pinpoint the sensation.

In the kitchen, Bill is sitting at the table. She's made coffee and is eating a sweet roll. She looks tired. She must have heard the whole thing, her bedroom being the first one down the hall off the kitchen. I hope she got *some* sleep last night, but up close I can see she is red-eyed and a little shaky. She quietly pats my hand.

Mom comes in looking and sounding overly cheerful, as though she can repair the damage by force of will. She is wearing her yellow linen slacks and a white blouse. She puts her apron on. "Would you like some pancakes?"

"I'm not hungry," I say.

"How about an egg, then? You need more protein." She fries an egg for me and one for Bill and says I can stay home from church if I want.

I turn to Bill. "Do you want to go to church? If you do, I'll drive you if Mama doesn't feel like going."

In the end we all skip church. I change into my work clothes. Mama says I can take the car. She won't need it.

Neither Bill nor Mama ever made me feel like I was a

burden, or that I was stupid or insufficiently loved or an unwanted mistake. Over the years, Mama has pointed out most of my shortcomings, but I never doubted that she loved me.

I tell myself words can't kill a person. If being raped didn't kill me, something my father said while drunk isn't going to, either. I'm fine. Really. I'm fine.

I didn't know my heart was broken. I only knew I was different now, changed in ways I could not comprehend, much less repair. I thought I would never be happy again.

Daddy gets up just before I have to leave for work. He is wearing his blue-striped pajamas and his blue bathrobe. He usually dresses before coming to the table for breakfast. Dark half-circles cup his eyes and he will not look at me directly. That's fine. I don't want to look at him either, and I certainly don't want to talk to him.

At least I can be grateful that my father's drinking is rare—usually only on special occasions and then never to the point of being really drunk. Last night was an exception. Some fathers get drunk on a regular basis and say horrible things to their kids or even beat them. Daddy doesn't do any of that. But I suppose he could stop being my father if he wanted to and I hate him for making me know that.

Over the next few days, I have difficulty concentrating and can't even read to escape. I go to work because I have to. I wonder what I'll do if he insists I move out. I wonder why he is so angry with me. Maybe if I contributed more to household expenses, things between us would be better. Why had I thought all the money I earned was mine? It kept anyone from having to give me spending money or buy me most of my clothes. But in families, everyone should pitch in. If I had figured that out sooner, maybe Daddy wouldn't dislike me so much.

I look for a better paying job, but with no luck. I offer

Mama my next paycheck. She won't take it. I put gas in the car. My dad continues to avoid me as much as possible.

When I tell Sheila what happened, she tells me her dad has said some really awful things to her too, especially when drunk. At least Sheila and I have each other.

"You can count on one thing," I tell her. "I'll never marry a damn drunk. I can promise you that." And no matter what my father says or does, I will never forgive him.

Two weeks later, it's my eighteenth birthday. When I come into the kitchen that morning, there are two birthday cards waiting for me on the table. Daddy is up earlier than usual for a Friday. He must have gotten off early the night before. As I sit down to breakfast, he is drinking his morning coffee. He wishes me happy birthday and says he has something to tell me. I wonder if he and my mom are moving. Since his news is rarely good for me, I am not anxious to hear it.

"There's this couple in Evansville," he says, "two of my best customers, who sometimes sponsor deserving high school students to go to college. If they like you, they are willing to set up a private fund at the college of your choice. What do you think about that?"

I don't know what to think. Who are these people?

I will have to be interviewed by the wife, Daddy says. It's mostly her money. I will also have to keep up my grades, of course.

"Isn't this wonderful news" Mama says.

I suppose it's wonderful. If they like me, I'll get to go to college. That means I have somewhere to go and some direction to go in. It means if they like me they will give me money that will change my life. I'll have options, which is what I said I wanted. It also means I will leave home, which is what Daddy said he wants. How did this offer of money for college come about? It probably started with my father telling one of his wealthy customers he has a daughter who wants to go to college and he can't afford to send her. Maybe he said I was smart and it would be a shame if I couldn't go. Maybe he said he really needed to get me out of the house and the only way my mother would hear of it was if I go to school. Maybe someone told him to talk to these wealthy people and he did. The only thing I know for sure is that he's acting like he and I never had a problem.

"Where would you like to go to college?" Mom asks. She, too, is ignoring the elephant in the room.

I don't want to go to a big university any more. I am in no condition to handle the anonymity of a campus with twenty-thousand-plus students. I might vanish completely.

"It's too late to apply to UK," I say. "I know some kids who are going to Murray State. That's the closest school. Maybe I can get in there."

"I hear that's a good school," Mom says. She thinks all colleges are good.

"What do you want to study?" my father asks.

"I might study acting, or English. I like to write."

Mother does not respond, but Daddy snorts, unimpressed. This was not the answer he was looking for.

"But I like science, too," I add, as a fast afterthought.

Daddy stubs out his cigarette and stands to go. "You better be a nurse then, or a science teacher or even an English teacher. That way, you'll have something to fall back on."

Afterward, I go out to the front porch and sit down. I wonder what Mama said to Daddy following his drunken outburst. Knowing her, she did not let him get away with it unscathed, though I doubt she will ever tell me what she said. This is shaping up to be a particularly unforgettable birthday.

I wonder if Ann Elizabeth realizes it's my eighteenth birthday. I wonder where she is and if she thinks about me on August fourth. I almost always think of her on this day.

Pee Wee comes ambling over and sits beside me. I put my arms around him and hug him. He licks my face and rubs his head against my arm. He smells like he's rolled in something dead, but I don't care. I feel like crying, and I don't really know why. I ought to be thrilled and relieved, but I'm not. I'm not anything and I still have to be interviewed by some rich lady I don't even know. Plus, I don't know anything about being interviewed and I don't know anything about going to college.

I'll wear my purple shirtwaist with the self-belt. I look good in that dress. It makes my eyes look lavender. I wonder what she'll ask me. I mostly don't want to sound like a fool. The more I think about it the more I worry. I hope she doesn't ask me about sororities and stuff like that.

The interview is short and seems to go fine, though totally perfunctory. I feel like I'm sinking. I can't seem to rid myself of the fog coating my brain. I am trying to focus on the next steps, one at a time, until I leave for school. I am so lost, I don't even wonder what will happen to my dog when I leave for school.

Bill is unusually quiet during these two weeks. It never occurs to me that my leaving home will be sad for her, or that it will affect her situation. Nor do I understand how much this rescue likely cost my father in terms of his pride and self-respect. He probably had to go hat-in-hand and ask for the money.

In writing this memoir and reflecting on the events of that summer, I came to understand the level of stress my father was under back then. Stress doesn't excuse or ameliorate his behavior, but it does explain it. He was trapped in another bartending job with a commute of over a hundred miles per day partly because of me. He had dropped out of school at fourteen and gone to work to help his mother and sisters. Compared to that, I must have seemed like a real burden, especially if he was thinking about four more years of paying for my clothes, school, food, and books. He had no education and was nearly fifty-two years old with no retirement. What would he and my mom do when they got too old to work? He had to be worried. My grandmother cost him money. He couldn't save a dime, and now he was supposed to send me to college? In most every way that counted, my father did the very best he could for me. Unfortunately, that did not include saying he was sorry. I wish it had.

More Trouble with Men

Not knowing anything about how college works—no one in the family has ever been, except Aunt Eva back in Topeka fifty years ago—I check biology as my proposed major on the Murray State University entrance form. I have no intention of becoming a nurse or a teacher, but I want to appear smart so I go for one of the sciences. I know the difference between being smart and merely trying to assume the appearance of it, but figure I'll worry about the substantive part later.

Since I checked biology, the academic advisor to which I am assigned is in the biology department. In addition to English, history, and physical education, he enrolls me in advanced chemistry, a five-credit-hour course for science majors, and a four-credit-hour algebra for science majors—for which, as it turns out, I am completely under-prepared. There are chemistry and algebra courses for liberal arts majors, which is where I belong, but neither he nor I understand that at the time.

MSU is over-crowded and late applicants like me are housed in the old football boys' dorm, which smells like one might imagine. There are four girls to a room, with two sets of bunk beds, two desks, two closets, and two chests of drawers. My roommates are Flo from New Jersey, Carol from Chicago, and Pat from Florida. Pat's clothes almost fill one of the closets and one of the chests of drawers.

For an only child with emotional issues who grew up in a quiet environment, I feel like I'm suffocating. I am also struggling in algebra and chemistry, and am suddenly painfully shy, afraid of walking across campus alone or of speaking up in class. Convinced strangers are laughing at me, that everyone knows I don't belong, I begin having panic attacks again, which I try to hide for fear of irritating my roommates. In short, I am a mess.

By Halloween, I am totally lost in algebra and almost lost in chemistry. I am increasingly depressed. I had thought I was academically and intellectually ready for college, but now I realize that is not the case. I am failing and can't help wondering if my father's low opinion of my abilities might be well founded. Nothing is turning out the way I expected.

I spend most of my time hiding in the library, reading. That makes my English and history grades adequate, but not good enough to offset nine hours of D's and F's. I manage to make one or two friends over the course of the first three months, but I am drifting and seem powerless to turn things around. I go home as often as possible, just to feel grounded again. It doesn't help.

One weekend in March, I catch a ride to Sturgis with an older student who is going on to Evansville. He drops me off at the Dairy Maid and while I am waiting for Mom to pick me up, a boy named Roger, from history class at Murray, sees me and comes over to say hi. We had been in a group that studied together for the midterm.

"What are you doing here?" I ask.

He says he's in town visiting his grandparents.

"I had no idea you had relatives in Sturgis."

"I haven't seen them in a while, so I hitched a ride. Too bad I don't have a car or we'd do something tomorrow night."

"Give me your grandparents' phone number," I say. "I'll ask my mom if I can borrow her car tomorrow night and we'll go to the movies. I'll call you."

Mom had a little gray Renault for running into town to shop, going to church functions during the week, or visiting the neighbors. She used it every day to drive the half-mile to my uncle's house to give his wife her daily morphine injection. Uncle C.K.'s wife Ethel was waging the end of a seven-year battle with the ravages of breast cancer. My uncle could not bring himself to give his emaciated and dying wife her daily shot, so my mom agreed to do it for him. Mom had given herself hormone injections for two decades and knew how to do it. To help both my mom and my uncle, Daddy bought her the little car, getting a really great deal on it from someone he'd met at work. However, he couldn't afford to insure it or replace it if something happened to it.

Ignoring all of that, I think only of getting out of the house almost as soon as I arrive. If my dad had been there, he would never have given in, but Mom was easier and so I pushed. She didn't want to let me borrow it, but she wanted me to be happy. At the time, I did not consider that she was still worried about my mental health.

Nevertheless, when I ask to borrow the car, Mom says, "No. Absolutely not. Nice girls do not pick up boys in their cars."

"That is simply too old-fashioned, even for you," I say.

"I don't care. The answer is no. It isn't fair of you to ask. I've only had the car a few months, and I love it. It's small and zippy, and I need it with your dad gone five nights a week. Besides, I have a bad feeling about this."

"Oh, Mother. Don't be so superstitious!" I badger until she finally gives in.

Roger and I go to the movies in Morganfield. On the way home, we're talking and I'm driving too fast for a badly banked curve with loose gravel on the shoulder. At the top of the curve, the rear end of the car starts to slide in the gravel, and without thinking, I slam on the brakes. That little Renault flips over like a pancake on a hot griddle. It slides down the hill on its roof, scraping the pavement and sending sparks flying. No one is coming toward us from the opposite direction, so we are not hit, as we easily could have been. At the bottom of the hill, the car rolls over into a ditch and rocks to a halt, right side up, perpendicular to the highway.

When I come to my senses and look around, Roger is in the back seat with minor scrapes and scratches. I am gripping the steering wheel with a piece of windshield stuck in my forehead and blood dripping down my face. The radio is still playing, but the gas tank and fenders are lying in the middle of the road about twenty yards back, fuel sloshing onto the asphalt. With all those sparks, I don't know how the car kept from catching fire.

I ask Roger if he is all right. He says yes, he thinks so. Suddenly, I'm out of the car and running. Roger stops me, slaps my face to stop the panic (I suppose he read to do that somewhere), and the next thing I know we are in the emergency room at the small local hospital back in Morganfield. I have no memory of how we got there. A nurse cleans up Roger's injuries and a doctor checks him over after pulling the glass out of my forehead and stitching the wound. Then I phone home.

"I told you so," Mom says, "but oh no, you just *had* to take some boy to the movies. Well I hope you're satisfied. You always were totally headstrong, stubborn, and self-centered." She calls my uncle and sends him to pick us up.

"Daddy will be furious," I say as we drive home. Uncle C.K. doesn't disagree.

We drop Roger off at his grandmother's house. When I tell him good-bye, I mean it. Surely there's no future for Roger and me since I had just tried to kill him. That night, as I try to sleep, I keep seeing the car flip over. Bill hears me crying and comes to my room. She pats my arm and whispers, "Don't worry. They won't stay mad long. They'll just be glad you weren't seriously hurt." Of course, she was right, but at the time I didn't believe her.

Between being academically underprepared for college, and being an emotional basket case, my freshman year was a disaster. Of the twenty-six hours attempted, I managed to end the year with seven hours of usable credits above a grade of D. Algebra was a total loss. After I wrecked my mother's car, I stopped going to most of my classes.

My father would disown me now for sure, I thought, and he'd be completely justified. All that money wasted. But when I call home to tell them I have flunked out, he is not angry. He doesn't threaten me or tell me what a disappointment I am. Instead, he tells me to come home. He says I can try college again next year. He sounds almost happy and very sincere and perhaps for me that has been the goal all along—to find out what my dad would do if I flunked out.

Within days, I realize that I am so humiliated and feel so guilty, I simply can't go home. I call a married friend from high school who is living in Indianapolis. She and her husband want to rent part of their house. So as soon as school is out, I catch a ride with a senior going home to Indianapolis. There I find a job as a shipping clerk in a plastics factory and spend the summer working, taking public transportation, and trying to save money to prove I can take care of myself. If I go back to school, I intend to pay my own tuition—for one semester at least, to see how I do. In Indianapolis, I am bored, homesick, and lonely, but I stick it out. Penance needs to be paid.

On August 4, Mama calls to wish me a happy nineteenth birthday.

"Why don't you come home?" she says. "We miss you."

"I miss you, too, but I have a job and I'm doing all right."

"Starting next week, your dad is going to housesit for a friend in Evansville," she says. "There's plenty of room; it's a big house. You could get a job in Evansville and live rent-free and save even more money for going back to college."

My father gets on the phone. "Whirlpool is hiring," he says. "My boss at the club says he'll see to it you get on there. They pay better than what you're making where you are. Come on home."

I do not require much persuasion and ten days later I'm on a Greyhound bus headed south to Evansville. Daddy will meet me at the bus station when he gets off work. Even though I've taken the latest bus they have, I will still have to wait nearly an hour at the terminal. The bar where Daddy works closes at midnight; the bus gets in a little after eleven.

"There's a nice café at the depot," Daddy says, "where you'll be perfectly safe until I get there, as long as you stay inside."

The day is a scorcher. I dress in a sleeveless white linen sheath with matching wide-brimmed straw hat, hot pink hatband, pink high heels and white-framed sunglasses. I'm going for that Audrey Hepburn look in *Breakfast at Tiffany's*. I sit alone and flirt, via the rear-view mirror, with the extremely attractive bus driver, a Cary Grant look-alike with a killer smile and blue bedroom eyes that he couldn't seem to take off me. I remove my hat and fluff my hair. I shift in my seat so I can dangle one leg into the aisle. I hope he doesn't run us off the road. I pretend to read and glance at him frequently, protected I believe, behind my large dark sunglasses.

When the bus pulls into its only scheduled rest stop along the way, the door swooshes open and the driver steps down onto the dirt to help the passengers disembark. As I climb down he holds my hand a moment longer than necessary and then gives it a slight, but unmistakable, squeeze before releasing it to assist the person behind me.

I sit at a table as far from the jukebox as possible and order a cup of coffee—more sophisticated than Coke, I think. I light a cigarette and strike what I think is an alluring pose.

"Mind if I join you?" It's the bus driver.

His name is Jeff. I'm not sure his smile actually extends to his eyes, but he is movie-star handsome—for an older man—and I am definitely flattered by the attention.

He orders coffee and stares at me until I am uncomfortable.

"Do you know how beautiful you are?" he whispers.

I shake my head and feel myself blush.

"You're like a frisky young colt," he says, "all soft and dewy-eyed, but so full of energy and life and curiosity. It's really nice to see."

I don't know what to say. I wonder if he's sincere. He *might* be.

"Is someone meeting you at the terminal in Evansville?" he asks.

"My dad, but he can't be there exactly when we arrive, so I'm supposed to wait in the café."

"I'd be happy to wait with you," Jeff says. "After a long trip, I usually stop in for a cup of coffee before heading home." He looks around. "That part of town, late at night. It isn't really safe for a young girl alone."

I mumble something about that not being necessary and thank him. Again, I am at a loss. He really is one of the best-looking men I have ever seen in person—and he's wearing a uniform. I know it's just a bus driver's uniform, not the army or the marines or anything like that, but still, it's pressed and creased and spotless. To my schoolgirl eyes, he looks quite dashing.

When all the passengers are back on board, the door folds shut and the bus begins backing up like a drunken pachyderm. Darkness has overtaken us, but I can still see Jeff eyeing me in the rearview mirror. This is the first time I am aware of attracting the attention of an older man and I am finding it intoxicating.

When we arrive at the depot in Evansville, Jeff finds me in the depot's café, second booth from the door, by the windows where I can watch for my father's car. When the waitress comes, Jeff orders a beer. "You should have one too," he says. "It'll relax you."

I order coffee. "I'm not old enough to drink," I say, "and I don't really like beer. I thought you needed coffee after a long trip."

He shrugs and unbuttons his shirt collar button. "I changed my mind. It's okay for a man to change his mind, isn't it?"

"Well, sure," I say.

"It's just that..." He lowers his eyes. "I know you'd never be interested in an older man, a lovely young girl like you. It makes me sad is all."

"Pardon me?" What makes him sad? And what did that have to do with his ordering beer instead of coffee?

"You have your whole life in front of you. I guess I'm jealous," he says. "I hope you'll enjoy your youth. Have some fun. Don't be afraid to take a few risks. That's what makes life worthwhile."

"When I go back to school next summer, I'm going to change my major from biology to English," I say. "That doesn't involve taking much of a risk, though. I used to want to be an actress, or a writer, but I'm probably going to be a high school English teacher—if I ever manage to graduate."

"That doesn't sound very exciting," he says. "But writers and actresses, now that's a different story. They have to know what life is all about to be any good at their craft."

"Oh, I agree." Here is a man, I decide, who understands. He sighs.

"What's wrong?" I ask.

He lays both hands open, palms up on the table. "I'm still grieving over the loss of my wife, I suppose." He stares past me. "After twenty-two years of marriage." He shakes his head and takes another sip of beer.

He seems so sad. I feel sorry for him.

"I'm so sorry," I say. "Was she ill a long time?"

"Oh, she's not dead. She left me for a younger man. Ran off with no warning." He leans closer and lowers his voice. "We never had children because, well, I can't. It's my fault. I'm sterile. When we found out, she said it was fine, but it really wasn't fine at all. She wanted children so she found someone else." He looks down at the table.

The poor man, I think. He just needs somebody to talk to.

"She always said I was a wonderful lover even if I couldn't make babies. But I guess she wanted babies more than she wanted me."

My scalp prickles and a warning light begins flashing faintly in my head.

"I feel like I can talk to you," Jeff says. "Like you'll understand." He moves to my side of the booth. I edge toward the window. This is past feeling icky, like there is quicksand underfoot just waiting for me to make a false step. I figure I am safe enough, though the place is not exactly packed. There are four other people here, including the waitress and the bartender.

"Do you think you could ever go out with somebody like me, someone my age, I mean?"

Do I look like I'm a complete idiot? Apparently yes, I do. I am such a late bloomer in so many ways, at so many levels. And though I am definitely naïve, I am not stupid, regardless of what old Jeff might think. Old Jeff is full of shit.

"Um, well, um, I have a boyfriend. He's a Marine," I say, which isn't exactly true. I had dated someone in

Indianapolis, a very nice boy who was home on leave from the Corps, but we'd only gone to a couple of movies and a picnic once before his leave ended. After that we exchanged a few letters, but no more.

Jeff gives me a sly smile and lays his arm across the back of the booth near my shoulders. "I'm sure you've had boys," he says, "What you need is a man. I have a room upstairs. Come with me." He stands, extends his hand, and nods in the direction of a side door toward the back of the café. "Come on. Let me make love to you. I know how to please women—and I'm safe. I can't make you pregnant. You've been with self-centered, inexperienced boys. Aren't you curious about what a man with a way with women can do?"

Wasn't that like a line from *Gone with the Wind?* I had absolutely no idea how to handle this guy. The truth was, I was nineteen with limited experience, and yes, of course, I was curious about men. But I had better sense, and taste, than to experiment with old Jeff. Or maybe I was just too scared.

"Um, my dad will be here any minute." The instant those words pass my lips I realize he thinks I'd have said yes if it weren't for my father's imminent arrival.

He smiles. "How about a phone number, then? I'll call you sometime."

"Um, well, I don't actually live in Evansville. We live about fifty miles from here."

He stands up abruptly, chugs the rest of his beer, and sets the bottle down with a bang. "Can't blame a guy for trying." He shrugs and leaves me sitting there as I finally get the full and oh-so-ugly picture.

Did old Jeff's approach ever work? Seriously? I bet he practiced it on as many unsuspecting young women as possible. Was his wife at home right now waiting for him with no clue what a sleaze bag he really was? I hoped she *had* run off with a younger man. Nobody deserved to be married to old Jeff. Eeewh.

I stared at my wavy reflection in the darkened window-pane. As far as I could see, I didn't look any dumber than any other nineteen-year-old. Of course, I was playacting a bit in my Audrey Hepburn dress and hat, and I did have that weak chin. Was that it? Was that enough to target me as vulnerable? Was that why old Jeff had zeroed in on me, why Bobby Joe had attacked me? Or was I somehow even more fundamentally flawed? Without any relatives with whom to compare myself, I couldn't tell if I was different or the same as most of the other female members of my family. Nor did I know how important genetic heritage was in this area. Maybe there were other family members who'd been preyed on. Or maybe it was just that I was the only young woman on the bus that night, the only other female in the car that other night. I simply did not know the answer to "why me?" If I was going to do well in life, I would have to be very careful, pushing most everyone away, for the foreseeable future.

I did not know it, but I was following a predictable course. Due to the trauma of the rape and being rejected by my father, I was suffering from a decreased ability to enjoy life. Years later, age and psychotherapy took care of that.

For most of my nineteenth year, I live and work in Evansville. The first job they assign me to at Whirlpool is operating a high-speed saw in cold water, mitering gaskets for refrigerator doors. The company is behind on a huge order and we put in twelve-hour shifts for the first month. When that job ends, I operate a punch press with both hands in a harness that snaps them back if I trip the press at the wrong time, which I do once. If not for that harness, I would have lost my right hand in that split second of miscalculation.

After the job at Whirlpool ends, I spray-paint Chevrolet emblems at Shawnee Plastics, breathing blue paint and

Carole's parents in front of the house in Evansville, Indiana.

standing on a wooden platform beside a vat of acetone. I cough up blue paint and have dreams of being chased by huge hydraulic punch presses trying to chop off various parts of my body. Nothing provides more incentive for going back to college than a year of working on an assembly line in some dirty, dangerous factory with a group of women who swear like sailors, hate and envy young people, and who have lost all hope of a better life.

The house Dad is taking care of is a large French provincial located on the east side of town, a block from the University of Evansville. The house belongs to George B., a man Daddy met through work, another of his "best customers." George was a local businessman and an occasional high roller.

He had recently moved his family to Florida, but didn't want to sell their Evansville home. When Dad moved into the house, my parents sent my grandmother to Grand Junction to live with my aunt Bessie. My mom closed the house in Sturgis and moved to Evansville, too. I did not get to say good-bye to Bill. She was already gone by the time I arrived back from Indianapolis. My dog Pee Wee also disappeared just before I came home.

Mama says she searched for Pee Wee for days and alerted all the neighbors. I want to go back to Sturgis to look for myself, but Mama says if he found another home, we should leave him alone since they can't keep him in Evansville anyway, and I cannot take him to college with me when I go back.

I know from experience that protests are useless and convince myself Pee Wee is happy with another family who loves dogs and will take good care of him. He is only eight years old.

Later I came to suspect my father had him put down, though I never asked and he wouldn't have admitted it if he had. I also wanted to believe my grandmother was happy and well-cared for in Colorado. She loved it there when she was younger. But I miss her.

Mama and Daddy like living in the big house, partly because the owner is rarely there and it is a beautiful home. However, one particular week at the end of the summer of 1963, after I have gone back to college at Murray for summer school, George comes in to town from Florida on business. He is at the house for two weeks and I am there, too, since I am between the end of the summer session and the start of the fall semester. I paid for summer school myself and made all A's on my way to digging myself out of the academic hole I'd previously gotten myself into.

On the last Saturday before I am scheduled to return to school, George and my father invite me to go with them to the races. We sit in a box seat courtesy of someone George knows, which apparently includes a large number of people. As I watch George meet and greet at the track, I find him charming, energetic, and self-confident to the point of appearing cocky. He is well dressed in a light blue summer suit and white shirt. He is also on the short side, five-ten or less, with hair graying at the temples and a wad of bills thick enough to choke the horses he's betting on. Clearly, he considers himself a player. And just as clearly, I can see how much my father envies him.

George claims to believe in luck. "Some gambling involves skill, but mostly, it's a matter of luck," he says. "Lady luck is either with you or she's against you. But sometimes, who you know helps." He and my dad both laugh; I have no idea what about and I don't much care. I do not believe in luck. Believing in luck is dangerous. My father never bet more than twenty dollars on a horserace in his life, not that I know of, but here he is, showing off for George, trying to run with the big dogs. I have never seen him act so out control, at least not when completely sober. He is betting fifty and a hundred dollars at a time, and barely breaking even. With every race the tension builds.

Prior to the seventh race, my father leans over, slaps a stack of bills in my hand. "Here," he says. "You place the next bet. Five hundred to win on Electric Velvet."

"Are you sure?" I say.

"Yeah. Go on. You're over eighteen. You can do it. Better get down there before you get shut out."

"Daddy. I just turned twenty."

He waves me off backhandedly. "You know what I mean. Go on. Have some fun."

I hesitate. I want to say I can't place such a large bet. I want to insist he come with me. Instead, I hurry to the pari-mutuel window, nervous with all that cash, and torn between wanting to do what he told me to do and wanting to protect my father from making a huge mistake that will make him angry and unhappy and make my mother furious. Electric Velvet has only won one of his last five races. Maybe George B. can afford to wager five hundred dollars on a single horse with no winning record to speak of, but my father can't. It would be terrible if he lost. He'd be devastated. Five hundred dollars is a small fortune. What is Daddy thinking? But if I spread the bet out on a win, place, or show ticket he'd have a better chance of winning something. If I bet it all to win and the horse comes in second, even by a nose, Daddy will lose everything. But if I split the ticket and the horse runs second or third, Daddy will still make money and he'll be grateful. I can picture in my head the scenario whereby I get to be the hero of the day—when Electric Velvet runs second. It does not occur to me that I might be showing off for George, too, a girl who knows about gambling and horse races. Lots of things do not occur to me, such as, it is not my money and no one in their right mind messes with someone else's wager.

I step up to the window, still arguing with myself, and shove the money through the opening and say, "Five hundred to win, place, or show on Electric Velvet in the seventh."

Then I watch the odds. Electric Velvet closes at six-to-one—a two-dollar wager yields a fourteen-dollar return. But a five-hundred-dollar wager to win at six-to-one would net around thirty-five-hundred dollars. With a split ticket, Daddy would only win roughly a third of that if the horse runs first. When I hand him the ticket, his eyebrow shoots up to his hairline.

"What the hell?" The gun sounds, and they're off.

Electric Velvet wins by two lengths. Daddy is on his feet, towering over me and screaming. "God-damnit! Can't you do anything right? You always think you're so damn smart. Like you know more than everybody else. Jesus H. Christ, I thought I could trust you to do one simple God-damn thing. Shit. I should have known better. Stupid fucking…! God-damnit!"

"I'm sorry. I was just…"

"Shut up. Just sit there. I don't want to hear it. God-damnit!"

With that bet, I had cost my father approximately two thousand dollars—tuition money for two whole years. Worse, I suspect, was the fact that I had robbed him of his victory celebration with George. He was so angry the cords in his neck were bulging as hard as bones. I was afraid he was going to have a stroke. He stalked off to claim his meager winnings and try to get himself under control. He did not speak to me the rest of the day. This was another car wreck. I couldn't seem to do anything right.

Back at the house later that evening, I am sitting up in bed reading when I hear a tap at my bedroom door. Assuming it's my mom, I say come in. My room is at the opposite end of the house from the other bedrooms.

The door opens and there is George. "It's just me," he says. He pushes the door closed behind him.

"I'm really sorry about what happened," he says. He stands with his hands folded in front of him, head down looking at the floor. "It was actually my fault. I suggested your dad let you place the bet. I thought you'd get a kick out of it. We should have told you we pretty well knew the horse would win, but your dad wanted that to be part of the surprise." Since it was not his money, George could be reasonable.

"I was afraid he'd lose it all."

George grimaces. "Yeah. I guessed that much." He shrugs apologetically. "I know the jockey. It was as close to a sure thing as there is in horseracing. We should have told you."

"I shouldn't have changed Daddy's bet."

George shrugs. "No, but then you're not a gambler."

The words on the page before me begin to swim. I shut my eyes, determined not to cry. I had already been sufficiently embarrassed in front of George for one day.

"Whatcha reading?" he asks.

I blink and show him the cover. "Drury's *Advise and Consent.*"

"Any good?"

"It won the Pulitzer a couple of years ago."

"Really? I'll have to read it." He has migrated to the

edge of my bed and sits down—uninvited. "So, have you been to the museum here in town?"

"No. Any good?"

He points at me. "Quick," and grins. "It's not a bad museum for a city the size of Evansville. You'd enjoy it. It covers art, history, and science. I'd be glad to take you. We could go tomorrow afternoon."

Before I can respond, the door to my room swings open and there stands my mother with her arms folded across her chest, fire shooting out of her eyes. From the set of her jaw anyone can see that her face is about to crack and fall off her skull.

"What's going on here?" she says.

"Nothing," I say, irritated by the unspoken accusation. "We were just talking about books and the Evansville Museum."

George had already jumped up like he'd been caught with his hand in a collection jar for crippled children.

"Yeah, well I know where talking can lead. George, you need to go on to bed. Just because we're living in your house, doesn't mean you can take advantage." She glares at him; I glare at her. Of all the times to decide to play angry mother hen protecting her chick. Damn it, I thought. I can take care of myself.

George excuses himself, gives me the "Oh-shit!-I-got-you-in-even-more-trouble" look over Mom's shoulder and backs gingerly out of my room.

"What do you mean letting a man in your bedroom in the middle of the night?" Mom is slicing the air with her hand like she's wielding a hatchet.

"He just came to say he was sorry about what happened at the track today. He felt bad for me. He sort of thought it was his fault, I guess."

"I bet he did."

"We were only talking. He was being nice after Daddy…"

She looks at me like I'm lying through my teeth. "He

was trying to get into your pants and you were encouraging him."

Even if she was right about George, she was dead wrong about me. I was not encouraging him. She didn't understand how upset I was. If George had been more obvious, I'd have shooed him out of my room already. But it didn't matter. I had not the slightest intention of allowing myself to be talked into bed by a friend of my father's. Did I attract predators like ants to a picnic? I must really look like easy pickings. I was going to have to work on that.

In October, while I am back at college trying to become a sophomore, Dad quits his bartending job to take a job with the Kentucky State Parks System—compliments of help from yet another of his "best customers." Mom and Dad move out of George's house, sell the family home near Sturgis, along with all our possessions—all our furniture, pots and pans, dishes, silverware and linens, my piano, everything except our clothes—and move to east Kentucky. I find out about it in a letter. For several weeks I don't even know for sure where they are as they are traveling to each of the existing parks in the state's system as part of Dad's orientation.

Now I have no home, and no room of my own anymore anywhere. My grandmother is two thousand miles away in Colorado and my dog, if he is still alive, is lost somewhere in the west Kentucky countryside. All I know is that I'm miserable again and not at all ready to be on my own.

I talk to my mom by phone, standing in the hallway of the dorm with girls passing and talking and music blaring in the background.

"Where are you, now?" I ask above the noise.

"We're at Jenny Wiley State Park outside of Prestonsburg, in east Kentucky," she says. "It is so beautiful here. You can come for a visit between semesters at Christmas, but not for Thanksgiving. Is there any place you can go for the holiday?"

"I'll ask my roommate if I can go home with her," I say.

She tells me that when Daddy completes his training, he will serve as assistant manager at a state park somewhere in eastern Kentucky, probably for a year. Then hopefully he will be assigned a park of his own to manage. She will let me know where, as soon as they know, but I should not plan on seeing them before Christmas vacation.

Clearly, I will never go home again. Suddenly I can't breathe. I feel like I'm treading water in the deep end. Over the next few weeks I suffer a series of panic attacks again and cannot rid myself of a sense that the floor is sinking beneath my feet.

When I was younger, I often felt like I had blinders on, as though there were things going on around me I could neither see nor understand. There was a whole world out there to which I was not privy, and I wanted to be. I wanted to understand how life worked, especially around people. Now, however, I was glad for those blinders. They allowed me to put one foot in front of the other and simply keep going regardless of extremes lurking at the periphery.

For Thanksgiving, I go home with my new roommate, a girl from Collierville, Tennessee. By Christmas, my father is serving as a manager-in-training at Cumberland Falls State Park in south-central Kentucky. I find someone going to Somerset, Kentucky, for the holidays and arrange to ride with her. Daddy meets us at a gas station in town and we ride the rest of the way to the park, just the two of us. My father is as happy as I have ever seen him. He loves his new job, and although the money is not great, he says, the benefits are.

At the lodge, I have a room all my own next to my parents. The old lodge once belonged to the DuPont family and was built at a time when it could only be reached on horseback. It has a huge stone fireplace along one end and large widows in the front. Everything is decorated for Christmas with garlands along banisters and across the mantel and a decorated Christmas tree that reaches to the rafters.

That night it snows several inches, and in the morning the pristine scene beyond the windows and front doors is breathtaking. Only a few deer and rabbit tracks disturb the surface of the snow. The park ranger offers to take anyone dressed for a hike to the falls to see it frozen. The ice contains all the colors of the rainbow, the result of mineral deposits in the water.

Several travelers on their way to Florida and Alabama for the holidays are trapped along with us and part of the hotel staff. We have a great time, playing board and card games, singing Christmas Carols, and putting together meals, which we share at one long table in the dining room. It is a wonderful two days before the snow melts sufficiently for people to continue their journeys. This vacation leaves me feeling that perhaps everything will be all right after all.

~ 21 ~

Kissing Bill Goodbye

In the spring, Dad is appointed manager at the newest park in the state system, Buckhorn Lake State Park near Hazard, Kentucky. He only served as an assistant manager for a few weeks before being given a park of his own.

Mom is to be in charge of the dining room staff. The park has not yet opened so my dad will have to arrange for the landscaping, the creation of a beach and swimming area, the new pool, and the hiring of most of the staff. He works long hours and is often frustrated, but he loves it. My parents' new life is exciting for them and I am glad. Mama is fifty-nine and Daddy is fifty-six. If they work for ten more years, they'll have a modest state retirement to supplement their social security. They can save a little money, Daddy says, living on the park itself. They will be all right.

During spring break, I visit Buckhorn Lake State Park for the first time. Daddy gives me the grand tour. Bulldozers are still scraping the mountainside prior to landscaping around the main lodge. Clouds nestle against the rim of the surrounding mountains and from time to time clumps of mist tumble along the treetops and roll onto the lake, blurring the line between air and water.

Buckhorn is a beautiful location and Daddy takes pride in the park there. He wants to make it the best in the system. He shows me where the beach and the swimming pool will be. After driving around the park and walking down to the lake, seeing the front of the lodge from below, we stop to sit on a picnic table and enjoy the view. He pulls a pack of cigarettes out of his shirt pocket and lights up. The afternoon air is warm. Daddy is in his shirtsleeves. I am fanning my face with a large leaf when out of the blue, he says, "I want to ask you a question."

My father wants to know what I think about something. I am thrilled. In my whole life he has never asked me anything more important than: "Where's your mother?" or "What's for supper?" He has never asked me anything remotely close to a substantive question. He never wanted to know if I thought there was intelligent life on other planets, or whom I believed would be the next president. Nothing. So for these and other reasons, this is monumental.

"Sure," I say. "What is it?" Knowing my father, I am fully prepared for disappointment. His big question might easily be, "What are your plans for when you finish college?"

He bends forward with his arms resting on his knees and gazes out at the water. He takes a drag from a newly lighted cigarette and exhales. "Do you believe in God and the hereafter?"

Needless to say, I am astonished. This is not just any question. This is *the* question, the one every human since the dawn of time has pondered. What, if anything, happens to us after we die? And *my father* wants to know what *I* think about that.

If I'd been younger, I might have simply said, "Of course." If I had been just a little older and wiser, I would have understood he was seeking reassurance, not an analysis of the human condition, and I would have said, "Of course." But that was not the case. I was a college junior, and opportunities to prove myself to my father did not come along every day. So, I took a deep breath and jumped on it—telling him what I actually thought.

"I don't know," I say. "No one does, not in the sense of having actual physical evidence—that kind of knowing. We don't know where the universe came from or why it exists, or even if there is a reason, and we definitely don't know what happens to us after we die—if anything. It's a matter of faith. People choose what they believe, usually based on the religious tradition they're born into. Faith is without proof or concrete evidence of any kind. That's why they call it faith."

He listens, but remains silent, smoking and looking out across the lake.

"As for religion, it doesn't seem likely to me that some human version of a Supreme Being visited a virgin on Earth and nine months later she gave birth to the Son of God. That sounds just a notch too much like a combination of wishful thinking on the part of men telling the story, and Greek and Roman mythology, which were also stories made up by men to explain how the world worked."

Now I was showing off, but I was still rather proud of my answer. It was honest, even courageous, I thought, not to mention mindful. But if I fancied this the beginning of a new dialogue between my father and me, a sharing between adults of their secret doubts, questions, ideas, hopes, and fears, my enthusiasm was short-lived. It would have behooved me to remember my father was a man of few words. He listened patiently, then grunted, shook his head in disgust, stubbed out his cigarette, and walked back to the lodge, slowly, with his hands clasped behind him. He was probably thinking something like, "Well, that was money well spent!" He never asked me what I thought about anything theoretical, philosophical, or substantive again.

He remained manager of Buckhorn Lake State Park for the next eight years.

During that time, I visited them in the summer and

over the Christmas holidays. When I called them, or when they called me, I nearly always talked to my mom. But my dad paid for the rest of my college and when I started my senior year he bought me a car—with the understanding that I would assume payments after I graduated and found a job, which I did.

Just before the last semester of my senior year, I travel to Grand Junction to see my grandmother. It's summer. Bill is ill and in failing health, but I am not prepared for how bad things really are. I have missed her terribly, but have written no more than a Christmas, birthday, or Mother's Day card since the last time I saw her. She turned eighty-five in January.

"She isn't even in a room," I say, when I see the hospital bed she's in. It is set up in a corner of the foyer of a small nursing home on the edge of town.

"It doesn't matter. She's blind," my aunt says. "She can't see where she is."

Of course it matters. How could you put your own mother in such a place and leave her there, alone, night after night? The least the staff could do is put a screen around her. I said none of this aloud, but my aunt reads my face.

"This is the only nursing home we could afford. I got to where I couldn't take care of her. I don't have the strength." Aunt Bessie rubs her roughened hands together and glares at me. "They'll put her in the first room that comes available."

She leaves then, so I can visit with Bill for a while. I sit on a folding chair by her bed in full view of every stranger who enters the building. I am angry. I hadn't seen my grandmother, the woman who raised me, for nearly two years. I was finishing college in Kentucky. She was ending her life in this awful place in Colorado.

I had planned to tell her about school and to read to her, but we can't really talk and she doesn't want me to read just then. In minutes, she is asleep. I sit beside her and wait.

She groans in pain and opens her eyes. I go to find a nurse, not understanding the differences between a nursing home and a hospital. "It's not time for her medication," I am told. "There's nothing I can do." I don't argue with the woman, but I should have. My grandmother is suffering.

When I return to Bill's bedside, she says, "I don't know why God is keeping me here. I just want to go on." I don't know what to say. I'm twenty-one. She's eighty-six.

"Would you like to get up?" I ask after a time, when she seems easier and a bit more awake. "I could take you to the sunroom."

"I don't think I can," she says.

"Sure you can." I fully believed I could help manage to get her into a nearby wheelchair and take her to the sunroom. I thought she needed to get out of bed and move around. I did not realize how weak she was, how feeble she'd become since I'd seen her last. I managed to get her on her feet, we took two steps, her knees buckled, and her legs gave way. If I had not been young and strong, she'd have fallen right there and hurt herself badly, bringing on even more pain and suffering. With the help of a passing orderly, I managed to get her back into bed, though we may have wrenched her back or an arm in the process.

While I'm in Grand Junction, I tell her about the young man I met this summer and think I might eventually marry. She smiles and nods. "Tell me all about him," she says. So I do.

"I met him on the first day of class, Shakespeare, earlier this summer…"

I got there early to get a good seat in the middle, about

three rows back. I am flipping through *The Complete Works of Shakespeare,* the most expensive textbook I'd ever had to buy, when into the room saunters a young man wearing cowboy boots, a cowboy hat, and Levis with a white tee shirt. He sits directly behind me and, as it turns out, can read Shakespeare with a semi-Shakespearean accent. He has just gotten out of the army in Texas and has a gorgeous tan that shows off his sandy-blond hair and green eyes. He reminds me of James Dean, good-looking, brooding, and intense. He is from a small town. He also lived in Detroit for a while. He likes the theater. He was an English major. We have so much in common...."

When I leave her that first day, she holds my hands in hers and tells me she loves me. Even then, I don't give Bill my full attention. I don't talk to her enough, or read to her enough, or sit with her as much as I should, though she never complains. I'm interested in seeing Charlotte's older brother, who still lives with his parent's on the adjoining farm. After speaking to him once, I am preoccupied with finding ways to encounter him at the mailbox, in church, at the grocery store. It's always wise to comparison shop. That's what Mama would say.

I don't even see Bill every day during those two weeks. My aunt and uncle are both still working and can't take me into town that often. Insulated by my age, I harbor the hope that Bill will "get well," regain her strength, and live until I can come back again. After all, Bill's mother, my great grandmother, lived to be ninety-seven.

When I'm ready to leave, my suitcase packed and waiting in my uncle's truck, I kiss Bill's soft and sagging cheek, refusing to believe this is the last time I will ever see her. She smiles up at me, her curly blue-white hair wreathed against the pillow. I clasp her hand and she squeezes mine lightly.

"I'll come back as soon as the school year is over," I say.

She does not respond. How could I have been so self-centered, so selfish, and so blind?

She died the following Mother's Day, 1965. My parents and I traveled to the funeral in Marysville, Kansas. She was buried near where she'd grown up, in a beautiful spot between two large cedar trees beside her mother and father and several of her siblings, on a hill in the rolling northeast Kansas prairie.

I marry J. Weldon Stice the following winter, three days after graduation. I wish Bill had been there.

With our degrees in English, we find jobs teaching for Job Corp in west Kentucky. I am hired to teach low-achieving young men to read and write and become fascinated with how hard my students work and how little progress many of them make. During that first year, I also realize my new husband has serious substance abuse issues and after ten months of less-than-wedded-bliss, I leave him.

I call my mother and move into a hotel. Mom comes from east Kentucky and together we confront my husband. The house is a wreck and he is passed out drunk in the living room. Mother says I cannot leave him in that condition. She helps me clean up the house and sober him up. He declares how sorry he is, and that he will do better. We remained married for nearly twelve more years.

During those dozen years, we achieved master's degrees and moved to Florida, where he works on his doctorate at Florida State and I taught elementary school. At the age of twenty-seven, I gave birth to our only child, Shelley. In the hospital, I checked her fingers and toes, smelled her baby scent, kissed her round face, and declared her perfect. My only regret was that I couldn't see her as clearly as I wanted to, even with my glasses on. As far as I knew, Shelley was the first person I had ever seen to whom I was biologically related. I was like every new mother, totally fascinated by each baby move, sound, and facial expression. I could hardly leave her long enough to cook and clean and kept her by my side as much as possible.

Mom came and stayed two weeks. I was very grateful for her help and terrified when she went home. When Shelley was two months old, my dad came for a visit. I was completely surprised he wanted to do that. It's the first time he had ever flown on a commercial airplane, but he said he wanted to see his granddaughter and he didn't want to wait till Christmas. He brought her a little red sleeper outfit. Red is his favorite color. I wished Bill had lived long enough to see my little girl. Shelley laughed at funny noises. She seemed to love everybody and almost never cried. My grandmother would have adored my daughter, though she, like my mother and father, would not have approved of my choice of husband.

When my dad left to go back home, I was almost relieved. Not only did he not care for my husband, he didn't like where we were living. It was a small rented house at the edge of town under the flight path for a nearby naval air station. It was terrible when the jets were practicing take-offs and landings, but it's all we could afford. I hoped then that before my father died, I would manage to amount to something he could approve of.

∼

PART 3

Losing Mom & Dad

∼

$\sim$ **22** $\sim$

A Question of Roots

Over the next decade, my husband and I finish our doctoral degrees and move to Nashville, Tennessee, where we both find college faculty positions, mine in teacher education, his in speech communication. In addition to being a teacher, Weldon is a frustrated singer, songwriter, and actor who wants to live in Music City.

We find an apartment near campus and within the month, he has auditioned for and won a part in a play with a local theater company that does musicals. For the next thirty-five years Weldon performs in community theater productions all over town and is well known and highly regarded for his singing and acting abilities. Unfortunately, he can't dance, so his options in musicals are somewhat limited.

Nashville is a good location for us. Only a two- to three-hour drive by car to both sets of our parents, we can dash home when we are needed. And the city is a fine place to raise our little girl. After two years there, we buy a house, and in another year we finally divorce, though we remain friends, especially after he finds Alcoholics Anonymous. Even when we are divorced, I never miss seeing any of his performances.

Coming to the decision that divorce was the only way forward was difficult. I did not want to give up on my family and I fought it longer than I should have, spending the next few years exploring various psychotherapies, learning about co-dependence and how to be a good single parent. My therapist diagnoses me as having difficulty adjusting to adult life. That sounds about right to me as I explore my "inner self" through insight group work, Primal Integration, Gestalt, Transcendental Meditation, and Transactional Analysis. I "work on" my childhood and the various traumas I'd experienced along the way. I explore such issues as why I married an alcoholic in the first place. One theory was that I was subconsciously trying to work out my relationship with my father.

By my mid-thirties, I also "work on" how I felt about having been sexually assaulted at seventeen, as well as how I coped with being adopted. In light of all that therapy, and the money it cost, at about the age of forty, I pronounced myself cured and stopped going.

Among other things, I believed I understood what being adopted meant in my life. I'd accepted it for what it was—just one more aspect of my identity—and had long since moved on. I was not an orphan. I was not abandoned, tossed into a dumpster, or left on a doorstep somewhere to live or die at the whim of fate. I had a wonderful family. Even though my mom and dad and I stumbled occasionally over the rocky road of the parent-child relationship, what family hasn't? My childhood was rich. I experienced a sense of extended family, I traveled with my grandmother, I lived in a variety of places. I had friends, cousins my own age, and pets. It was mostly really good, and I had a handle on the few aspects that weren't. My career was adequate and I loved the work. My daughter was wonderful, although I resented the fact that she looked more like her father's side of the family than like me, apart from her blue eyes and wide forehead. In other words, I considered myself a fairly well adjusted, normal adult, most of the time.

I still didn't like being the child who was given away at birth, just as I would not have liked having juvenile-onset diabetes or any number of other difficulties with which people have to cope. Being adopted was a blessing in my life. I was quite clear about that. And that was all in the past, ancient history. There was nothing I could do about any of it now, anyway. It was what it was, is what it is, end of story.

But what I thought was ancient history turned out to be merely buried history, like some prehistoric mastodon silently preserved in a peat bog to be unearthed at just the right moment, which arrived for me one evening in the spring of 1977.

I am with old friends, a couple I've known since my freshman year in college. They live in Nashville and that night we are watching the final episode of Alex Haley's *Roots* on TV. I have recently redecorated my living room with pale blue-gray walls trimmed in ivory. It's cool, clean, and calming without feeling cold, a pleasant space—not quite like being under water, but close.

I am seated on a new upholstered sofa, light blue flowers on a creamy beige background. My friends have each taken one of the new blue and beige wingback side chairs. On the coffee table between us we have glasses of iced tea sweating on coasters and a large bowl of popcorn. My daughter is spending the night with a friend from her second-grade class. The cat is asleep on my lap.

Near the end of the program, Alex Haley, a seventh-generation descendant of a young boy kidnapped into slavery in 1767 Gambia, is listening to the village historian recount orally the litany of the tribe's history. Alex is bored and has almost stopped listening when, suddenly, there he is, Kunta Kinte. In the space of a single heartbeat Haley's lifelong search is over. He has found his ancestor—his connection to the past and to all the human beings from whom he is descended since the beginning of time.

My throat tightens, my eyes sting. Suddenly, I am crying uncontrollably, deep sobs from some place in the center of my being that I didn't even know was there. It comes on so fast I have no time to try to control it, much less prevent it. Tears and snot stream down my face. I'm breathing in gasps and can't stop crying.

"What's wrong?" Sharon asks.

I can't speak and don't really want to. Jim grabs a box of tissues and hands it to me. Sharon offers me some tea. I wave the glass away. They sit beside me for a while, ask what they can do, and eventually mumble their apologies and flee into the night. Not that I blame them. I am bordering on hysteria.

I sob off and on for the rest of the night. What the hell is wrong with me? I have roots. They might not be genetic roots, but I have them. When I think about it, I start to cry again.

Whether I liked it or not, I wanted what Alex Haley had wanted, what most every non-adoptee already had. I wanted to know the people to whom I am related by blood and from whom I am descended. I wanted to know where I came from. I wanted to find my biological relatives and trace my roots.

All I knew about my genetic heritage for sure was my birth mother's name, Ann Elizabeth Pugh. When I was born, she was eighteen or nineteen and unmarried, according to my grandmother, who also told me everyone called her Elizabeth. That meant Elizabeth had been born around 1925. She had red hair and blue eyes. My birth father was an older married man named Jimmy. He had a son around five years of age when I was born. That meant the son had been born in 1938, give or take a year.

They were from Tennessee, Knoxville or Memphis. And Jimmy had family in Detroit, at least he did in 1943, and they lived near Daddy's niece Jenna Lou on Santa Rosa Street.

Most likely I still had blood relatives there and in Tennessee somewhere. But my mom and dad would be very upset if they found out I was actively searching. Besides, I didn't know where to begin. I looked up Pugh in the phone book and found an A.E. Pugh. Could that be her? Would it be as simple as making a single phone call?

I dialed the number. From the sound of the voice that answered, I knew she was a very old lady who could not have been my natural mother. She might have been my grandmother, but what if she didn't know about me. I could not spring that on such an elderly person, and definitely not over the phone. I apologized to the ancient, rickety voice, saying I was sorry to have disturbed her, that I had misdialed, and hung up. Now what? I didn't have a lot of free time to learn how to look. Even though the desire was raw at that point, I reluctantly put it aside and got on with my life.

In the spring of 1980, when I am still visiting my parents for fun, a critical piece of information falls into my lap. I am thirty-seven, Mom is seventy-five, and Dad is seventy-two. They are living in Calvert City, Kentucky, a little more than a two-hour drive from Nashville.

This weekend, I'm in Kentucky to take Mom shopping in Paducah. Always very careful about her appearance, matching tops and pants mostly, Mom still dresses and puts her makeup on first thing every morning. Today, she is after new shoes and a raincoat.

Dr. Zhivago is playing at the local movie theater and she

has agreed to go with me. Dad will stay home and watch a ball game. But *Dr. Zhivago* is my favorite movie and Mom has never seen it so it's my treat, even though I've probably seen the film at least twenty times. Mom doesn't like the movie as much as I do and falls asleep toward the end.

The next day, after breakfast, as I am preparing to return to Nashville, Mom says, "I have something for you. I was waiting for you to come home. I didn't want to just put it in the mail." She disappears into her room and reappears with a small, white envelope. We are standing in the dining room, my overnight bag on the floor between us.

"Mary Williams left this here when she and her husband stopped by on their way to Florida a couple of weeks ago. She wanted you to have it."

"Who is Mary Williams?" I've heard the name but can't place her. Mom has at least four friends named Mary.

Mom hands me the envelope. "An old friend from Detroit," she says. "Mary grew up on Santa Rosa down the street from Jenna Lou."

Ah. Inside the envelope is a single black and white snapshot.

"That's Elizabeth," Mom says, pointing to the younger of the two women in the picture. "It was taken when she was pregnant with you. She was just eighteen, poor girl. Wasn't she pretty? And that's Mary," Mom says, pointing to the other woman. I stare at the photograph, transfixed. The two women in the picture are sitting on the back porch steps of a white clapboard house. The younger woman, squinting into the sun, has my hands, nose, legs, and ankles. Her hair must have been dark red. Mom's friend, and Jenna Lou's neighbor from forty years ago, Mary Williams, now an old lady, knows all about who I am and where I come from. I wish I could talk to her.

Mom pulls a tissue from the pocket of her slacks and blows her nose. "One of your father's brothers found this

At right is Carole's biological mother, Ann Elizabeth Pugh, age 18, pregnant and in Detroit.

snapshot at the bottom of a shoebox full of old photographs when they were cleaning out the place where your biological father had been living. Jimmy died a few months ago. The family asked Mary to make sure this picture went to you."

Mom sounds like she's about to cry. I don't know if she's emotional because she remembers how hard it was for Elizabeth during those days, or because she hates dealing with the fact that Elizabeth is my birth mother.

"That was very nice of them," I say. "I met Mary once, didn't I?"

"Yes, she and her husband visited us when we were living at the lake."

So my natural father was dead. All hope of ever finding and meeting him was abruptly ended. I felt the loss, not intensely, but rather like part of my shadow was leaving me, moving away to a place where I could no longer see it. Who had he been? Where had he lived and died? Was he a good person? Did he have friends and family at the end? What had his life been like? Am I like him in any way?

"How did Jimmy die?" I ask.

"Mary thought he died of colon cancer, but she wasn't exactly sure," Mom says. "It could have been a heart attack, though he did have cancer. Maybe she said prostate." Mom scratches the side her head. "I can't remember."

Everyone's lack of attention to details when it comes to my biological heritage is maddening. What he died from is important—to my daughter and me. And I would have liked having a photograph of him. Why hadn't they sent one? How could it have failed to occur to them I might like to know what he looked like?

"Did you ever find out his full name?"

Mom hesitates, as though deciding how much to say. "They called him Jimmy. James Donaldson was his name. Mary said he was just seventy when he passed away. That's all I know."

So I would have been a Donaldson if my birth parents had married. Donaldson was Scotch or English. Pugh was Welsh and, long before that, French. Anyway, I was mostly a Brit. That made sense to me.

I study the photograph again. Elizabeth looks fairly miserable. I guess I would have looked miserable, too. Who are you, I wonder? And where are you? You don't even know he's dead, do you?

I tuck the envelope into the bottom of my purse. It is likely to be the only photograph I will ever see of her and I want to keep it safe.

Mom walks me out to my car. "Mary's mother was named Virginia. I don't remember her married name. She was Jimmy's older sister. Elizabeth stayed with them in Detroit until you were born. Mary's mother would have been your aunt, so Mary is your first cousin on your father's side."

"Grandma told me about Elizabeth staying with some of

his relatives. I wish I'd known Mary was related to me when they came to visit us."

"I should have told you, I guess, but you were still so young." Mom sighs.

Not that young. "Did Mary say anything else?"

"She told me her uncle, the one who saved Elizabeth's picture for you, said he was sorry the family had not made up with Jimmy before he died. They cut all ties with him over what he did—I mean with Elizabeth and to his wife and son."

"That was pretty harsh. And they never spoke to him again?"

"Evidently not."

"What happened to his wife and little boy? Did Mary know?"

"She didn't know much about Jimmy's wife. I think her name was Gladys, but she thought the boy was very bright and had become an educator or a lawyer, a professional of some sort."

Here was another approximation of accurate information. But at least now I knew my natural father's last name and roughly when he died. I wish Mom had asked a few more questions. According to her, Mary said nothing about the kind of man my biological father had been. Either what she knew wasn't good or she actually didn't know much.

When I got home, I took the envelop with the snapshot from my purse and wrote a note on the back. "Jimmy Donaldson. Died at the age of 70 years, in the fall of 1979." That meant he was born around 1909.

Until recently, my biological father had been alive somewhere, probably in the south, maybe even in Tennessee. Now I would never be able to meet him, but maybe someday I'd find his son. I have a half-brother out there somewhere, more than one, according to my grandmother. Maybe I will live long enough to meet them. Had Jimmy and his son been close? Was he at the funeral? Maybe one day he will tell me about our biological father. I want to find him, but he could actually be living anywhere, and since I don't even know his first name, I'd have to plow through lots of Donaldsons born in Tennessee around 1938. I don't even know for sure he'd been born in Tennessee.

I could have looked for Jimmy's son anyway, but if I found and contacted him, my parents would very likely find out. So I continued to let information come to me. And it did, but very slowly.

Nearly nine years later, in the spring of 1990, while I was still living in the house in Nashville and teaching at Tennessee State University. I had a paper accepted for presentation at an international conference on literacy to be held in Stockholm, Sweden that summer. I had to have my passport renewed since I'd let it expire, and I couldn't find a copy of my birth certificate. I looked everywhere, in the lock box at the bank, in my private papers at home. No luck. I wrote to the state of Michigan requesting another copy, and after three correspondences and one long-distance phone call, I received, in error as it turns out, a photo-static copy, white on black, of a document registering my live birth. On it was more information than I had ever seen before.

Mother—Ann Elizabeth Pugh; Residence—Hazel Park, Michigan; Place of Birth—Nashville, Tennessee; Age—18, Occupation—Factory worker; Father—James Hugh Donaldson; Residence—Knoxville, Tennessee; Place of Birth—Knoxville, Tennessee; Age—35; Occupation—Bus driver.

Jimmy was a bus driver? Images of a man in a gray uniform driving a city bus and a woman with her hair tied up in a scarf, working on airplane wings, sprang to mind. So

CERTIFICATE OF BIRTH
MICHIGAN DEPARTMENT OF HEALTH
Bureau of Records and Statistics

State File No.
00 11520

Carole Faye Pugh   Local File No.

| If so, born 1st, 2d, 3d | No. mos. of pregnancy 9 | Is mother married? No | Date of Birth August 4, 1943 |

USUAL RESIDENCE OF MOTHER:

Wayne   State Michigan   County Oakland

Township

Village or City   Hazel Park

Detroit

Warren Diagnostic Hospital   Mailing Address 347 West Pearl, Hazel Park
(If not in hospital, give street address)

FATHER   MOTHER

Hugh Donaldson   Full Maiden Name Elizabeth Pugh

Age at time of this birth 36   Color White   Age at time of this birth 18

Knoxville, Tenn.   Birthplace Nashville, Tenn.

Occupation (and Industry) Factoryworker

Bus Driver

Children of now living 0   No. of other children, born alive, now dead 0   No. born dead 0

certify that I attended the birth of this child, who was alive   on above date at 4:30 P.M.
(Born alive or stillborn)

BY LAW:
child been treated with one and cent solution of silver nitrate?

Signature _______________

Dated Aug. 5, 19 43   Physician
(Attending physician, midwife, father, etc.)

blood tested for syphilis?   90 East Warren, Detroit
Date April, 19 43   Address

state reason   Filed 8-19 1943 Olive Cook

I hereby certify that the above is a true and correct reproduction of the certificate on file in the Michigan Department of Public Health, Lansing, Michigan

CERTIFIED BY:

George Van Arburg
APR 25 19

Certificate of live birth from the state of Michigan giving the names, addresses, and occupations of both biological parents.

---

much for any residual girlish notions of movie stars and secret trysts or international intrigue. I laughed. My mother was Rosie the Riveter and my father was Ralph Cramden.

Elizabeth was from Nashville. That bit of information, I had not expected. I had been living in Nashville since the summer of 1974. I didn't know what to make of this situation. I'd always felt at home here and assumed that was because it was a mid-sized city, friendly, easy to navigate, and beautiful. Now I wondered if it was because I could have grown up here. This could have been my hometown. Maybe I had relatives living right here. This also raised another fundamental question: If Elizabeth was seventeen and living in Nashville when she became pregnant with me and James Hugh Donaldson was thirty-five, married, the father of a son, and living in Knoxville, how the hell did they get together? Elizabeth might have been a college student at the University of Tennessee in Knoxville. Maybe she babysat on weekends for extra money. That would have been one way they could have been thrown together.

I had my own sleazy bus driver example of what might have happened. Talk about the universe revealing itself. Please tell me my biological father had not been as smarmy as old Jeff. An even worse thought struck me and I did the math. When I was nineteen, James would have been about fifty-five. I didn't think old Jeff had been that old, but the coincidence was definitely creepy.

In the early 1990s, after they moved to Florida full-time, my mom's health began to fail. She started having a series of tiny strokes that finally ended in a pacemaker implant. In addition to her weakened heart, her eyesight was worsening significantly. She had lost the ability to drive years earlier and now could no longer see to read or watch TV. She had advanced osteoporosis and a bowel obstruction resulting in a colostomy. Mom turned eighty-eight, and Dad was eighty-five. In the spring of 1994, five years after my dad's heart attack and two years after surgery to repair an aortic aneurysm, much to my relief they decided to move back to west Kentucky. Having them nearer would make life easier for everyone. Trips to Florida two to three times a year were costly and time-consuming.

As they were settling in, I was helping them unpack and happened to see Mary William's Florida phone number in my mother's address book. I had not been looking for her, but there she was. I jotted the information down and when I got home, I called her.

She knew who I was. I thanked her for the snapshot she'd given me several years earlier. She said she'd been glad to do it. We chatted about her health. During our conversation, I asked if she knew any of her Donaldson relatives who might be living in or around Nashville. Mary said she had lost touch with most of them. All of her mother's immediate family had passed, but one niece lived in Dixon, a town only forty miles west of Nashville. I might call *her*, she said. Mary gave me the woman's name and number and we hung up, promising to keep in touch. That was the second and last time I ever spoke to her. I should have asked her more questions when I had the chance. Did she have a picture of Jimmy? Had he driven a bus all his working life? What did he die of? Where had he been living? What happened to his son? What did she know about Elizabeth?

Why hadn't I asked her even one more question? I couldn't believe I had been so ill prepared. I suppose I was afraid she'd tell my mother if I asked too many questions. I determined to call her again later, but she died several weeks after that and I lost my only contact on my natural father's side except for this cousin in Dixon. After learning that Mary Williams was gone, I called the woman in Dixon. I told her who I was and that I thought we were cousins. I explained how I got her name and number. She sounded skeptical. She told me she had bought into a retirement facility. Yes, she had been born in Anderson

County, near Oak Ridge, in east Tennessee, and that her father was a Donaldson. She vaguely remembered Mary Williams. Other than that, she didn't know what I was talking about. She didn't even know she had an Uncle Jimmy, so she had nothing to say to me. She was wary and unwilling to even meet me. I was disappointed, but if she didn't know she had an uncle named James Hugh Donaldson, even the photo-static copy of my birth certificate would be of no help. We never spoke again. What kind of family did I come from that this woman didn't even know about her father's youngest brother? They had treated him worse than if he had actually been arrested for a serious crime. They had treated him as though he never existed.

I decided to stop picking away at locating my biological relatives. I could not launch a full-fledged search while my parents were still alive. If they found out, they might be worse than upset. At their advanced ages, they would likely be devastated, and they did not deserve to feel the fear of being abandoned or rejected in the time they had left. Besides, I didn't know how to follow the paper trail and I had too little concrete information to go on. Maybe there were school pictures, marriage licenses, driver's licenses, addresses, phone numbers, death certificates, but how to find them, where to start? Actually, I thought it was all too late anyway, that the ones who might know about me were likely all gone, and that I'd never be able to find any of them.

By then, I was in my fifties. My birth mother would only be sixty-nine or seventy, so more than likely she was still alive. But she could be anywhere, and she might have married two or three times by now. Or she could be gone already. And even if I found her, or some of her siblings or her other children, there might be nothing but more disappointment and denial down that road. I was fairly certain her other children, and probably their father(s), did not know about me. So once again I decided I had to let it go for a while longer.

238

Gone Fishing

It's the fall of 1993. I have sold my house and moved into a condo. My daughter graduated from college and has started working. Mom and Dad are moving back to Kentucky from Florida. They have bought a place on a hill overlooking the Ohio River within three or four miles of where we'd lived when I was in high school. The spot is near the cemetery where most of Daddy's family is buried. I wish they had found somewhere else to relocate. My memories of that stretch of river are not pleasant. But the view is still beautiful and three old family friends live nearby to help look after them.

Daddy bought a detached garage, paved the driveway, and landscaped the place, which is shaded in back by a huge old catalpa tree in which hummingbirds love to nest. They will enjoy their view of the river, their shaded backyard, and those little birds for the next five years.

Now that they are living in Kentucky again, Daddy misses going to the dog track the way he could in Florida. When he discovers the dubious joys of riverboat gambling, he perks up. Until he is too feeble to make the trip, he goes to the riverboat at least once a month, usually with a neighbor-lady who drives. On my fifty-third birthday, I take him at his request, and we spend the day together. Another

Carole's mother and father, August 1983, at their fiftieth wedding anniversary party.

neighbor comes to stay with Mom while we're away. Mom is nearly blind now and cannot be left alone.

We are in my car, about halfway to Evansville, when Daddy gives me five hundred dollars cash in a birthday card and says he expects me to gamble with it. Having been down this road with him before, literally and figuratively, I try to give the money back.

Daddy says he knows I won't spend my own money to gamble with. He says I'll enjoy myself more if I'm spending someone else's money, so this is my big chance. He grins at me. We both know what we are each remembering, but neither of us names it.

"Daddy, you know I hate gambling. To me, I might just as well drop the money in a toilet and flush it repeatedly."

"You just don't like taking risks," he says. "You remember Mildred Sayles?"

"Sure."

"She comes up here every month. About five years ago she hit the dollar slots for twenty-six thousand. Bought a new car. It can happen."

"How much does she usually lose each month?" I ask.

"Around five hundred but when that's gone, or she gets tired, she leaves."

I keep my eyes on the road. "You know, if she loses all five hundred most months, she's already lost back every penny of that twenty-six thousand. Then if you add all the money she lost before she won the twenty-six thousand, and what it costs in gas each month to drive here, you have how much money she's handed over to that damn casino."

Daddy thinks about that for a minute and laughs. "Yeah. I expect that's about right, but she can't lose back the thrill of winning it in the first place. She got her name and picture in the paper. It was fun. You never know. It could happen again." He looks at me like he knows I am incapable of comprehending that kind of fun.

Even at eighty-eight, barely able to walk, with his jug ears, his chain-smoking, mottled and blood-blackened skin that hangs on him so every bone beneath shows through, he can still enjoy himself. He finds modest gambling entertaining.

"You're right, Daddy. No one ever accused me of taking too many risks or of having too much fun."

"That's all right. You have your own way of doing things," he says.

I'm so shocked I nearly run off the road. I never thought I'd hear anything remotely close to such a compliment from my father. That doesn't change the fact that I would not enjoy gambling away five hundred dollars, no matter whose money it is. I try another tack.

"You know, Dad, I never win at games of chance. I'm not lucky in that way. I'm lucky in other ways, but not at gambling. I just never win."

"Oh," he says, as though I have finally uttered something that makes sense. "Well, you can play the quarter slots while we're here and keep whatever you don't spend."

"Okay I can do that. But I'll play slowly. The people who sit in those little rooms somewhere watching the players on closed circuit monitors won't like me taking up a spot. I'd bet on that and win."

"You can play as fast or as slow as you want to," he says.

I am amazed, not so much because he says it, but because I still want to hear it. At my age, and after all these years, I continue to try wresting some degree of recognition, validation, and acceptance from my father. I suppose I ought to find that a sad state of affairs, but I don't. This is a rare and precious moment. Daddy has acknowledged that I do things my way, implying my right to do so and that, reading between the lines, maybe I'm even good at some of them. Only later does it occur to me that perhaps he is searching for validation and acceptance from me as well. I could have said how glad I am that he has found something enjoyable to do. Surely he knows that. Surely he knows how much I love him.

The following spring, the Ohio River floods. I have to drive over the hill past the cemetery to reach their house because, at the lowest dips, high water has cut off the main road in two directions. As I pull into their driveway, I notice Dad has a brand new golf cart sitting by the garage. It's a beautiful sunny Saturday morning and he is on the back porch smoking.

"When did you buy that?" I ask, joining him to watch "his" hummingbirds do battle with wasps and with each other around the four feeders hanging from the porch rafters.

"Last Wednesday," he says, flicking ashes into a nearby coffee can.

"You drove all the way to Calvert City? By yourself?"

"That's not a hard drive," he says. "And they helped me load it."

"What was wrong with the old golf cart?"

"Uh, it had some problems." He shrugs, without looking at me. "I just wanted a new one. Like it?"

Later, when Daddy is in the bathroom, Mama whispers to me, "Ask Lou what happened with the old golf cart."

Lou, their nearest neighbor and old family friend, has come over with her daughter to visit. The daughter suggests she and I go for a short walk around the neighborhood while her mom and my folks talk.

When we're out of earshot, she asks me how my father is doing. I can tell she is not inquiring about Daddy's general health.

"I think he's okay," I say, cautiously. "Why?"

"Because he almost drowned on Monday."

"What?"

"He didn't tell you?"

"No, he did not. What happened?" We have stopped in the middle of the road, but with the flood there is no traffic.

"He went fishing in the backwater down there." She points to the dip in the road at the bottom of the hill where the river now sloshes at least five feet of sludge and debris over the pavement. "He backed his old golf cart up to the water's edge and then sat on the rear end to fish. But when he got ready to leave, he forgot it was still in reverse and backed on into the river up to his neck." She shakes her head. "So there he was in that dirty old floodwater, standing on his golf cart to keep from drowning. He wouldn't leave the cart because he knew if he did, he'd lose every bit of fishing tackle he owned."

"How long was he in the water?"

She cocks her head at me. "Over an hour. He took a chance someone would come along and see him."

"Oh crap."

"That's why I'm telling you. My sister Sandy and her husband spotted him. They saw his head sticking up out of the water and fished him out, then went back for the cart. It was ruined, of course. Saved his tackle box and his fishing poles, though."

I almost cry. My poor mother, nearly blind at ninety-one and alone at the house, would have been unable to find the phone and call for help. What if he had drowned? What if Mama had tried to get outside to call to him? They had always been so vigorous, these hard-working, strong-willed, independent, "handpicked" parents of mine. What was I going to do?

"I guess I need to hire someone to see about them," I say.

"Try hospice," she suggests "They have more volunteers than people who need them around here. And your mom and dad definitely need them."

$\sim$ *24* $\sim$

Mama's Hawk

On Mama's ninety-third birthday, we walk outside for what turns out to be the last time. She holds onto my arm and we walk slowly, carefully, up and down the driveway enjoying the fresh, warm air.

Daddy has hung red geraniums in pots on the back porch and planted purple petunias along the walk. Mama can still see colors at the edge of her field of vision. She can't see my face, the macular degeneration having advanced well beyond what the doctors predicted, but she is willing to let me lead her. As we walk, we talk. She tells me she doesn't want me to grieve for her when she's gone, that she has had a long, full life. Her life spanned nearly all of the twentieth century. She has lived to see marvelous things. She's even gotten to hold her great grandson, my daughter's little boy. "Our baby" she calls him. She is satisfied.

"I will grieve anyway, and I'll miss you for as long as I live," I say. "You still miss Grandma, don't you?"

She nods. "Your grandmother was such a sweet person. I've missed her so much over the years."

"Are you looking forward to seeing her again and your father and Grandma Johnson? All the people you've loved and lost?" I fully expect her to say yes. After she retired, Mom never missed a Sunday at church until age and infirmity prevented her going. All my life I was comforted by the knowledge that she and my grandmother both believed and were not plagued as I was by information, rational doubts, and rampant questions.

"To tell you the truth," Mom says, turning her face up to the sun the way Bill used to, "lately I've begun to think this is all there is. This one life is all we get."

"What?" I feign outrage. It's all right for me to have such thoughts, but I don't want my dying mother to have doubts. Not now. "But Mom, I am depending on you to be there to meet me when I die. You can't tell me now you don't believe in an afterlife. You and Grandma always believed. She was a devout Baptist and she raised you. This is *so* not fair."

Mama laughs a little and shrugs. "Oh well, never mind," she says. "It's all too complicated for me."

In July 1998, I am with my daughter and her family in Florida for a week. My one-year-old grandson seems to love the water.. While we are there, Mom's brittle hip bone breaks. When the call comes, I leave my daughter and her family at the beach and hurry home to be with Mom in Kentucky. She undergoes surgery, develops pneumonia in the hospital, survives that, and comes home, though she never walks again. After this trauma, sometimes she doesn't recognize me or my dad or even know where she is. I don't know how much longer she can survive.

The journey from Nashville to my parents' house in west Kentucky takes roughly two hours and forty-five minutes. I have been going there almost every weekend for a couple of years and spending longer stretches during the summer. Now that she is completely bed-ridden and almost totally blind, I dread every visit, watching her body cave in around her, trapping her in a cage of frail bones beneath parchment-thin, bluish skin that bruises and tears and bleeds almost daily. Worse is the massive bedsore along her spine.

I am sitting beside her when she draws her last breath. It's January 5, 1999. She is nearly ninety-four years old. The hospice nurse had phoned for me to hurry back, that Mom had slipped into a coma earlier that morning. I had been back in Nashville only two days, the semester having just started, and hadn't yet unpacked from my Christmas visit. I suppose I knew there was no point.

When I arrive, I whisper to her that I am here. I want to hold her, but she is so frail I'm afraid of hurting her, or worse, of waking her up. So I let her go where she lay curled on her side, in a coma, panting, her shallow breaths growing steadily fainter and fainter. Though I am touching her, I am actually looking the other way when the panting ceases. I had not wanted to see her take her last breath. When I turn back, she is perfectly still. I think her breathing is just so faint I can no longer see it. I stare at her for several seconds before I realize it really is over. I will never hear her voice again, never have another chance to tell her about something I am doing or to make her laugh. My grandson will not remember her at all, but thankfully my daughter will.

As terrible as the finality of death is when it comes, I would not call her back for anything. I doubt she weighs seventy pounds. The bedsore on her spine, which the nurses drained and re-bandaged almost daily, is the size of my foot. Memory still conjures up the smell of that infection.

Before waking my father, I kiss my mother's forehead and hold her cooling hand. I stroke her face and tell her how much I love her. I thank her and tell her how glad and grateful I am that she had wanted to be my mother. I spend about fifteen minutes alone with her saying good-bye. It is not yet midnight.

Then I go to wake my father. "Daddy." I barely touch him.

His eyes open. "Is she gone?"

"Yes, Daddy. She's gone." They have been together since 1929 and married since 1933. Like me, he had not wanted to see her final moments. While he sits with Mama, holding her hand and saying his own silent good-byes, I phone Debbie, the hospice nurse. When she arrives we wash and dress Mama's body the way family members used to, with clean cloths and warm water, long gentle strokes to wash away all that fear and suffering, loneliness and death. Then we dress her in her best pajamas and robe, the green ones with the matching slippers. She had lived up every ounce of life her body had to give.

In the days between her death and funeral, I meet with the funeral director to purchase the casket and plan the event. I write her eulogy. She had grieved for the loss of her life out west (she had wanted to be cowgirl). She adored my father, but had married him as a rational choice, because she knew he was a family man. She struggled with her dread of growing old and was vain about her appearance until well after she could no longer see herself in the mirror. When she was a young woman, she had driven from Detroit to Los Angeles and back with a girlfriend—at a time when there were few if any decent roads. She loved to tell stories about her adventures on that two-month trip. She'd passed up a chance to become a silent screen actress and a dancer while she in California. She had loved horseback riding and wanted to go to college to learn to teach algebra.

We bury her during an ice storm. Sheila, my old friend from high school, comes to the funeral, but due to the weather, there are only a handful of other mourners, even though country folk set great store by funerals. I worry that Mother will be hurt or disappointed by the small turnout. My unwillingness to admit it no longer matters

Mama demonstrating her riding prowess, summer 1948, in Grand Junction, Colorado.

is interesting, but I don't have the time or inclination to reflect on it. I had bought a pink linen pantsuit to bury her in, knowing pink was not her favorite color. But against the silver of the casket and the soft gray lining, with her white curly hair, she looks lovely and at peace. I know what music she wanted played. I cover the casket with a variety of flowers rather than roses only, just the way she had asked.

After the funeral, I stay with my father for two more days. He and Mom were together almost every day for seventy years and I hate to leave him, but I have to get back to work. I have no choice and he will not come with me. Their house is less than a mile from the cemetery. Later that spring, neighbors tell me he rides his new golf cart up the hill to her grave every day and sits there smoking cigarettes and talking to her—sometimes for an hour or more, they say. He lived nine more months without her

During their six years back in Kentucky, I probably drove there and back a hundred times. At first I listened to books on tape, but that turned out to be unsafe, so I took to counting things to keep alert. Interstates are great sleep-aids. In the winter I counted hawks, mostly red tails and a few others, Kestrels, Harriers, and Coopers. Hawks are easily spotted perched upright on bare tree limbs or fence posts, looking for the slightest movement that signals the presence of small furry prey. On each trip I'd average twenty or more sightings, mostly in the distance, though occasionally I'd see one on the ground nearer the highway with its talons closed on lunch.

Two days after the funeral, on my way back home, driving southeast on Interstate 24, I found myself sobbing and talking to Mom as though she were sitting in the car beside me. "I'm sorry the funeral was so small. It was just the ice storm. I hope you liked the flowers and the pantsuit. You really looked beautiful in the pink. I tried to find something green, but I couldn't. I wanted to hold you while you were dying, but I was afraid I'd hurt you, or wake you up." I was apologizing for all my shortcomings, as well as things over which I had no control. I told her again that I loved her very much, saying the things then that I had wanted to say while she was still living but couldn't because I believed she wouldn't want me to.

I knew I needed to pull myself together, but I was alone, and there wasn't much traffic, so what did it matter? I knew what was happening. I did not want to let her go. At one point I began laughing at myself.

"Mom," I said out loud, "if you're hearing any of this, the least you could do is scare up a hawk just to let me know you're there."

I told myself I wasn't really serious. Still, I began to look, just in case. I mean, who knows for sure, right? First to the left, then right, then left again—and in no time, there he was, a huge Northern Harrier up ahead, lifting off from a treetop in the middle of a field. He headed directly for my car. If he kept coming, on our present trajectories, we'd actually collide. I was certain of it. I slowed down. On he flew—straight for me. I was mesmerized. I glanced behind me. The road was clear. With my mouth hanging open, I stared as the large raptor paced his flight to match my speed. The distance between us closed until he reached the edge of the median, alongside and slightly above my car. As I hit the brakes he flipped up his right wing exposing his pure white underbelly to the afternoon sun. Then he rolled over and soared away. He had flown so close that I could see the clear blue of the cloudless winter sky between the splayed black feathers of his wingtips. In all the years I'd made that trip, I had never come so close to a hawk in flight. In the years since, I never have again.

With His Boots On

Three months later, after a doctor in Evansville unceremoniously tells my dad he's terminal unless they amputate his left leg at the knee, or possibly the groin, Daddy and I discuss his options. We are sitting at the kitchen table. The hospice nurse has explained the situation to him in gentler terms than the doctor employed. Plaque build-up in his femoral arteries from decades of smoking and his heart attack a few years ago have weakened his heart, so the blood no longer circulates properly to and from his lower limbs. He has a small spot of gangrene on his ankle. My father is shocked. He had not expected a death sentence so quickly after losing Mama.

He refuses to allow the doctors to amputate. He always said he wanted to die with his boots on and he sees no reason to change his mind now. Debbie, the hospice nurse, and I try to make sure he fully understands the situation. He says he does and he wants to let nature take its course.

"We can make adjustments, Daddy. Are you sure this is what you want to do?"

"What, for a few more months of life confined to a wheel chair, on morphine, if I survive the surgery? No thank you. Absolutely not."

As the reality sinks in and we each grapple with what we think lies in store for him, I have to go into my bedroom, bury my face in my pillow, and sob as quietly as I can, knowing how uncomfortable he is with any kind of emotional display. I don't want him to die. I don't know how bad the end will be, but I'm sure it won't be easy. There is no pulse even in the groin in one leg and the other is dead from the knee down. That spot of gangrene will not be the only place where it breaks out, the nurse has told him. And it will never heal.

Mother nearly lost her leg and her life from infection when she was three. Now Daddy's leg is going to kill him.

Before she leaves that day, Debbie tells me that Daddy knew I was in the bedroom crying and asked her why. She said, "Because she loves you and she's upset."

I am surprised by that, and wonder if he still does not fully understand what's happening to him, or if he never believed I loved him. He has not always been a kind and gentle parent. But a few ill-chosen words, spoken under the influence, in a time of serious stress in his life, shouldn't cancel out years of hard work, support, and sacrifice. He parented me better than he had been parented. I'm quite clear about that. In almost every way he had done the best he could for me. I knew that, too.

Between my mother's death and when we learn my dad is also terminal, he asks me another serious question. The way he says it sounds rhetorical, but I suspect he wonders how I will respond. He's balancing his checkbook at the kitchen table—something my mother did almost all their married life. He performs the task accurately, though it takes him three times longer than it would have taken her.

"What in the world would we have done," he says without looking up, "your mother and me, if it hadn't been for Social Security?"

"It would have been hard," I say. "You'd have had to live with me. We would have planned differently, saved for it, I suppose. I might have bought a different house or made an apartment in the basement of the one I had.

That's what people used to do and that's what we would have done. You would not have been without a roof over your head and food to eat, that's for sure. You and Mom would have been reasonably comfortable, I think. Without having to pay Social Security taxes, we'd have had more money to work with, I suppose." I didn't say I would have hated such an arrangement and neither did he, though we both knew that was the case.

I know the precise point my father and I crested the divide between us and began to like each other, even love each other, again. It happened when I returned to college and was successful, my marriage notwithstanding. When I became independent, he was free to pursue a new job, achieve his own degree of success, and save money for their retirement.

By the time we learn he is dying, we each understand that my adoption fifty-five years earlier has enriched both our lives. Would I have preferred him to say so directly, however awkwardly he might have expressed it? Absolutely. But to him, such sentiments were better left unsaid. It's the way he was raised.

The following Saturday, I arrive at his house around noon. Fortunately, my ex-husband is with me. He helps me from time to time with my parents and with our grandson as part of his twelve-step program. On this day, we find my dad on the floor by the sofa. He has fallen and is too weak to get up. He's been there for more than two hours, and is in serious pain. But helping him up is not so easy.

When we try to lift him by his arms, I'm afraid we will break a bone or dislocate a shoulder, or tear his skin. "Hurry up," he says, twisting around to sit on his other hip. The last thing I want is to prolong his agony, but neither do I want to make a bad situation worse.

"Wait a minute," I tell him. "Let me think about this."

I ask Weldon to get down on his knees and together we

make a basket with our arms the way children do, which Daddy is then able to scoot onto so that we lift him gently, almost effortlessly, onto the sofa. Aside from being relieved and having the pain subside, he seems genuinely impressed with that little bit of problem solving. I had figured out how to help him without hurting him further and he is grateful, though he never says so directly. Instead, he complains that I did not arrive sooner.

The scene reminded me of a time years earlier when he and I were fishing. I was in my thirties at the time. He accidentally shoved a fishhook through the pad of his left thumb and wanted me to cut his thumb open so he could pull the hook back out the same way it went in. I was appalled. He was bleeding and wiggling the hook around under the skin pulling on it. "Wait a minute," I said. "Just wait a minute. Let me think. Do you have a pair of wire cutters? All I have to do is cut the hook in two and you can pull out both halves without hurting yourself any more than you already are." He stared at the hook and realized the solution was in fact that simple.

What amazed me was not that he'd gotten excited and couldn't quite figure out the best course of action. What amazed me was that he didn't seem to feel the pain of having a rather large fishhook embedded and wiggling around in his thumb. I wondered at the time if he had been so damaged in his life that he no longer experienced some forms of emotional or physical pain. His young life had been very hard. I knew that.

The week before he died, we were having breakfast, when out of the blue, he told me that he was sorry for some of the things he'd said and done when I was growing up. "I guess I didn't give you as good a childhood as I could have."

After all we'd been through, the last thing I wanted was for him to die thinking he had failed me in some way. "You

did fine, Daddy," I said. "You gave me a great childhood."
And that was it. That sparse apology, and my sparse reassurance, was as close as we ever came to talking about the things that he knew had been hard for me. And I never told him I understood why he did what he did or said what he said. Over the years we had found a way to stay father and daughter, not because we knew what we were doing or how to be close. We didn't. But we didn't want to lose each other, either. He was the only father I would ever know or have, and I was his only child.

I'd known he was sorry for some of the hurtful and damaging things he'd said to me when I was young. I knew he was proud of the adult I'd become. I'd seen it in his eyes, in his thoughtful actions, his comments about me and my work, to my mom and others, in the pride he'd shown when he told the neighbors about some accomplishment or when he displayed the books and articles I'd authored. All the same, I was gratified that he had finally tried to put some apology into words. That was difficult for him.

In the end, my father and I were both cowards. We had been silent too long. He was reared in a time when men hardly named their feelings or spoke of private matters. They kept their fears, hurts, and doubts closely guarded secrets, and dealt with them internally, if at all. And he had made it clear over the years he would not talk about feelings. So when we wanted or needed to speak, before it was too late, there were no words, no established pathways, no portals or open channels of communication to make it happen. Twice in my life he asked me what I thought or how I felt about something. So when I wanted to question him, to learn more about his life, his concerns, regrets, hopes, fears, to give him a chance to finally say whatever was on his mind, whatever he felt and thought about his life and impending death, or the truth of his relationship with me or with my mom, or to reminisce so he would not feel so alone, our voices were aborted. I could not bring myself to ask him a single question and backed away from anything remotely personal or emotional. For one thing, I knew I'd cry, and he would have hated that, I thought. So all I could do was talk about the weather.

I told myself that was the way he wanted it. And yet, if I had it to do again, I want to believe I would force the issue. I hope I would. But I didn't then, when it counted, and that remains a lifelong regret. He died shortly after midnight on the first day of October 1999.

The funeral was held in the lovely little Methodist church his parents had attended for years and from which his mother had been laid to rest sixty years earlier. My father's funeral was one of largest they'd ever had in the neighborhood—standing room only. I buried him near his mother and father and beside my mom in the cemetery overlooking the river.

~ 26 ~

Re-searching

Gradually I begin to think about resuming the search for my biological family. In the spring of 2003; I am approaching sixty and my daughter is thirty-three. She had expressed an interest in helping find my biological roots, though it had never occurred to me she would care. But of course, they were all her relatives and ancestors, too.

First, we visit the state archives. On that particular visit, I locate Jimmy's son, or the man I am fairly certain had been Jimmy's four- or five-year-old son at the time I was born. This man is the right age. He is James Hugh Donaldson, Jr., and he and his wife are living in east Tennessee. He has children my own daughter's age. I could have contacted him then, but I didn't. I'm not sure why. I suspect his mother and father divorced over the affair James had with Elizabeth. No boy wants to lose his father. What if James Sr. was some kind of dead-beat dad? I might be stumbling into a hornet's nest of resentment even this many years later. Or what if he didn't know about me? What if he had grown up loving and revering his dad? It was not likely, but it was certainly possible.

I tuck his phone number and address away and tell myself I can call him any time. If he'll talk to me, that will be great. He is the first half-brother I knew about and I had known about him since I was a young girl. If he won't talk to me, I will have lost nothing. I want to call him, but keep

258

putting it off. I even consider driving to east Tennessee and knocking on his door. I always wondered which side of the genetic code I most resemble. Maybe James Jr. and I look enough alike, even though I have Elizabeth's coloring, that he will recognize our connection. Maybe face-to-face, he'd talk to me. I would want to know if I had a half-brother or -sister out there somewhere. I did want to know, but I am painfully aware that he might not.

Because his father, our biological father, was the guilty party, the perpetrator so to speak, I couldn't bring myself to contact him. James Sr. was the grown-up, the one who had probably destroyed his family and hurt a young girl and set me adrift in the world. Elizabeth had seen to it that I had a family. As my mom and grandmother always said, she did the best she could under the circumstances.

James Sr. had done the best he could for himself. Though in all fairness he had not abandoned Elizabeth when he found out she was pregnant. But James's relationship with my birth mother could easily have cost James Jr. his father and left him to be reared by his mother, and perhaps a stepfather. Reminding him of his childhood might be hurtful. So I delay and waffle and come close, but don't do it.

One night, about a year after I locate James Donaldson, Jr., I dream of Jimmy Donaldson, Sr. The dream is both vivid and tactile. In the dream, he phones me. I don't want to talk to him, but my daughter makes me take the call. I feel the cold receiver against my ear and hear Jimmy's raspy voice, a bit higher pitched than a typical man's voice, with an east Tennessee accent that is unmistakable. He says he's sorry he was not there to raise me. He asks me if I had a good life. He wants to know if I would have helped take care of him when he was dying of cancer. I tell him yes. That seems to please him. As we say good-bye, he promises to call again.

During that second trip to the state archives, I also found his death certificate. At least I think it's his. It is for a James Hugh Donaldson—born in 1909 in Tennessee, died in Louisiana on November 11, 1979—listed as unmarried and childless at the time of his death. The name and dates work. If that was my birth father, he may have lived a lonely life. He may have been a drunk sleeping in doorways in the French Quarter for all I know. I want to know more, but there is no other information.

In the 1930 census, I also find an Ann Elizabeth Pugh born in Nashville in May 1924, one of ten children, mother Nancy Ann Cone, father Elijah Paul Pugh. That must be her. Her siblings are mostly boys with odd names. There is also an address for them on New York Avenue. I know exactly where that is. I ran out of time and had to stop. Though I was determined not to wait ten more years to resume the search, I did wait another two.

In the spring of 2005, because my daughter is a high school government and American history teacher, she takes her advanced placement students to the state archives to show them how to do research. Afterward, she tells me she has learned a little more about how to use the archives, so a few weeks later, she and I go back together.

Seated at a long table with volumes from the 1930 census stacked in the middle, I read while Shelley goes in search of sources. We quickly find the families of Elijah Paul Pugh and Nancy Ann Cone Pugh. Since the 1940 census has not yet been released and will not be until sometime after 2010—seventy years after the fact by law—I cannot find out about the family after the '30 census. Elizabeth is listed as the first daughter born to her parents after six boys. She has a sister named Geraldine. Her brothers' names are Mabry, Manfred, Willoughby, Clyde, Doris, and Dudley.

New York Avenue is in what is now considered north Nashville—the dodgy part of town near the Cumberland River, the Tennessee State Penitentiary, a huge lumberyard, and an old chemical plant. I used to live less than three miles from there and have driven within a block of the place most every day for years.

Shelley and I search for any of Elizabeth's siblings that might still be living and find that Willoughby appears to be the last boy to die. He passed away in 2000. At the time of his death he was living less than two blocks from where my daughter had been living since 1997. Once again, we are close, but too late. We look for marriage licenses or death certificates for Elizabeth and her sister Geraldine, but find none.

How could I be absolutely certain that this Ann Elizabeth Pugh was my Ann Elizabeth Pugh? Without a photograph to compare with the one I had, or some form of human acknowledgment, I still had no independent confirmation. The data fit, but that was circumstantial, not positive proof.

Shelley had an idea. If Elizabeth was living in the house on New York Avenue as a teenager, we knew which high school she would have attended. Her picture had to be in one of the yearbooks.

We call the school, which is now an adult learning center. The secretary is very gracious and tells us they have yearbooks going back to the 1920s. We are welcome to come and see them whenever we want. The following Saturday, with the black and white snapshot of eighteen-year-old Ann Elizabeth Pugh in my purse, my daughter and I go to the old school. A man leads us to the basement where the yearbooks are stored. An adult class is going on, but we can sit at a table in one corner, if we are quiet.

We pore over the collection of yearbooks from 1935 through 1945, but find no trace of Ann Elizabeth or any of her brothers or sisters.

"How can that be?" Shelley says as we leave the building, disappointed. "They had to go to school here. There wasn't another high school for miles."

"Unless they all went to a parochial school? Would there have been a private Christian school back then?"

"Not likely. And they wouldn't have been able to afford it if there had been one."

We had stumbled on one other bit of archival information about Ann Elizabeth, an address in an old Nashville phone book from 1944, the year after I was born. Elizabeth had lived on Nevada Street for one year and worked at an enamel factory, according to the record. Nevada Street runs two blocks behind the old high school. After locating the house on New York Avenue, which is still standing, we find the house on Nevada Street, too.

"So after she had me, she left me in Detroit and came back to Nashville. My grandmother always said she stayed in town, got married, and had two boys. I guess that wasn't true." I wonder what else wasn't true.

"Why did she live in a room in a house near the school if she wasn't there to finish and graduate?" Shelley says. "It doesn't make sense."

I agree. I know why my grandmother thought Elizabeth stayed in Detroit. When I was in my twenties, my cousin Mona told me that Elizabeth and my mom accidentally ran into each other at the doctor's office once when I was around five years old. Mom and I arrived at the doctor's just as a red-haired woman with two little boys, a toddler and a new baby, were leaving the waiting room. After they left, the nurse asked my mom if she had recognized the woman. My mom said no, and the nurse said, "That was Carole's mother. That was Elizabeth."

Apparently, my mom freaked out, fled the premises, changed doctors, and never went back. According to my cousin, Mom lived for years in fear of running into Elizabeth, or of her finding us.

"Maybe Elizabeth came home to Nashville," Shelley says, "got married, and returned to Detroit with her new husband, where there were still good jobs. The war wasn't over for another year."

"I suppose that's possible."

I had always wondered if Elizabeth was still living in Michigan somewhere, but a search of marriage licenses in Wayne County turned up nothing. A search of marriage licenses in Tennessee also failed to yield any further information. After 1944, I could not locate a thread to pick up her trail or that of Jimmy Donaldson. No mention of an Ann Elizabeth Pugh existed in any document I could find—no address for her, no driver's license, marriage license, or death certificate existed for her in Michigan or in Tennessee, no address for James and Gladys Donaldson was listed in Tennessee anywhere. I would have to wait for the release of the 1940 census to track them further and time was running out. I was in my mid-sixties and nearly ready to retire. No matter what I did or where I looked, after 1944 Ann Elizabeth Pugh and James Hugh Donaldson, Sr., were nowhere to be found. Why had the paper trail on each of them simply ended? As far as I could tell, they might as well have been abducted by aliens.

PART *4*

Relative Strangers

~ 27 ~

Becoming Alex Haley

Snow fell overnight, whitewashing the wooded hilltop beyond my living room windows and frosting the streets with ice. Schools are closed all across the area. I am about to put the coffee on when the phone rings.

"Whatcha doing?" It's Shelley.

"Looking out the window at the snow."

"Want some company? I'll bring the X-Box for *your* grandson. We can hook him up to the TV in the guest room and you and I can visit. It's going to be a long, boring day." He must be giving his mother a hard time this morning. He is always *my grandson* when he's being a handful.

"Sure," I say, "but be careful. They've salted, but the road up this hill looks pretty slippery."

I put the coffee on and get dressed. Thirty minutes later, Shelley arrives with Reilly in tow. After we settle him with his X-Box, I pour the coffee. "Come into my office," I say. "I have an idea. Last week I saw this ad for two weeks free on Ancestry.com. It's been five years since I looked there. The internet has expanded a lot in the last five years. Let's join and see if we find anything new."

"We haven't got anything else to do," Shelley says with a shrug. The wet-bar-turned-office-cubby is a squeeze, but once we're seated, we're comfortable enough. She sips her coffee and watches.

Ten minutes later, I am a member of the website.

"Now what?" Shelley says.

"Let's put Elizabeth's name in and see what happens." I type Ann Elizabeth Pugh into the box.

Almost immediately, I receive a message saying the name Ann Elizabeth Pugh is cited on a family tree managed by a woman named Rachelle. I can't view the tree without her permission. To obtain such permission I have to contact her directly. Her email address is attached.

Shelley looks at me. "You going to do it?"

"Absolutely. Why not? I mean, what's the likelihood this woman actually knows Elizabeth personally? She's probably just a name on some distant branch of the family."

Shelley lifts her eyebrows at me. "I guess we'll find out."

"We've come this far," I say. "I have to contact her."

I type, *"I'm looking for the descendants of Ann Elizabeth Pugh. Her name appears on your family tree. Would you allow me to view the tree?"* and hit send.

I finish my coffee and glance at the screen. Rachelle is online and has already responded. *"Of course you can see the tree. How are you related?"*

Shelley sits up straighter. "What are you going to tell her?" Like me, Shelley has not actually contemplated contacting real people.

"I'm not going to lie. I have to tell her."

"I know you want to know, but I just think you ought to be careful. You don't know any of these people." Shelley holds up her hands. "I'm just saying…"

"How can I be careful?" I take a deep breath and forge ahead. "Okay, how about this?

I type, *"Let's make sure we are each talking about the same person. The Ann Elizabeth Pugh I'm looking for was born in 1924-25, in Nashville, Tennessee, to a rather large family. She had siblings with some pretty unusual names like Mabry, Manfred, Dudley, and Willoughby. Do you think that's the same woman as the person listed on your family tree?"*

Rachelle responds immediately. *"Yes, that's her. How are you related?"* Now what?

It does not occur to me to ask Rachelle how *she's* related. I am convinced that after all this time, the connection has to be distant. I don't believe she will be close enough to really care who I am or how I am related—except out of curiosity. She probably expects the same, that I will say I am an in-law of one of the older brother's grandchildren or something of that sort with an interest in genealogy. But of course, I'm not. So I write back.

"I believe she is my birth mother. I was born in 1943 in Detroit to an Ann Elizabeth Pugh from Nashville, Tennessee. She was only eighteen at the time and unmarried. I am seeking her children or any living siblings. What can you tell me about her?"

This time the response is *not* instant. Shelley and I stare at the blank screen. "She's either thinking about it or trying to check it out," Shelley says. "She might decide you're some kind of nut."

"What was I supposed to do? I either had to tell her or lie or sign off." I hold up my hands. "I'm just saying…"

Shelley laughs. "Whatever." She hugs me. "Don't worry. It'll be all right."

We check on my grandson, who is seated on the floor wearing headphones. He waves without looking at us. We leave him and put our empty coffee cups in the sink. When we recheck the screen, perhaps thirty minutes later, Rachelle has written back.

"Elizabeth was my mother-in-law. I am married to her oldest son. But we don't know anything about a Detroit connection. Are you sure?"

I stare at the screen. Wow. Is she really married to my half-brother? If so, I might get to meet one or more of my illusive half-brothers after all, and a new sister-in-law. I like that. But she referred to Elizabeth in the past tense. She must be gone. I am not surprised, only sorry. If still living, Elizabeth would be eighty-five or eighty-six. Was I sure their Ann Elizabeth was my biological mother? Not completely. I mean, it had to be her. But I still had no independent confirmation. That's what I was looking for.

"Okay. My turn! What do I say?" My daughter, who has remained by my side the entire time, is staring at me rather than the screen.

"Calm down, Mom. You need a glass of water. Take some deep breaths; take your time."

I might be breathing a little fast at this point. My face might be a bit warmer and pinker than usual, but I am fine.

I type, *"No, I'm not positive. I have a birth certificate with her name on it and Nashville as her birthplace and her age. I also have a photograph taken of her when she was pregnant with me in Detroit. If I have my daughter scan these two documents and send them to you, would your husband be willing to look at them, at the photo especially, to see if he thinks it's his mother? It is only a small black and white snapshot taken sixty-seven years ago, but he might be able to tell."*

Rachelle replied in seconds. *"Of course he will look at them. Send whatever you have and we'll get back to you."*

The entire exchange with Rachelle, from the first communication I sent to her last note assuring me her husband would look at the photograph and birth certificate, has taken less than an hour. Nothing is definite yet, but I feel like I have just stuck my finger in a light socket. My whole body is buzzing.

Shelley has a few errands to run so she and my grandson leave. The roads have cleared. She takes the snapshot and birth certificate with her to scan when she gets home.

I do not expect further developments that day, and try to go about my business and keep calm. I will find out Rachelle's husband's reaction to the photograph when I find out. In my excitement, I have forgotten to even ask his name. I've waited sixty-six years; I can wait another day or two. In the meantime, I clean up the kitchen and sit down to watch TV, but can't stay focused. I read a little, but can't concentrate. I go to the store, do a couple of loads of laundry, answer some emails, and am about to shut my computer down for the night when a message from Rachelle pops up. Expecting another question or a request for additional information, I open it, totally unprepared for what it says.

"It's true! You have found your birth family. Call me." She has included her phone number.

And just like that, there they are. I am Alex Haley. I have found them. The date is February 22, 2010.

For more than six decades I have imagined and longed and given up and started in again and again and again. Now, in the space of a single day, a heartbeat really, I have reached back in time and touched my roots. I stare at the screen as the enormity of what just happened hits me. Sixty-six years is a long time to be an only child. Now there will be answers, and people, maybe even people who look like me and my daughter and my grandson. Their Ann Elizabeth Pugh was my Ann Elizabeth Pugh. What should I do now? Who should I call? I have to call Rachelle, of course. How did she *know* it was true? Talking to Rachelle might be easier since we are not blood relatives. I don't even know where she and her husband, my half-brother, live.

By that time, I am walking in circles around the dining room table on the verge of hyperventilating. I have to call Shelley. Where is the phone? Until the moment I try to locate the phone, I had not realized I was crying.

By the time I reached my daughter I am babbling. I try to tell her what has happened.

"Mom, are you all right?"

"Not really. I can't sit down." I also can't get a deep breath, but I don't tell her that. Still, she can hear that I am losing it.

"I'll be right there," she says. It is after ten o'clock at night.

When she arrives, we phone Rachelle. She is still up and expecting my call.

"You have two brothers and one sister," she says, "but the bad news is Elizabeth is gone. She died in 1994."

"I thought that must be the case." How I wish I had found her in time. "But I have a sister? Really?" I can't believe it. "Where is she?"

"Kentucky, where your other brother lives, too. You have a brother Stewart, my husband, and a brother Lee, and your sister is Becky. And Elizabeth has three sisters still living. Two of them are in Nashville."

"You're kidding." For years I had joked about having relatives all over town. Now, it was no laughing matter. "How did you know it was true?"

"I called Stewart, he's out of town, when I got your message about looking for your birth mother and at first he said no way. We'd never heard anything about it. Not a word or a hint, and definitely nothing about Detroit. So I called Becky and asked her."

"Oh dear. Was she shocked?"

"Well, she didn't believe it either. So she called her Aunt Geraldine in Portland. Aunt Geri's the oldest. She's eighty and was the closest in age to Elizabeth."

I did some quick subtraction. Geraldine would have been twelve when Elizabeth left home pregnant with me.

"Aunt Geri knew about you. She may be the only one of the sisters who did."

"What did she say?"

"I'm going to let Becky tell you all that. She's the one who talked to Aunt Geri. And they both want you to call them, when you feel up to it. Do you have paper and a pen? I'll give you their numbers. You also have an Aunt Betty and an Aunt Christine there in Nashville. Aunt Chris is in Gatlinburg right now, but Aunt Betty wants you to call her, too."

They all want me to call them. After a lifetime of not knowing, and they all want to see me and talk to me. My hand is shaking and I am crying again. I try to write the names and numbers, but can't quite manage it. Shelley writes for me.

My brother Stewart, who until then believed he was the oldest of his mother's children, was eight years younger than I; Becky was sixteen years younger and Lee was in the middle. Stewart was in advertising after having majored in philosophy and modern dance at Berkeley in the late sixties, Rachelle said. Even in my agitated state I laughed out loud at that. Philosophy, and dance, at Berkeley, in the sixties! Oh, I definitely wanted to meet him.

From Rachelle I learned that Stewart was named after his father. He and Rachelle had two grown boys, both in college, the older one in law school. Stewart already had a son, Isaiah, when he and Rachelle married. Isaiah and Shelley were born about two months apart. Elizabeth helped raise Isaiah until Rachelle and Stewart married. Like Bill had helped raise me, I thought.

"By the way," Rachelle said, "everyone called her Liz or Sugar, Shug, or Shuggie for short."

"For me, she is Elizabeth."

"I understand," she said. "Lee works in Louisville, and Becky works for the U.S. Post Office. Becky has three children. Lee has one daughter and a grandson there in Kentucky." She told me Aunt Betty and Aunt Christine both had children and grandchildren, some of whom lived in Nashville. I had first cousins living nearby and nieces and a nephew in Kentucky and three nephews on the East Coast.

Shelley kept up with the notes as I talked to Rachelle. "When you hang up, we'll redo these," she whispered.

Rachelle was a social worker by training and told me she had dealt with this sort of thing once or twice before. She said I should proceed slowly, at my own pace. I could call her anytime I wanted to talk. When we finally hung up, I felt like a lifeline had been severed. I tried to take her advice, but I wanted to know everything immediately. Slowing down did not feel like an option, even though I couldn't digest all the information I'd already been given. I reread Shelley's notes and then I called my sister in Kentucky.

I could hear in her voice that she'd been crying. "Why didn't she tell me?" Becky said. "Why didn't Mama tell me? I thought we were so close."

It is one thing to consider how you might upset or hurt someone. It is another thing to know your actions have done just that. "Oh honey," I said. "Times were so different back then. No one talked about things like unmarried pregnancies. She was trying to protect herself and you. And once she'd lied and put it behind her, how could she go back?"

"But I, we all had a right to know—we have a sister."

"I would have liked that, too. Maybe she thought after all this time I would never show up."

"That's what Aunt Geri says," Becky said. But no one could have predicted the internet.

"Tell me about your conversation with Aunt Geraldine."

Becky sniffled and then relayed the entire conversation she'd had with our eighty-year-old aunt: "I told her I had something to ask her. You have to tell me the truth, I said. Did Mama have a baby before she married Daddy? There was a pause on the other end of the line and then Aunt Geri started to cry. She said, I promised your mother I would never tell. I promised. I told her you have to tell me, and she did. She said Elizabeth went to Detroit and had a little girl and gave her up for adoption. I had not mentioned Detroit or that you were a girl. So then I really knew for sure it was all true."

There was the independent proof for me, as well. The piece of the puzzle I had been waiting for most of my life. It was a good thing I was already sitting down because suddenly my whole body relaxed. I had not been conscious of being afraid they might not be the right Pugh family, or that they would not accept the truth if they found it, but I had been seriously tense over something.

Becky and I wanted to meet as soon as possible. She said would come to Nashville the next weekend. She suggested we meet at a restaurant on Saturday evening around five-thirty. Shelley and I agreed. "We'll be there."

We sounded alike, Becky and I. I wondered if we would look alike. We said good-bye and I phoned the next number on the list, my aunt Betty.

Like me, she was retired and free to meet during the day. We decided on lunch in a couple of days. We would both bring our daughters. Shelley would be attending a conference that day and could get away for an hour to join us. Aunt Betty's daughter Kris worked part-time and could be there as well, though she might be a little late.

Over the next few days I would meet an aunt, a first cousin, my half-sister, and more. My mind would not shut off. That night I went through scenario after scenario, what I'd say, what they'd say, what Elizabeth would say if she knew, what my own mom would say. I listed all the questions I wanted to ask. I didn't go to sleep until dawn.

Aunt Betty and I arrived for lunch at almost the same time. We recognized each other instantly. She said I looked like Elizabeth. I thought Aunt Betty looked like a slimmer version of me. We both had dark brown hair with streaks of gray and cut it pretty much the same shape and length. We both had blue eyes and the same shaped nose. We could easily pass for sisters. Aunt Betty was only seven years older than me. Neither hers nor Aunt Christine's name had been listed with the rest of the children on the 1930 census because they hadn't been born yet, along with at least two more boys, Frank and Roy. Aunt Betty laughed. "Mom had run out of weird names for the boys by the time those last two came along."

Aunt Betty and I spent the next two and a half hours talking, picking at our rice and refried beans, and laughing, or tearing up, then laughing again, looking at the few pictures she'd brought. Our daughters came and went. Aunt Betty and her daughter Kris look alike. My daughter Shelley and Kris's daughter April are nearly the same age and know many of the same people in town.

Aunt Betty said her brother Roy had an interest in the family genealogy and had started collecting names and photographs before he died, some of which helped Rachelle with the family tree. Roy had lived most of his adult life in South Dakota, where his family still lived.

Cousin Kris said she knew about me because Betty, her mom, had told her years ago. Aunt Betty said her sister Christine told her and swore her to secrecy. So actually, all three of Elizabeth's sisters knew about me. I was going to meet Aunt Christine on Saturday when I met Becky.

Before our daughters left, Aunt Betty told me a little about her parents, my biological grandparents.

"My daddy, Elijah," she said, "your grandfather, married Mama when she was just fourteen. He was twenty-one. He had a peg leg he made himself. Did you know that?"

"No, I didn't. Really? How did that happen?"

"He accidentally shot himself when he was sixteen. He was out hunting and set the shotgun against a tree or fence

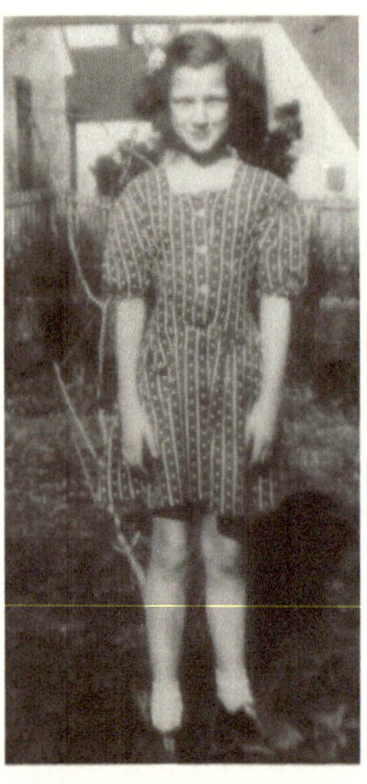

LEFT: *Aunt Betty, age 10.* RIGHT: *Carole, age 7.*

post and it fell over and discharged. That was the story, anyway. Hit him in the leg below the knee. A neighbor lady heard him, I guess, calling for help. She found him and got him back to the house. She took off her petticoat and tied it around his leg to stop the bleeding. Somebody fetched a doctor and that old doctor took Daddy's leg off at the knee. Saved his life."

"That's horrible," I said.

"I'm sure it was terrible, but it didn't seem to slow him down much." Aunt Betty said in her cigarette-raspy voice.

I wanted to take it all in, old family stories that were new for me. I thought about my mom nearly losing her leg as a little girl and my dad, who would have lost his leg if he'd let the doctors operate. I asked Betty to tell me more.

"There were thirteen of us kids. I was the baby, the last child my mama ever had. They were amazing, our parents. Mama fed and cared for all of us children in that little house over on New York Avenue. Daddy worked fifty-five years at the same job and almost never missed a day of work. After he retired, two different companies tried to

Carole's natural maternal grandparents, Nancy Ann Cone and Elijah Paul Pugh, when they married.

hire him. They asked him to help train new workers."

"I bet they did. What did he do?"

"He worked for a stove company. I guess you'd call him a tool and die maker. The factory was originally within walking distance of the house, but then they moved it down to Franklin, and after that Daddy had to ride with another man or take the bus to work. He had to be up really early, like four in the morning, to go all the way out to Franklin."

"That could not have been easy, especially with an artificial leg."

"No, but it was probably better than staying home with all us kids." She laughed again. Aunt Betty likes to laugh.

"Mama's name was Nancy Ann Cone and Daddy's mother was an Elgin. Daddy called Mama Annie. She was born out in the Antioch area south of Nashville. Her daddy owned a lot of land out that way, along Smith Springs over to Blue Hole Road. He didn't want Nancy Ann to marry Elijah Pugh, but when she did he gave them the house on New York and a couple of acres so they never had a mortgage payment or rent to worry about."

"Tell me about Elizabeth."

"She was the first girl that lived after six boys. She was really sweet and very shy, almost backward when she was young. I never did understand how such a thing could have happened to her." I assumed she was referring to her pregnancy and my birth.

"What did Elizabeth die of?"

"Non-Hodgkin's lymphoma. She was diagnosed when she was just fifty-nine. Not too long after Stewart and Rachelle married. She lived eleven years fighting that disease. I was with her when she passed. I used to go see her when they lived in Kentucky. I'd clean house for her when she couldn't hardly lift a finger she was so sick and weak."

Was non-Hodgkin's lymphoma inherited? I would have to look it up.

"Tell me about her husband and her children," I said.

"Husbands," Aunt Betty said. "She was married twice. After she came back from having you, she lived with my brother Manfred and his wife Sarah for a while, trying to finish high school. Sarah just died not too long ago. She was way up in her nineties. Manfred was the oldest boy. He's been gone a long time."

"Do you think your parents ever knew about me?"

"Mama did, but I don't think Daddy did. Sarah knew it, though."

"Was Sarah mentally competent toward the end?"

"Sharp as a tack till the day she died," Aunt Betty said. "Sarah saw Liz naked getting out of the shower once and saw her stretch marks. "Liz said there was this boy but he was killed in the war and she gave the baby away. I think that was the story she told Sarah."

"If I had been a pregnant teenager in the middle of World War II that's exactly the story I would have made up: He was a soldier. It was very sad and tragic and I don't want to talk about it!"

I wondered if that was the story she told her husband. No wonder she didn't come looking for me. I guess I outed her about Jimmy Donaldson, the thirty-five-year-old married man and father of one she's been with.

"So tell me about Elizabeth's husbands."

"The year Liz worked and lived with Sarah and Manfred she went to this school downtown for people who wanted their high school diplomas. She started dating one of her teachers and married him. He had some kind of weird name, Baxter Maxey, I think. He was really handsome. Looked a lot like Kirk Douglas. He had four grown children. They were all such pretty people. But he turned out to be an alcoholic. They weren't married even two years, I don't think. He'd pass out in the front yard, laying out there for the neighbors to see. Mama was mortified. Liz divorced his sorry you-know-what."

"She didn't go back to Detroit?"

"No. Never. Not to my knowledge."

The fact that both Elizabeth and I had married older men who drank did not escape my notice.

"Liz was working at a grocery store out at the edge of town when she met Stewart Sr. He fell for that red hair of hers." I thought of the red-haired lady in the doctor's office when I was a child and wondered who she was, because clearly she was not my birth mother.

"Stewart? That's Becky's father, right?"

Aunt Betty nodded. "Yes. Liz and Stewart Sr. married pretty fast, but then she didn't have Stewart Jr. until 1951, I think. She had Lee three years later and Becky five years after that."

I hung on Betty's every word. "Were they happy?" I asked. "Elizabeth and Stewart Sr.? Was she happy? In most of these pictures she isn't smiling."

"She was self-conscious about her teeth. They were really crooked. But I think she was very happy. Stewart was in the Navy, you know, and gone a lot when the children were growing up and that was hard. They lived out in California. Stewart Sr. outlived Liz by ten years, but while they were together, they seemed to get along and enjoy each other. He was outgoing and funny, and he was good to her. They had a nice house. She always had a nice car. She loved to garden and quilt. Sometimes, when Stewart would be at sea for a year or eighteen months, she'd bring the children to Tennessee, to our mother's house to stay for a while. Next time, I'll bring more photographs so you can see all of us kids. I just grabbed these few. I should have brought more. I wasn't thinking."

"That's all right. We have time."

After Aunt Betty left, I sat in my car and cried. I'm not sure what I was crying about. My own sense of loss, I suppose.

That afternoon I called Aunt Geraldine in Oregon. We didn't talk long. I thanked her for telling Becky what she knew. She said she was there the morning Elizabeth left home to go to Detroit with Jimmy. She said Elizabeth told her not to tell anyone until they all got up and then to say she'd gone to the city to work in an airplane factory and she'd send money home when she could. A few years later, Elizabeth told Gerri she just couldn't bring another baby into that house. "She said she just could not do that to our mother."

"I understand," I said, and having seen that little house, I did understand.

"Did you have a good life?" Aunt Geri asked.

"Yes. I had a very good life."

"I asked Elizabeth once what she was going to do if you showed up looking for her, and she said she'd cross that bridge when she came to it."

I couldn't help wishing again that I'd found her before she died. At least I could have assured her that she'd done the right thing giving me to my adoptive family. Still, I will always wonder what she would have said, how she would have handled it. Would she have been hesitant at first, but then happy? Would she have been angry, wanting me to go away before anyone in her family saw me or found out? Would she have thrown her arms around me and burst into tears? Maybe she'd have fainted. She might have felt disloyal to her other children if she allowed herself to like me. Who knows? But I would have risked it, of that much I'm certain.

~ 28 ~

My Half-Siblings

That first meeting with Becky and Aunt Chris passed in a blur and yet I remember it as though it happened in slow motion. I arrived at the restaurant late, having accidentally driven past it not once, but twice.

When I finally park and go inside, the hostess leads me to a room at the back where several people are seated around one long rectangular table. The room seems crowded and I have the sense that there is not enough light. I can't focus on any one face. They all look up when I walk in. I see my daughter. She beat me here. One or two of the others are standing. I know that, but all I want is to see Becky. "Where is she?" are the first words out of my mouth. Everyone seems to know exactly what I mean. "Here she is," and "She's right here." Voices of people I can barely see, and do not yet know. Finally, there she is, my half-sister Becky, sixteen years younger and maybe an inch shorter.

We hug. I cry. All I can think is I have a sister. This is my sister.

We sit beside each other. She brought me a gift. I show her my birth certificate and the photograph of Elizabeth taken in Detroit back in 1943. Becky looks a little like my daughter, with her square jaw and long hair, except Shelley is smaller and twelve years younger. Becky has our high, wide forehead, or we have hers, and the same large blue eyes.

Other people at the table comment on how much Becky and I look alike, and how much I remind them of both Elizabeth and Elizabeth's mother, Nancy Ann.

In addition to Becky and her husband David, there is my aunt Christine and her husband Roger, her son Marty (my first cousin), Marty's son Caleb, and Marty's wife Brenda. I feel Marty start to sob when I hug him and that makes me cry again.

Someone tells the wait staff about the sisters who have just met and that most of the people at the table are cousins and aunts and nieces who have just found each other. Word spreads throughout the restaurant and occasionally someone comes to the entrance and peers in and smiles. People from the kitchen come by to see us and say hello.

Shelley is sitting on the other side of Becky. Aunt Christine sits next to me. She is soft spoken and sweet, probably like Elizabeth. She doesn't look a day over sixty, though she is actually seventy-eight. Becky suggests, in a whisper, that maybe Aunt Chris might have had a nip and a tuck or two.

Aunt Christine confesses she's known about me since she was a child, that her sister Geri had told her, but then pledged her to secrecy. "She probably figured I'd forget all about it because neither of us ever mentioned it again."

So they all knew, all three sisters, and still they had not told Becky even after both her parents were gone. I suppose they were afraid to, afraid Becky would be too upset, afraid she'd try to find me and wouldn't be able to. Or that she'd find something she would not want to know.

Aunt Christine says Elizabeth and Geri shared a bed in the house on New York Avenue, so Geri knew exactly when Elizabeth packed a bag and left in the wee hours of that winter morning back in 1943.

Aunt Chris pats my arm. "When I was older, Liz told me it was her problem and her fault and she took care of it. That's about all she ever said on the subject. But honey, if she'd brought you home we would of all helped raise you. It would have been fine."

"That's really sweet of you," I say, "and I'm sure it's true. But back then it would have been really hard. Your parents wouldn't have been able to hold their heads up. They'd had enough problems with all those boys. Elizabeth would have been looked down on. And there were so many children already. It was better the way she did it. I had a great family—wonderful parents and grandparents, lots of aunts and uncles and cousins. They mostly all loved me and I loved them. It was fine. Elizabeth handpicked my mom and dad. Did you know that? She interviewed several couples and selected my folks because they were from the South and also I think my dad looked a lot like your daddy, from the pictures I've seen."

"I'm glad you had a good family," Aunt Chris says. "That makes me feel better."

Aunt Christine is the second youngest sibling Elizabeth had. She's a tiny person, pretty and energetic. She tells me a little more about my natural grandparents. "Elijah Paul and Nancy Ann had five girls and nine boys. There was one girl born before Elizabeth, but the doctor dropped her. She lived only two days. Broke our mother's heart to lose her first baby girl like that."

"I'm sure it did. That's terrible. According to Aunt Betty, those first six boys gave your parents a very hard time."

"They did. Two of them got into serious trouble with the law." She was talking about my biological uncles. "The local police shot and killed one of the boys when he was only ten or twelve, and Willoughby spent some time in prison for robbery."

One of the boys was a kind of savant. He couldn't speak

plainly, but he could play the piano the first time he ever saw one. "Dudley could play anything he heard as soon as he was big enough to sit on a piano stool," she said. "But the smartest boy was Clyde. He made straight A's in school, read all the time, and never gave our parents a moment of trouble. He drowned in the Cumberland River when he was fifteen trying to save a friend who also drowned."

Aunt Chris shakes her head. "Mama and Daddy had a lot of sorrow in their lives."

Aunt Betty had also talked about the boy who drowned. She said her father was never the same after that. I can't imagine surviving that much grief.

The people my aunts told me about, grandparents, uncles, cousins, were my blood relatives; I carried some of their tendencies in my DNA. But they did not exist as living, breathing individuals for me the way they did for Aunt Betty and Aunt Chris, in their memories. The pain and anguish Elizabeth's mother and father had endured in their lives was etched into the lines of their faces, and carried as weights on their shoulders. I saw it in the photographs I was given, and wondered what they would say to me if they could.

In pictures of Elizabeth's mother, Nancy Ann, I saw elements of my face and my daughter's face, especially when Nancy Ann was young. There were pictures of a young Elizabeth, too. Like me, she had almost no eyebrows and had to draw them on with an eyebrow pencil. Becky told me later, when she was growing up, there were little red Maybelline eyebrow pencils all over the house.

In some of the pictures of Elizabeth, she seemed so familiar and yet such a stranger. In photographs of some of the other relatives I saw genetic connections. Clearly Shelley's square jaw came straight from the Pughs. But for all the similarities and familiarities, there was a hollow ring to it as well. I didn't *know* any of them. Their faces did not spark memories of younger versions of themselves, or remind me of what they sounded like when they laughed or cried. I was not part of the events of their lives, nor were they a part of mine—and they never would be. My memories were different. There were unexpected and even weird parallels and similarities, but the paradox was still there. I was from them but not of them, like them but not like the. Relationships are made in the details of daily living. They are not instant, nor do they exist just because of shared DNA. I was always more startled by the similarities than by the differences anyway.

Becky filled me in on some of the family members I had not yet met. "Your half-brother Lee has a daughter, Lori, and a grandson named Lucas, who is only two years old."

"I think someone told me that and either Shelley or I wrote it down. I'm going to need a spreadsheet to keep everyone straight. Who is Lori?" I was totally overwhelmed with all the names.

"Your other niece, your brother Lee's daughter."

I nodded. "Oh yes. Got it. And her husband is Josh?"

"Yes, and one of Stewart's sons is also named Josh. Stewart's oldest son is Isaiah. He's married and has three children"

I glance across the table at David. "I'll be calling you for help with all these names." He grins and threatens to test me on them the next time we meet.

Becky's daughters are in college and her son is a high school senior. They wanted to come visit, but Becky wanted to meet me herself, alone the first time, so her children stayed home. We decide that the very next weekend if the weather cooperates, Shelley and I will drive up to Kentucky to meet them and we'll bring my grandson.

Aunt Christine's husband Roger and daughter-in-law Brenda tell anecdotal stories about members of the family.

Becky and I laugh. It's uncanny how similar we sound. Aunt Betty said we sound alike on the phone, too. She said I sound like Elizabeth, but that I remind her most of her mother Annie.

"It's in your face and mannerisms," she says.

I ask Becky to tell me about her father and bothers. "I've talked to Rachelle several times, but I haven't spoken to Stewart yet.

"My dad was the life of the party. But Stewart Jr is more reserved."

"Rachelle has invited Shelley and me up there to meet them."

"Maybe we can all three fly up," Becky says. "I haven't seen him in quite a while. They have a big house and with the boys away at school, they have room."

"If Shelley is going to go it has to be her spring break. That's Easter weekend."

Becky agrees to take the time off and go, too. We talk with our heads together while everyone else chats and eats. In an odd way, Becky reminds me a little of my best friend from high school—almost as though Sheila had filled in a place in my heart where Becky would and should otherwise have been.

"You grew up in California, right?" I say.

"We were all three born and raised in California, near San Francisco," Becky says. "Dad was stationed there. When he retired, they bought some land in Kentucky and Lee and I moved there with them. Stewart Jr. was already at Berkeley. I was a sophomore in high school; Lee was just starting his senior year."

"I moved to Kentucky when I was a sophomore. Bad timing for Lee."

"We were not happy about it, I can tell you. Were *you* happy about moving to Kentucky in the middle of high school?"

"Not exactly, but I didn't like the school I had been going to. It's a long story. And I met my best friend on the first day. She made the transition bearable. If it hadn't been for her, I would have been miserable."

"That's so funny," Becky says. "I made a best friend on my first day, too. What a coincidence."

"What year was that?" I am trying to construct a timeline of significant events in my head.

"The summer of 1974," Becky says, "August."

"I moved to Nashville in August of '74. I'd just finished my doctorate and I'd gone to California looking for a job that spring. I was staying with friends in Fresno. I thought I wanted to live in California. Shelley's dad and I were separated at the time. Then someone called me about a tenure-track position at the state university here."

"I wondered about that," Becky says. "Were you looking for us then, when you decided to live in Nashville?"

"No. Not at all. Shelley's father wanted to live here— frustrated musician. I didn't know Elizabeth was from Nashville until 1990. I knew I had relatives in east Tennessee, but that's all."

"That is so weird. You could have landed anywhere. Why Nashville?"

"Close to my parents, good job." I shrug. "Life just worked out that way."

"So where in town do you live?" Aunt Chris asks. She'd been listening to the conversation.

"A condo in Bellevue, but I raised Shelley in a house in the West Hillwood area."

"We have a house in that area," she says. "On Clematis. You know it?"

"Of course. My house was on Belton, a block over. And I had good friends from college who lived on Clematis for about five years in the late '70s. I spent lots of evenings there playing bridge. Which end of Clematis?"

"My house is the very last house at the end toward the interstate. Of course when we bought it there was no interstate. We lost half our acreage when it came through."

"Then your house and mine were *really* close."

As it turns out that was an understatement. Aunt Christine's house was only one block from where I had lived from 1976 to 1993. The two houses actually face each other at opposite ends of a short connecting side street. Her house was across the street and two houses down from where my friends had lived. The short side street between Aunt Christine's house and mine is over a hill. Had that street been flat, we would have been looking at each other's front doors all those years.

"I moved out toward the end of the '80s," Aunt Christine told me, "but my oldest son Lynn still lives there." She nodded at Becky. "Becky's been there lots of times, especially when she was in college at Lipscomb."

"Becky lived in Nashville and went to college here, while I was living in the house on Belton?"

"I was at Aunt Christine's every other weekend from 1977 to '79."

"We had a family reunion at the house in the summer of 1982, I think it was." Aunt Christine says. "Elizabeth was there. Of course, Liz was there more than once over the years. Were you living in your house on Belton in 1982?"

My face is very hot. "Yes. Shelley was twelve and in middle school then."

An image of Elizabeth standing on her sister's front porch, looking west toward my house, comes to mind. Had I unknowingly seen some of them, or passed them on the street? What would Elizabeth have thought if she'd known when she came to visit her sister, or when she came to that family reunion, that the daughter she had given up forty years earlier, and six hundred miles north, lived less than the length of a football field away? What would she have done if she'd known she had a daughter and a grand-daughter just over that small hill? Why hadn't we somehow known? Because life just doesn't work that way.

I had noticed Aunt Christine's house and thought the people who lived there must be unfriendly because the windows were always covered and I never saw anyone come or go. My friends who had lived on that street were the couple with whom I'd watched *Roots*. My aunt and I had probably seen each other at the grocery store. Of all the places to live, first in Nashville, near where my birth mother's family had grown up, and then only a block away from an aunt to whose house my birth mother and my brothers and sister came regularly. What were the odds? All the coincidences I was encountering were beginning to sound a little strange.

Two weeks after meeting Becky, Shelley and my grandson and I drive to Kentucky to meet Becky's three children, my nieces and nephew and Shelley's first cousins. We also meet my half-brother Lee and his daughter Lori and her family.

Becky and David's house, which Stewart Sr. and Elizabeth purchased and lived in after they retired, sits along a winding two-lane road at the edge of a small town south of Louisville. The surrounding land is on a plateau with an expansive view of beautiful rolling Kentucky farmland.

Becky and David have three dogs, two Boston terriers and a Doberman. In no time, my nine-year-old grandson is on his back on the floor being licked to death by the smaller Boston. The other Boston is standing on his chest and my grandson is giggling uncontrollably. Within the first hour, both the Boston and the Doberman take up residence on him as he sits on the sofa in the back room watching TV. He loves animals as much as I did when I was young.

Two of Becky's three children are here, but her oldest daughter is still at work. Jesse, Becky's son, has us in stitches with stories about what high school is like these days. David makes margaritas, which I drink while we look at more family photographs and Shelley and Ashley, Becky's middle daughter, compare notes about their common stomach and digestive tract issues.

Becky shows me around the house. Elizabeth and Stewart Sr. lived there until a year before she died. Several photographs of her hang on the walls. Looking at them, I try unsuccessfully to feel her presence. I wonder again what she would say if she knew I had found them.

Standing next to my sister in the hallway, I say, "Tell me something about Elizabeth that I don't already know." We walk into the front room and peer out the living room window.

"Well, Mom loved the movies. She read movie magazines more than she read books. And she used to bite her fingernails. Not like me, I rip mine off," Becky says. "She chewed hers. Then one day she just stopped, sometime in her late thirties. I wish I had."

I glance at my polished nails. "I used to bite mine, too," I tell her. "I quit when I was thirty-eight." Becky nods. "It's a family thing. After she quit biting them," Becky says, "her nails grew in really thick and strong," Becky looks down at my nails again. "Yours, too?"

"Like bear claws."

Becky nods again. "Oh, did I tell you her favorite movie was *Dr. Zhivago*? I bet she watched it thirty times or more over the years."

We gaze out the window without speaking. The number of similarities among people who share DNA is not surprising when they come scattered across a lifetime. But when those connections are compressed into a matter of days, they feel mysterious, and no doubt are endowed with greater significance than they deserve. Shelley is equally floored by some of the parallels. I seem to want to laugh and cry simultaneously. I don't really understand why.

"How about another margarita?" David calls from the kitchen.

Good thing I'm not driving.

When Becky's oldest daughter comes home from work, I am standing in the middle of the den watching my grandson being chased by the dogs around the back yard. He is having a great time when Bethany comes bounding up the porch steps. I hear her and turn just as she pops through the door. Suddenly, we are face to face. She gasps and bursts into tears. Bethany was twelve when her grandmother Elizabeth died and she remembers her vividly. No one in my whole life ever reacted to me that way, to the fact that I look like someone they loved. I hug Bethany and we both cry a little. I apologize to her for the shock.

"No," she says, "it's all good. Mom told me you look like Grandma. I just wasn't prepared for how *much*."

I call my grandson to come inside and meet his cousin Bethany. He comes to the back door. "I can't come in," he says.

"What do you mean, you can't? Why not?"

"We'll call the dogs," Becky assures him. "They'll come, too."

"Yeah," my grandson says, "but, um, that's not it." He screws up his face like he is trying to figure out how to explain a delicate situation.

I lean closer to him. "What is it?"

"Well, you know that stuff that looks like mud, but it isn't mud?"

Becky and I glance at each other. "Uh, yeah."

My grandson sighs. "I just stepped in it." Everyone

laughs. Look at us, I think, already making stories that might be shared within the family for years.

My brother Lee arrives with his family. We hug, but then he doesn't say much. I am afraid he's angry with me for finding them. But as the afternoon wears on I decide he's shy and reserved, like his mother. After meeting Aunt Christine's husband Roger and Becky's husband David, and hearing tales about Stewart Sr., Shelley says all the Pughs tend to be quiet, but they marry people who aren't. Shelley's father is an extroverted, loud teller of jokes, spinner of yarns—and that's when he's sober, which is most of the time now. Certainly both Aunt Chris and Becky's husbands are outgoing, warm, charming, lively, friendly, and very funny.

That evening, as we prepare to leave, Ashley hugs me and whispers, "I'm so glad you found us. My mom needed a sister."

"Me, too," I say. "And nieces and nephews aren't bad, either." I love being their Aunt Carole.

On the way home, driving down Interstate 65 in the dark, Shelley asks me how I feel. My grandson is in the back seat plugged into his iPod.

"I don't know. Happy, overwhelmed, sad, maybe a little pissed off."

"Really?" She glances over at me. "Why pissed off?"

"Because I would like to have known them longer, that's all. I feel like I do know them in ways I actually don't. I have no shared memories with any of them and that feels empty. Some of them seem so familiar, especially Becky and Aunt Betty, but there's nothing underneath that feeling. It's sort of like the reverse of what Alzheimer's patients must experience. And I'm not going to have much time with any of them, either. It's too late."

Shelley snorts. "God, you're like living with Eeyore. Stop with the negative vibes already. Just tell yourself, better late than never."

She's right, of course. I am grateful to have found them. I will make time to be with them and enjoy the time we have. Regret is counterproductive.

Nevertheless, I am filled with a sense of regret, and of time running out. I finally decide to do something I should have done ages ago. I find the phone number for James H. Donaldson, Jr., and place the call. He answers, but when I tell him who I am and that I believe he is my half-brother, he says three things:

"Why are you looking after all this time?"

Not wanting to go into all the reasons, I hem and haw. I don't tell him I just found the other side of my genetic family. I don't tell him I've had his address and phone number for years. Instead, I say, "I want to know about my biological father's side of the family before it's too late."

"I'm sorry. I can't help you," he says. I ask if he knows of any of his Donaldson relatives who might be willing to talk to me.

"I do not wish to continue this conversation," he says, and hangs up.

Maybe I didn't handle the phone call well. I was not even prepared for his first question. I suppose I hoped he would react the way Elizabeth's family had. But he didn't. He might have thought I was trying to scam him in some way. I decide to write to him, giving him my information and asking him to please contact me if he changes his mind. He never has, and I have to respect that, but I keep hoping.

Perhaps when he said, "I can't help you," he meant it literally. Given that the Donaldsons disowned James Sr., totally, and given the fact that James apparently died un-married and "childless" in Louisiana back in 1979, James Jr. may not know much more about his father and that side of his family than I do. Still, I would have liked to meet James Hugh Jr. and his daughters. They are our genetic family, too.

On Friday evening of Easter weekend, Shelley and I fly to New York City, arriving at LaGuardia from Nashville five minutes before Becky, who is coming in from Louisville. Stewart and Rachelle pick us up first, finding us on my cell phone. "We passed you, I think. We're coming around again," Rachelle says when she calls. "We expected you to look older."

"I'm having a second childhood," I say, "so I look young-er than I really am."

Rachelle and I have swapped a few photographs, one I found of me when I was sixteen that looks a little like Stewart when he was a teenager. I think I look like Elizabeth when she was young, but I don't have a recent photograph of myself, so they are looking for us blind. Rachelle sent me one of Stewart and his two sons taken a couple of years earlier, but I have no idea what she looks like.

Suddenly, I spot him, my half-brother, walking toward me down the sidewalk beside the American terminal. Stewart and I hug, somewhat awkwardly, but he is warm and smiling. And then, finally, I see Rachelle, a short bundle of energy with an open face and lively, intelligent eyes. If not for her and the family tree, I never would have found any of them. And she has helped me in other ways, as well. For all of her generosity, I am extremely grateful.

Shelley and I pile into the back seat of Stewart's BMW, with Rachelle at the wheel, and take off to find Becky at the Delta terminal. Instantly, we are in a traffic jam and

*Sister-in-law
Rachelle.*

we're still at the airport. Let me just say Rachelle is an experienced big-city driver and leave it at that.

I spot Becky first. "How did you do that?" Stewart asks. "You've only seen each other twice."

"I recognize the high forehead," I tell him. "Shelley and I both have one just like it."

Three months ago, this encounter was the farthest thing from my mind. I never would have predicted such a gathering. I have to keep telling myself that Shelley and I are in New York with my brother, my sister, and my sister-in-law.

The following morning, Stewart is outside taking his morning run. He is preparing to climb Mt. Kilimanjaro with his three sons later that summer as a birthday wish from his oldest son, Isaiah, who will turn forty in July. Rachelle and I are in the kitchen talking over coffee, seated on tall chairs at the large island in the middle of the room. Floor-to-ceiling windows behind her provide a view of their tree- and flower-lined backyard. Becky and Shelley are not up yet.

Rachelle wants to add my birth father's name and information to my branch on the family tree, so I tell her what I know and she enters the data on her laptop.

"Oh," she says, "I wonder if you've ever seen this. You haven't mentioned it." She closes out of Ancestry.com and opens the photo gallery on her computer. "Come around here so you can have a really good look."

I walk to her side of the counter and stand beside her while she clicks on the photograph of Elizabeth when she was pregnant with me to bring it to full-screen size. I have never seen the picture enlarged before.

"Do you notice anything in this picture we haven't talked about?" Rachelle asks. I study the enlarged image wondering what I've missed. Elizabeth and Mary Williams look like they might have been going to, or coming home from, church. Both are wearing heels and coats over dresses. Mary has on a large dark hat. Elizabeth is squinting slightly into the sun.

Rachelle touches the bottom of the screen and then I see it, clearly outlined. It's the shadow of the man taking the picture. He's wearing a cape-shouldered overcoat and hat, very 1940s. Rachelle and I look at each other. "Jimmy Donaldson," we say simultaneously.

That is as close to seeing his likeness as I will probably ever come. How ironic. The man forever in the background, literally caught in shadow.

Drawing Conclusions

After lunch we watch home movies of Becky, Lee, and Stewart when they were children. I see their grandmother, Nancy Ann Cone Pugh, taken probably fifty years earlier as she comes down the sidewalk toward the car one Easter Sunday all dressed up for church. "Good grief!" I say. "I walk just like her."

Becky laughs. "Join the club."

We are sitting in Stewart and Rachelle's den chatting, relaxing with our feet up, drinking Cokes and cups of herbal tea. Becky and I are seated on their blue flowered sofa looking at the TV screen mounted on the wall above the fireplace. The entire wall of floor-to-ceiling bookshelves is filled to overflowing with books. The colors in this room remind me of the colors I used in my living room in the house in which I raised Shelley, the one a block from Elizabeth's sister Christine.

Stewart is seated in a large, comfortable-looking chair to the left of the fireplace. I ask if he thinks his father knew about me

He shakes his head. "I've wondered about that, too. I don't know. He and my mom were really close. Surely he did. I mean, how could she keep such a secret all those years?"

"Except," Becky says, "Daddy was the one who couldn't keep his mouth shut. Mom was *really* private. Don't you think if he had known, he would have told us, especially after she died? I was with him almost every day for ten years. If he'd known we had a half-sister out there somewhere, he would have said. He wouldn't have been able not to."

"You got a point." Stewart slips off his shoes and puts his feet up. "Maybe he didn't know exactly, but he had to know something."

Becky lays the magazine she's been reading onto the coffee table and picks up her glass of Coke. "She might have told him she'd gotten pregnant by her first husband, the drunk, and lost the baby."

Stewart shrugs. "That's possible. He knew she'd been married briefly once before. So had he. But if that was the story she told, why didn't we ever hear it?"

"So much for that idea," Becky says.

Rachelle turns to me. "What do you know about James Donaldson?"

"Not much." I tell them what I know. "Elizabeth stayed with his older sister and her family until I was born. That's my understanding."

Stewart picks up the book he had been reading earlier and flips the pages. "How in the world, as shy as she was, did she ever get mixed up with a married man from Knoxville? It just doesn't make sense."

"I've asked myself that same question and I asked Aunt Betty and Aunt Chris, too. Jimmy drove a bus for the interstate bus line. He probably had the Knoxville-to-Nashville run. Back then, before interstates, it would have taken all day to drive Highway 70 through all those small towns. So he'd have to spend the night in Nashville and drive back the next day. And according to Aunt Chris, Elizabeth's first job was in the café downtown at the Nashville bus depot. She was sixteen when she started there."

Stewart exhales. "Well, that explains a lot. Donaldson must have had a room near the depot because he wouldn't have had a car there in Nashville. And she certainly didn't."

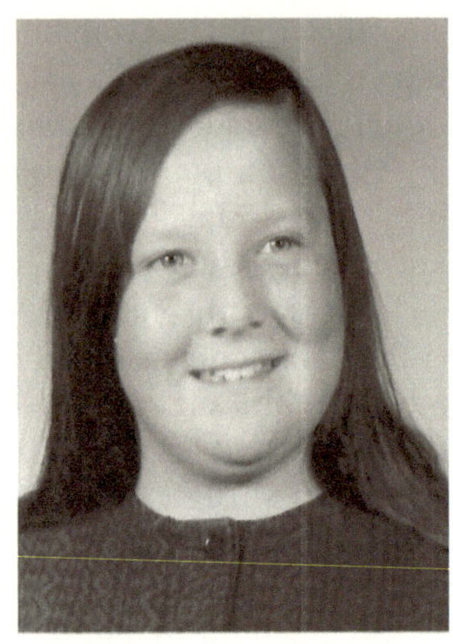

LEFT: *Daughter Shelley, age 8.* RIGHT: *Carole's half-sister Becky, age 12.*

I wonder again just how much of a predator Jimmy Donaldson was, if he was a total creep, or just lonely. "Maybe they fell in love," I say.

"Maybe she thought it was love," Rachelle says.

"Whatever happened, with their age difference, James was definitely the guilty party," I say. "He was probably a good-looking, smooth-talking man who paid attention to her. And she might have been curious about sex and figured an older married man would know what he was doing. I mean, being raised in a small house with all those boys, how could she not be curious? She probably didn't have anywhere near enough time or attention from her own father—not with him working so hard and all those other kids. And she was so shy and quiet. They all say that."

"That is an understatement," Rachelle says. "She was really an introvert."

"Pugh is Welsh, you know," Stewart says. "The Welsh are a poetic, passionate people. But like Rachelle says, Mom was *so* reserved. I still have trouble seeing it."

I nod. "That's what Aunt Christine said, too. She said Elizabeth was almost too shy. And yet, here I am."

"But she was also intelligent, wasn't she?" Shelley says.

Stewart smiles. "Yes, she was. It's a shame she never got to finish high school. She quit school after eighth grade to go to work and help out. But she could work any cross-word puzzle you gave her. She was very smart."

I look at Shelley. "So that's why we never found any school pictures of her in the yearbooks we scoured. She quit school just like my dad. It never occurred to me that was the case. And it must have been true for all her brothers and sisters, as well. None of the older ones ever went to high school.

"I like crossword puzzles," Shelley says, having returned to the magazine she'd been reading.

"Me, too," Rachelle says. "And Becky plays a mean on-line Scrabble."

I tell them I want to play Scrabble with them online when I go back home. "We can do it through Facebook," Rachelle says.

"Being smart, Elizabeth might have been really hungry for somebody to talk to," I say. "You know what I mean? Along comes this attractive older man who could carry on a conversation and who pays particular attention to her. He might have lied about being married or done the 'my-wife-doesn't-understand-me' routine. Most young girls in that situation would be easy targets."

Shelley looks up over the top of the magazine. "And we know this, how?"

"My mother told me," I say. Shelley doesn't know how true that is. I sip my tea. "I can't help wishing Elizabeth had told someone so we were not all left guessing."

Becky sets her teacup on the table. "I don't think she ever told anyone the whole truth. I called her best friend from their years in California, Helen, and her husband Nick. I figured if anyone knew it would be her. She and Mom were really close. All those years when Dad was gone for months at a time, Mom always said if it hadn't been for Helen and Nick she would have lost her grip. They came to Milwaukee to be with Mom at the end. Anyway, Helen was totally shocked when I told her about you. Mom never said a word to her about it. I think it hurt Helen that Mom didn't tell her. When we were kids, we called them Aunt Helen and Uncle Nick. That's how close we all were," Becky says.

Stewart reaches down to pet Maddy the family lab curled contentedly by his chair.

"Mom *never* let her guard down," he says. "Dad would drink almost every weekend and have people over to party until Mom got sick with lymphoma. She never joined in. She liked to make sure everybody had what he needed, but she didn't drink herself. But there was this one time. Dad talked her in to having a few. I was about twelve and listening from the stairs. Mom was laughing and having a great time."

"Where were you, at twelve?" I ask.

"In the house in Concord, California," he says. "That one night, after everyone left, Mom was washing her hands at the kitchen sink and dropped her wedding rings down the drain. She got so upset. I'd never seen her so upset. She said, "I knew it. You can't let yourself go. Not even once. Something bad always happens." Dad got the rings out of the drain the next morning. That was the last time I ever saw her take more than one drink and not even that very often. I didn't know of anything bad that had ever happened to her, so I didn't know what she was talking about." He shifts in his chair. "Now I do."

"If her capacity for drinking was anything like mine, all Jimmy had to do was give her a couple of beers and sweet talk her. I always was a cheap date."

LEFT: *Carole, age 12.* RIGHT: *Half-brother Stewart, age 16 years.*

Rachelle laughs. "Your sense of humor is a lot like hers."

Later, after dinner, we all go down to the beach, where we can see the north shore of Long Island across the sound. The sun is warm, but there's a soft breeze off the water. Stewart and I walk slowly down the wharf and back.

"Do you think she worried about having a baby and giving it away?" I ask. I appreciate the way he almost always pauses and considers my questions and then gives me an insightful answer.

"Looking back," he says, "I do. So many things make sense now, things she said that at the time blew right past me. My first son was born when I was nineteen. In fact, he's just about a month older than Shelley, so I guess we were on a similar track. Anyway, when it became clear that Isaiah's mother couldn't really take good care of him, Mom insisted that I try to get full custody and bring him to her house. She helped me raise him. He lived with her and my dad for over a year once when his mother ran off and left him. Then when Rachelle and I married, he stayed with us most of the time. But he and Rachelle didn't get along at first. Mom was so upset by that."

We walk in silence for a few minutes. Then Stewart says, "Now I understand better what was driving her and why she was so fierce about wanting to keep Isaiah with her.

"I'm sorry if it bothered her. She did the very best she could under the circumstances. I wish I could have told her that."

"I'm glad you had a good family," he says.

"No one is perfect. Certainly they didn't get a perfect daughter, but they loved me and they were really good to me. You want to know something weird?"

"Something else?"

"Right." I laugh. "Anyway, about fifteen years ago, I wrote the text for a children's picture book. It was published in a shortened version in a children's magazine. It's about a really smart Scottish Fold cat that lives in a library and learns to read and then goes out in the world to find himself. He ends up winning the blue ribbon prize at a cat show."

"Yeah?" Stewart seems to be waiting to see if this anecdote has a point.

"At the time, I thought the story was autobiographical, about me, but look at how it fits your life. By the way, my cat's name was Stuart—spelled differently. I used the clan spelling, but I called him Stuart from the beginning and never wavered."

After Shelley and I return to Nashville, I email Stewart and Rachelle individually and thank them for the weekend, for their generous hospitality and all the fun we had. In my note to Stewart I tell him I think that if we had been reared together, we would have been good friends.

Later that evening, I received the following response:

"I can't tell you how wonderful it was meeting you and Shelley. In some ways it feels like there had always been a part of the family missing and somehow I'd always known it was missing and this weekend I was finally able to find it. Will see you soon in Nashville. Love, Stewart."

He could not have said anything to me that would have meant more.

Since meeting Becky, Stewart, all their children, Aunt Betty, Aunt Christine, cousin Marty, his boys, and all the rest, I feel as though I know myself a little better. I always felt different from my adopted family. Not that I fit perfectly in my natural family either, but I am like some of them in so many ways. That is a first for me and I love it.

Marty told me once that Stewart was always different. "You just knew he was going to do something unique. He was always so self-directed."

I wonder if that translates into shy, stubborn, willful, and headstrong.

While I love these new relationships, I am also experiencing a distinct sense of guilt, a feeling of disloyalty, as though my adoptive mom and dad and the family they gave me and the history I learned of their families were not enough. They were wonderful in almost every way. It wasn't that. I simply wanted to know who *I* was. I have to suppress that inner critical voice that says I should not have needed to know, that I should not have wanted to look for my biological family, and therefore I am ungrateful. That voice is there and I hear it. Being adopted did not cast much of a shadow over my young life, but finding my roots has definitely brightened my old age.

Oddly enough, or perhaps not oddly at all, what I want most is to share these new relatives with my mom and dad and grandmother. I want to tell my mom, "Mama, I found them. And wait until you meet my aunt Christine. She's a lot like you. And Daddy is going to love Aunt Betty. She'll remind him of his favorite cousin, Versay. And you will both be crazy about Becky. Everybody loves Becky and her husband David." I want to tell my dad, "Wait till you meet Stewart. He is quite impressive. Talk about a self-made man. Everybody thinks the world of Stewart." I want to tell Bill, "Elizabeth died at seventy after eleven years of battling cancer. Isn't that sad? You remind me of her mother, Nancy Ann, in pictures and in the stories about her. She loved her church. I bet you two would have been big buddies." I want to make each separate family into one big extended family, and in my mind, I suppose I have done just that.

$\sim 30 \sim$

Except My Name

In June, Aunt Christine and her husband Roger host a family reunion at which twenty-eight of my genetic relatives show up. Before the reunion, Stewart and I find time to go to dinner, just the two of us. I asked him ahead of time if he would come a day early so we could spend a little time together, and without fanfare, he just made it happen. I love talking to him and wish we had more time, lived closer. I feel the same way about Becky.

Becky and I have been together several times, though not as often as we would like. Last fall Rachelle, Becky, and I took a long weekend trip together. We had so much fun we decided to try to do something like that every year. I could have lived without knowing any of them. I did live without it. But this is so much better.

When we were planning the reunion, Aunt Christine and I met for lunch at a nearby restaurant and soon we were talking about Elizabeth. I took the opportunity to ask questions I had not yet asked anyone else.

"Did Elizabeth marry Stewart Sr. in Tennessee? I never could find a marriage license for them."

"No. They eloped to Georgia. Then they went out to California pretty quickly after that."

That explains why, in the state archives, the paper trail on Elizabeth ended in 1944.

"What do most members of the family die of?"

"My dad had stomach cancer," Aunt Chris says, "and at least two of the boys had cancer—one died of lung cancer. But most had heart attacks, I think. Mom just dropped dead while she was out shopping one day. Heart attack, I guess. She was seventy-five. Daddy was seventy-five when he passed, too."

"Do you have any idea how Elizabeth contracted non-Hodgkin's lymphoma since she died relatively young?"

She looks up from the salad she's nibbling. "I always thought it was because Liz used this real strong deodorant, Mitchum. I think she liked it because it was unusual, but I was afraid maybe that was what caused it, that it was too strong. I don't know."

What a totally unexpected connection. It made me sorry all over again that I had not found them in time to meet my biological mother. Perhaps because we were so much alike, when the shock of my finding her wore off, it would have been all right. She might even have been glad.

"Liz gardened a good bit, too," Aunt Chris says, interrupting my wondering, "and probably got exposed to a lot of fertilizers and bug sprays and weed killers, and then where we grew up, down by that chemical plant, some days the air was so bad it made you sick to your stomach. But why would it kill her so young and not any of the rest of us?"

I wonder the same thing.

Aunt Chris shares more family photographs with me, pictures taken at the reunion she had hosted at her house back in 1982. It still strikes me as so utterly strange that Shelley and I were just a block away at the time.

I look through an album of photographs of all the brothers and sisters, some of which I have not seen before. I show Aunt Chris my birth certificate and the one snapshot I have of Elizabeth when she was in Detroit. While I look at the faces of my dead uncles, she studies the photo-static copy of my live birth record.

"How did you get your name?" she asks.

I laugh. "Mom and Dad almost named me Cindy Lou after my dad's mother, Lucinda, but in the end they named me after my mom's favorite actresses, Carole Lombard and Fay Wray, which is really weird because I didn't even know my mom liked movie stars that much when she was young."

Aunt Chris gasps and claps her hand over her mouth. "Oh, honey, your adopted parents didn't name you. Liz did."

"What? What do you mean?"

"Look here." She points. "If they named you, why does it say Carole Faye Pugh at the top of this birth certificate?"

Unbelievable. I had never paid attention to my own name. Of course I had seen it, but the significance had not registered. In the two decades that I'd had this document, I had been looking at Elizabeth's name and the information about her and at Jimmy's name and address. On the record of adoption I'd seen when I was thirteen it said Baby Girl Pugh. But here it was—my full name—Carole Faye Pugh, recorded before the adoption was official.

Aunt Christine pats my hand. "Elizabeth must have named you, and your parents kept the name she wanted you to have."

"Maybe Elizabeth had them put that name on my birth certificate because Mama told her that's what they were going to call me."

Aunt Chris shakes her head. "No. Elizabeth adored the movies. We went whenever we could. Her very favorite actresses were Carole Lombard and Alice Faye, not Fay Wray. She thought Carole Lombard and Alice Faye were the most beautiful women she had ever seen—and funny. She just loved them."

I am speechless. I'd spent decades worrying and wondering what my name would have been if I had not been

LEFT: *Biological mother, Elizabeth, at about age 30.* RIGHT: *Adoptive mother, Venda, at about age 35.*

adopted, only to discover that I had my name all along. Bill's words came back to me. "Your mother named you after her favorite actresses." Bill just didn't specify which mother.

Did Elizabeth give me names she hoped would bring me a happy and fulfilling life? Perhaps naming me after movie stars was the frivolous act of an immature, star-struck teenager, but I don't believe that, not now that I know her a little through her other children and her sisters. I believe that in naming me after her favorite movie stars, she was telling me she loved me and wanted me to have a wonderful life, a life she could not give me. My name was her third and final gift, after giving me life and people she hoped would be good parents. I choose to believe that in those two names lay all her good intentions, her hopes and dreams for the child so like her, the one she would never know, the child she had no choice but to leave behind. She had given me all she had to give. That has to be enough.

Last fall, Rachelle sent me a quilt she'd found packed in plastic at the bottom of a trunk. It was "Made by Liz," the tag said. It is the first object I ever received that belonged to my biological mother. It's in shades of browns and blues that match all the colors in my den, as though it were designed intentionally for the space.

This past Christmas, Aunt Christine, who has been diagnosed with a very slow progressing melanoma in one eye, gave me a fancy doll named Elizabeth. The note said, "This is the doll your mother never got to give you." Aunt Chris also gave me two bracelets that had belonged to Elizabeth. They are costume jewelry, but very pretty. I had the missing stones replaced and gave one to Becky. When my daughter remarried, I wore mine to the wedding.

Rachelle also sent me a CD video of her wedding when she married my brother. On the CD, someone is interviewing the guests, including Elizabeth. I have listened to it many times now. It's like time travel; I can see her animated face and hear her voice, very much like her sister Christine's, quiet, gentle, dignified, sweet, clearly thoughtful. But under that soft exterior, I think, lies a determined, self-directed, and perhaps even stubborn personality. She said she was familiar with more traditional church weddings. Stewart and Rachelle married at home. She said a justice of the peace had married her and Stewart Sr. She said she married her husband because she loved him and that they had three wonderful children together. I heard her say *we*, not *I*, have three children, and once again I wondered what she'd think if she knew that years later her first child would be seeing and hearing her say that.

The expressions on her face bloom and fade and change, and I have to admit, I do not see myself in her image, though others say they do. Neither do I hear myself in her voice. I do think we looked alike in some earlier photographs, when we were each five years old or twelve

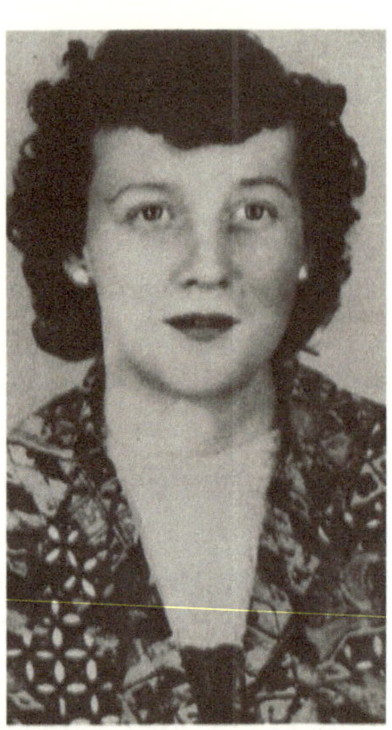

LEFT: *Carole, age 8. One of the pictures that seems to resemble a young Ann Elizabeth.* RIGHT: *Ann Elizabeth at age 15.*

or twenty. Perhaps at those times we sounded more alike as well, but then our paths diverged.

During one of our lunches at our favorite Thai restaurant, Aunt Betty told me something else I did not know. After five or six years of marriage, without children, Stewart wanted Liz to see a doctor to see if anything was wrong with her. So she did. "I don't know what Liz told that doctor," my aunt said, "but he also tested Stewart and found that he had a low sperm count. So Stewart Sr. began treatments and after that, Stewart Jr. was born. Stewart Sr. and Elizabeth had been married eight years at that point."

How could he have known about me and still believed the problem they were having conceiving was hers? Becky was right. Her dad, Stewart Sr., did not know. Aunt Betty disagrees. She believes he knew eventually but promised Elizabeth he would never tell.

Lately, I find myself considering the main "what if." What if I had not been given away at birth? What if Elizabeth had reconsidered and kept me?

I would probably have been fine being reared with my natural mother and her family, and maybe she and James would have ended up together, though probably not. If I had not been adopted, I would have escaped the likes of Bobby Joe and Mr. Fink, but I might have encountered worse. Every community has its predators. If I had not been given away I might have grown up with siblings. I might have gotten to live in one place for a long time with friends I could have kept forever, but I might not have. Such things are unknowable. No one would have said they wished they'd never adopted me, but then who would have straightened my crooked teeth or sent me traveling every summer or to college eventually? If my natural mother had kept me, she might have ended up wishing I'd never been born, and even if she hadn't said it, she might have thought it and I would have known. Children always know.

Answers to other questions remain equally unclear. Elizabeth was not the lady in the doctor's office with the baby and the toddler when I was five. The nurse was wrong, or my mother misunderstood. But was Elizabeth the lady in the scarf with the dark glasses watching the children play at recess when I was in Mrs. Hope's first grade? She was married to Stewart Sr. by then and living near San Diego. He was at sea for months at a time, during which she sometimes came back to Tennessee to her parent's house, so it's possible since Stewart Jr. had not been born when I was in first grade. Elizabeth might have taken a wide detour on a trip to Tennessee from California, but somehow I doubt it.

If she did look for me at some point back then, to make sure I was all right, it would not have been without considerable expense and difficulty. And it might have risked her secret. Still, it is something I think I would have wanted to do were I in her position, so I can't completely rule it out. But what would she have done if I had not been fine? What could she have done?

It occurred to me, once I knew when her other children were born, that my grandmother was right. Elizabeth was married and had two boys by the time I was thirteen, though Becky would not be born until a month before my sixteenth birthday. But Bill said Elizabeth was living in Michigan, which was not true. Had my grandmother misled me intentionally or was she misinformed? Did my parents and grandmother know something about Elizabeth back then that they never told me? Was someone in Jimmy's family keeping them informed? Or were they in contact with someone who knew Elizabeth? I will never know.

According to Aunt Christine, toward the end of Elizabeth's life, on a day when she still felt well enough to be outside working in her garden, she stood up, looked off into the distance and said, "Why am I still here? I shouldn't be." Aunt Christine didn't know what she meant but it sounded to her as though Elizabeth thought she did not deserve to have survived. Aunt Chris thought it might have had something to do with guilt over giving me away. I certainly hope that was not the case. Surely, she was referring to all the chemotherapy she'd had to endure and how sick and tired she felt by then.

Once I asked Aunt Chris, "Do you ever wonder what Elizabeth would say if she knew Shelley and I had found you, or that we lived so close to you all those years?"

"I think about it a lot," she said. "Liz missed so much in her life by not knowing you and Shelley. It's such a shame, really."

Elizabeth and I were always connected by our private awareness of one another's existence. I was always hers and she was mine. If I could, I would thank her, assure her that my life has been good, and that she'd made the right decision—one that was wise beyond her years. I am certainly grateful to her for that. I am also grateful to Aunt

Geraldine who verified my existence to Becky so I could finally know half of my genetic relatives before time ran out.

When Becky and I are together, dressed in jeans and hoodies, we look like a pair of hobbit sisters. We even walk alike, a bit like emperor penguins. We laugh alike and Rachelle says we sound alike on the phone. I wish we all lived a little closer.

Sometimes when I'm with Stewart I have the illusion that I have known him longer than I have, or that I know him in ways that are not possible. After three-fourths of a lifetime lived apart, we seem to be considerably more than relative strangers. Shelley says it helps that we all look a little alike and I'm sure that's true.

The summer after we met them, Shelley and I returned to New York with my grandson and Becky, for Stewart's sixtieth birthday. This time, Stewart's three sons were all there and I finally got to meet my other nephews. I see so many similarities between Shelley and Stewart's sons, between Shelley and Becky's daughters, and between my grandson and all four of my nephews. Rachelle told me Josh does not like heights and Becky said her children and Isaiah's children have anxiety issues. Shelley, Josh, and Ashley are intense about eating well, what foods to avoid, the proper diet, organic foods, nothing processed.

"It would have been nice, growing up," Shelley said, after we left, "if I had known Isaiah and Josh and Travis and Jesse and Ashley and Bethany. I would love to have known I had a first cousin like Isaiah. We are only two months apart and we are so similar. I'm a lot like Josh, too. But Travis is reserved like you and Elizabeth, isn't he? It really wasn't fair, was it, that we didn't know them before now."

"I should have put more effort into finding them," I said. "I gave up too easily. I didn't believe I would ever find any of them or that they would accept me if I did find them. You know I don't handle rejection well."

She snort-laughed.

"I really didn't think it would matter to anyone but me. That was selfish and extremely shortsighted on my part. I'm sorry."

"It's okay," she said. "You found them. That's what counts."

"Elizabeth didn't want me to find her—and my mom didn't want me to look. That's mostly why I skirted around it for so long. I waited until I thought all the principal players were dead and all I would find would be collateral connections and information."

"It would really have hurt Nana, wouldn't it, if she knew you wanted to find them?" Shelley called my mom Nana.

"Yes," I said. "She would have been devastated."

All those years, as I was searching for information about my biological family, I always thought if I found them I'd have the sense of a chapter in my life having closed or having come full-circle, but that is not how this new, extended family experience feels. Rather, it is more like a dormant taproot has awakened. I am able, through them, to experience what most every non-adoptee always has—I meet my adult self in them. I relate to their stories, and to stories about the ones who are already gone, Elizabeth, her parents, and all eight uncles. I see aspects of myself and my daughter and grandson in their faces, or at the oddest moments, in some expression or gesture or bit of inconsequential information. Because of knowing them, I am increased.

Clearly, Elizabeth did not want her husband, children, or grandchildren to know about me. Had I found them sooner, it might have been all right—love has long arms—but it might not have. I think, given a little time, she and I could have bridged the gap of secrecy and lies, but I don't

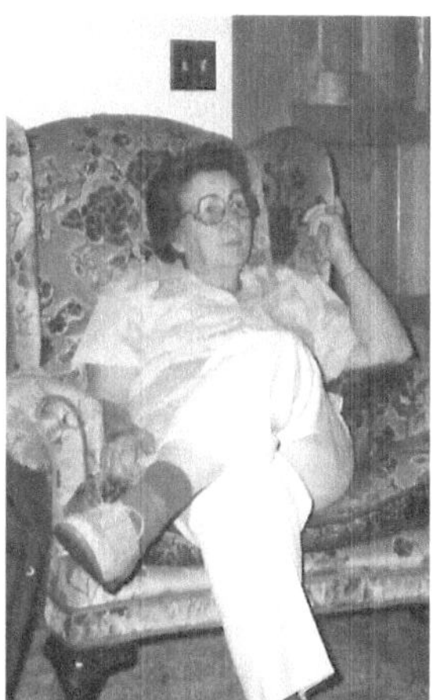

LEFT: *Carole's adoptive parents in the late 1980s.* RIGHT: *Carole's natural mother, late 1980s.*

know that for sure. I do not know how she would have handled it with her husband. It was a lifetime built on a lie of omission. Both my sister and brother believe it would have been fine, eventually. I am afraid it would have been a disaster. Stewart and Becky think their father would have been okay with it, but again I am not so sure.

Perhaps everything happened as it should have happened. More than sixty years after I learned I was adopted and my questions began forming, I have most of the answers I sought. I now know the people I come from. When I found them, I believed I'd learn everything except the name Elizabeth would have given me. I never suspected that it had been staring me in the face for years. Everything in my life was different from what it would have been had I not been given away at birth—except my name.

In searching for them I was seeking information, but I found so much more. I landed smack in the heart of a large and far-flung family. And after all this time, that is the most amazing part.

One-year-old Carole with Mama and Daddy.

Figuring out who I was as an adopted child meant I had an added layer of unknowns with which to cope. I tried to tell myself that was simply all there was to it. But life was a little more complicated than that. Back in the twentieth century, fewer working class couples adopted children than they do today. There were no organizations to offer support, no readily available information about the psychology of the task ahead or the appropriate language for talking about it with the adoptee or the rest of the family—not to mentions friends and neighbors. Many parents did not have the tools they needed for helping themselves cope, much less the insights they needed to help others. Ignorance of some things may be bliss, but generally speaking, information is what saves us.

Today, adoption is better understood and better supported. For one thing, it is usually acknowledged that adoptees need information about their birth parents.

As a young child, I wanted to be wanted. I wanted to know about my "real" mother. Thankfully I had a grandmother who supplied me with many of the details. Growing up an only child, I wanted to know my siblings. But during my late teens, I thought, if they don't want me, then I don't want them, either. When I became a mother, I wondered how Elizabeth could have possibly coped with the loss of her first-born child. And as a middle-aged adult, I wanted to know who my birth family was and where I came from. Most relationships are not simple and how one adoptee reacts may be vastly different from how another responds.

While I was almost totally my mom and dad's daughter, and Bill's granddaughter, my connection with my birth mother was always there. Of course, I was also my own person, even if I didn't fully understand that when I was young. We all always belong mostly to ourselves. Nevertheless, and no matter what else is true, I still wish I could have met her, my red-haired, blue-eyed, shy and private, introverted, movie-loving, crossword-playing, flower-growing, quilt-making, highly responsible birth mother. I came so close.

Epilogue

In May 2012, I traveled to Portland, Oregon, to meet my aunt Geri, the only one of Elizabeth's three surviving siblings I had not met. Stewart and Rachelle took me since he had not seen Aunt Geri in several years.

Geri and her husband James (Uncle Jimmy) were in their early eighties and nineties respectively. Aunt Geri suffered a bad fall the year before and had mild brain damage so she couldn't always say the precise word she wanted to use, and Uncle Jimmy had recently undergone open-heart surgery, but they both seemed in relatively good health and spirits. According to Becky, Aunt Geri is the sister who looks and sounds the most like Elizabeth.

Aunt Geri and Uncle Jimmy were very sweet and I loved meeting them. I also met another first cousin, Donna, and two of Donna's grown daughters. Donna is the daughter of Elizabeth's brother Frank, who died years ago. Meeting them meant I have now met more than forty-five people to whom I am genetically related.

While I was there, Aunt Geri told me the story of the morning Elizabeth left home to go to Detroit. "No one knew the real reason until later," she said. "Liz told me about it when she came back to Nashville the following year, but she wrote our mother a letter and told her she was pregnant.

She said it was her fault and her problem and she was taking care of it. I don't think our daddy ever knew."

I am willing to bet that was true.

At breakfast the next morning, over coffee and pancakes, Uncle Jimmy asked me where my house in Nashville was exactly, relative to Aunt Christine's house. I told him it was one short block away, over a small hill, and that our houses actually faced each other. "If the street were flat, we would have been looking at each other's front doors all those years."

He nudged Aunt Geri. "That's what I thought," he said. "Arthur and I took a walk over that hill once when Geri and I were visiting Nashville." Arthur was Aunt Christine's first husband. "You were in the front yard, and I said to Arthur, that woman looks exactly like Elizabeth. Arthur said Elizabeth was nowhere around. 'She's living in Kentucky,' he said. When we got back to Chris's house I told Geraldine about you and we walked over there, but you'd already gone inside."

The hairs on my arms were standing up and my face felt flushed. Why didn't they knock on the door? If only…

"When was that?" I managed to ask.

"Back in the late '70s," he said. "A couple of years before the family reunion."

By then, every blood vessel on the surface of my body had dilated. I couldn't believe it. Elizabeth and I had unknowingly come even closer to finding one another than I could have ever imagined. I glanced at Aunt Geri for confirmation.

She nodded and smiled.

On our way out of the restaurant, I noticed my reflection in the glass. Others see Elizabeth's face in mine, but I can't. I can only see me. I wonder what Mama would say if she knew how close I'd actually come to meeting my birth mother.

Ann Elizabeth and I were separated the day I was born. Seventy years later, I still lament the unfairness of never having met her. When I was a child in Michigan, she was mostly living in California, but from the summer of 1974 on, she was living less than two hundred miles from Nashville and less than fifty miles from my husband's sister in Kentucky. A few times, Elizabeth was just over the hill from my house, and once we missed the chance to meet because I left my front yard a few minutes too soon.

Whether we were separated by a thousand miles or a thousand feet, we were always connected. Such connections may flow unseen, but they exist. Of that much I am certain.

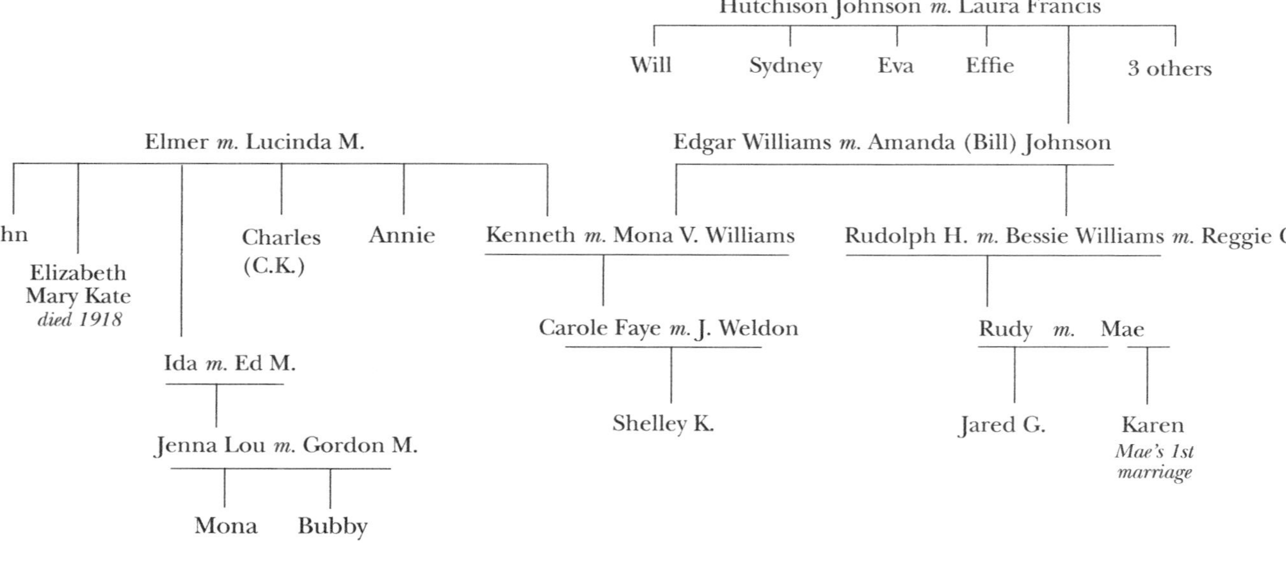

Kirchner Family in Michigan and Kentucky (Adopted)

Hutchison Johnson m. Laura Francis
Will   Sydney   Eva   Effie   3 others

Elmer m. Lucinda M.
Edgar Williams m. Amanda (Bill) Johnson

John
Elizabeth
Mary Kate
died 1918
Charles (C.K.)
Annie
Kenneth m. Mona V. Williams
Rudolph H. m. Bessie Williams m. Reggie C.

Ida m. Ed M.
Carole Faye m. J. Weldon
Rudy m. Mae

Jenna Lou m. Gordon M.
Shelley K.
Jared G.
Karen
Mae's 1st marriage

Mona   Bubby

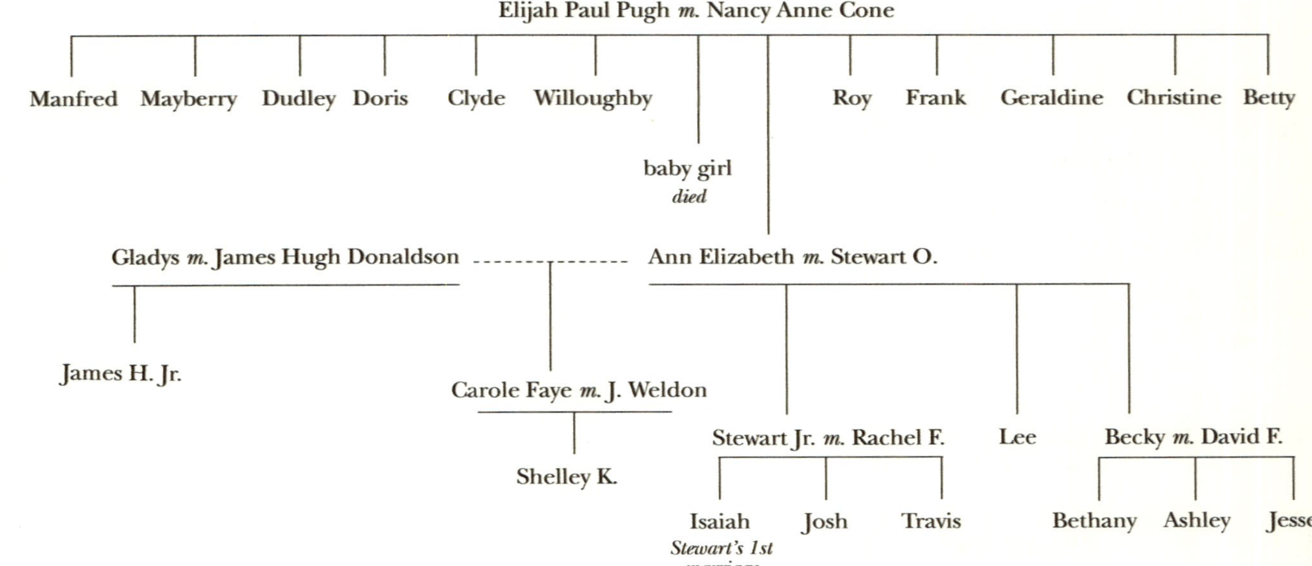

Pugh Family in Nashville, Tennessee (Biological)
Elijah Paul Pugh m. Nancy Anne Cone
Manfred   Mayberry   Dudley   Doris   Clyde   Willoughby   Roy   Frank   Geraldine   Christine   Betty
baby girl
died
Gladys m. James Hugh Donaldson
Ann Elizabeth m. Stewart O.
James H. Jr.
Carole Faye m. J. Weldon
Shelley K.
Stewart Jr. m. Rachel F.
Lee
Becky m. David F.
Isaiah
Stewart's 1st
marriage
Josh
Travis
Bethany   Ashley   Jesse

Acknowledgments

First and foremost, I wish to thank my sister-in-law, Rachelle. Had she not put the family tree on Ancestry.com, I likely would never have found any of them. From the first time we made contact, she has been my friend and supporter and for that I will be forever grateful.

To my brothers, Stewart and Lee, and to my sister Becky, to all my nieces and nephews, aunts and cousins who welcomed us with open arms, thank you. Your reactions to my showing up in your lives uninvited prompted me to write about the experience in the first place.

I am also most grateful to my daughter, Shelley, who demonstrated an interest in finding our roots, helped me search, and traveled with me, both physically and metaphorically, from our first trip to the state archives to our most recent visit with the family.

To my friends, colleagues, and mentors among my various writing groups, your patient reading and careful listening, your insights, suggestions, and criticisms were enormously helpful. The memoir is infinitely better because of each of you.

I am especially grateful to Darnell Arnoult for suggesting the title and for pointing out which photograph I should use on the cover. I began working on the memoir in her workshop.

Finally, I am deeply indebted to Judy Goldman, Kelly Prelipp Lojk, and Nora Esthimer for your encouragement and guidance, your developmental editing, copyediting, and publishing expertise, respectively. I simply could not have done this without you. Thank you all.